Using Microsoft Windows Small Business Server 2003

JONATHAN HASSELL

Apress®

Using Microsoft Windows Small Business Server 2003

Copyright © 2005 by Jonathan Hassell

ISBN-13 (pbk): 978-1-59059-465-0
ISBN-10 (pbk): 1-59059-465-7
Printed and bound in the United States of America (POD)

Lead Editor: Jim Sumser
Technical Reviewer: Jim Kelly
Editorial Board: Steve Anglin, Dan Appleman, Ewan Buckingham, Gary Cornell, Tony Davis,
    Jason Gilmore, Jonathan Hassell, Chris Mills, Dominic Shakeshaft, Jim Sumser
Assistant Publisher: Grace Wong
Project Manager: Kylie Johnston
Copy Manager: Nicole LeClerc
Copy Editor: Ami Knox
Production Manager: Kari Brooks-Copony
Production Editor: Kelly Winquist
Compositor: Dina Quan
Proofreader: Liz Welch
Indexer: John Collin
Cover Designer: Kurt Krames
Manufacturing Manager: Tom Debolski

Distributed to the book trade in the United States by Springer-Verlag New York, Inc., 233 Spring Street, 6th Floor, New York, NY 10013, and outside the United States by Springer-Verlag GmbH & Co. KG, Tiergartenstr. 17, 69112 Heidelberg, Germany.

In the United States: phone 1-800-SPRINGER, fax 201-348-4505, e-mail orders@springer-ny.com, or visit http://www.springer-ny.com. Outside the United States: fax +49 6221 345229, e-mail orders@springer.de, or visit http://www.springer.de.

For information on translations, please contact Apress directly at 2560 Ninth Street, Suite 219, Berkeley, CA 94710. Phone 510-549-5930, fax 510-549-5939, e-mail info@apress.com, or visit http://www.apress.com.

Contents at a Glance

Contents

About the Author

JONATHAN HASSELL is an author, consultant, and speaker residing in Charlotte, North Carolina. Jonathan's previous published works include *RADIUS* and *Learning Windows Server 2003* for O'Reilly Media, and *Hardening Windows* for Apress. His work is seen regularly in popular periodicals such as *Windows IT Pro Magazine, SecurityFocus, PC Pro*, and *Microsoft TechNet Magazine*, and he speaks around the world on such topics as networking, security, and Windows administration.

About the Technical Reviewer

JAMES F. KELLY is the owner of Blue Rocket Writing Services, Inc., an Atlanta-based commercial/technical writing company. Jim has been in the IT industry for 10+ years and holds numerous certifications. He still repairs his parents' PC for free, however.

Acknowledgments

This book was written by me, but I can state with certainty that others had an equally crucial role in the production of this work. A dedicated team of editors and production specialists put my words through the grinder and lo! out popped a professional book—for that, they all deserve praise and gratitude. First, my sincere appreciation goes to my editor, Jim Sumser, for his role in this work. Jim is a fabulous, flexible, and understanding guy, and I'm thankful for my opportunities to work with him. Also thanks to Kylie Johnston, Ami Knox, and Kelly Winquist, all at Apress, who corrected my mistakes, kept me on schedule, and generally made me aware that I am "the weakest link."

Also thanks to Jim Kelly for his timely and helpful comments upon reviewing the manuscript. While he worked to point out mistakes and deficiencies in coverage, any errors and omissions that remain are mine and mine alone.

And finally, but certainly not least importantly, my significant other Lisa remained rock-steady throughout the entire process, and I think she deserves the most thanks of anyone.

Introduction

Allow me to first say one of the most important things I'll tell you in this book—thanks! Months of work went into producing this book, and I really appreciate your spending your hard-earned money (or your small business's hard-won capital) on this work. I hope it exceeds your expectations.

With that out of the way, let's look at what you'll find inside this title. Small Business Server is such a large topic, mainly because the product you're interested in is many faceted, with lots of places to poke and prod. I've tried to cover all of the basics, some of the intermediate topics, and a few of the advanced features of SBS in this book.

In Chapter 1, you'll find a general introduction to the premise and promise of SBS 2003, including its components, how it can work for you, business opportunities that it creates, and a list of frequently asked questions. Consultants and business owners alike will find the information within this chapter useful. Chapter 2 oversees the actual installation process for SBS, including initially formatting the disk, installing Windows Server 2003, and adding the SBS-specific components to the mix. Then, Chapter 3 looks at initial configuration of SBS services, including adding users and computers, sharing printers, configuring the alerting services, setting up the fax components, and generally "moving into" your new SBS server.

Then the detailed part of the book begins. Chapter 4 delves into the innards of Windows Server 2003, the foundation upon which the rest of SBS is built. You'll learn how to manage file and folder sharing, set permissions appropriately, configure disk quotas and offline files, and set up shadow copies. Next, in Chapter 5, you'll look at the combination of Outlook 2003 and Exchange 2003 for managing communication and personal information in your business. The chapter starts by going through Outlook 2003, showing you how to use some special features and alerting you to some productivity-enhancing methods you and your users can adopt. Then it goes into Exchange Server 2003, the messaging engine itself, and shows you how to manage its internal operations. Chapter 6 details Windows SharePoint Services, the collaboration and document management system built into SBS.

The next part of the book goes into further detail about the features of SBS that may not apply to all businesses. Chapter 7 discusses in depth the very important topic of network security, and Chapter 8 takes a look at the various remote access features in SBS like virtual private networks and Outlook Web Access. Chapter 9 is a special chapter focusing on SBS's built-in faxing components. Chapter 10 demonstrates the health and performance monitoring capabilities of SBS, and finally, in Chapter 11 you can learn how to find the needle in the haystack by using Windows Server 2003's Indexing Service.

So, you've got a comprehensive user guide for Small Business Server, the ultimate Windows solution for businesses like yours. I hope you enjoy the material herein and find it useful.

CHAPTER 1

■ ■ ■

Introduction

Once thought to be only a remotely useful product to a market perpetually relegated to niche status, Windows Small Business Server 2003 has overcome its obstacles and finally come into its own: a respectable offering for businesses of up to 75 users who need a solution to help them protect their data, work more efficiently and quickly, reach more potential business leads and manage them around the clock, and focus on their work rather than on keeping their PCs running.

SBS 2003 was released in late 2003 to a growing small business market. According to the United States Small Business Administration, there are more than 22 million small businesses in the US alone—and those are only ones that have registered with the SBA. As the Internet and computers become ever more a part of our daily lives, small business owners are seeing increased revenues and more flexibility to integrate technology into their organizations.

SBS 2003 is a perfect fit for most small businesses. In this chapter, I'll provide an overview of the benefits of the product, its editions and the features of each, the requirements, and answer some common questions about its purchase, deployment, and administration.

Top Benefits of SBS

There are nine key points about how SBS improves technology and computing in the small business sector: by providing centralized storage; enabling simple backup and restoration; integrating simple yet effective security; increasing reliability of computer systems; improving the ability of users to remotely connect to their home networks; creating a larger, richer collaborative environment; adding better support for line-of-business applications; improving the configuration and deployment process; and improving the upgrade path for business systems.

Let's take a look at each of these in more detail.

Centralized Storage

How many small businesses have employee data, business reports, sales and marketing information, and e-mail spread across all of the machines in the office without any kind of organizational system? What if a user needed to access the latest proposal that Mary was working on, but Mary is out of town and her computer is password protected? A centralized storage solution, where all business documents and application files are stored, allows everyone in the office to go to one place on the network to find anything they're looking for. With SBS, the user who needed Mary's proposal can simply look on the server for the appropriate document and begin revising it while she's out of town.

But take that scenario a step further—what if the proposal that this user is trying to access is highly confidential, and only appropriate for viewing by the executives within the small business? Again, with SBS, the business can put limits on exactly which users can see what documents, so sensitive information remains privileged. You can also audit access to certain files and programs to determine what users are performing what actions on your systems.

Simple Backup and Recovery

Take the office scenario mentioned previously and consider this: what happens if one of the employees has a dead hard drive? How often was that computer backed up, if ever? If so, to where was the data backed up, and in what format? Can the data or the media be read on another computer on the network? You can begin to see the multiple problems associated with having data distributed across multiple PCs, particularly when it comes to disaster prevention and recovery. SBS comes with a technology called Volume Shadow Copy that enables the server administrator to take "snapshots" of the state of the server's disk at different points in time, creating multiple backups of any files and documents on the server at the time. These multiple backup versions are made available to users and employees through Windows Explorer, the regular file management interface, so they can easily recover lost data when they accidentally save over an important file or hit the Delete key too quickly. What's more, modern server applications can hook into the Volume Shadow Copy service and use it to make more quick and efficient backups of their internal data—Microsoft Exchange Server, the e-mail and groupware application bundled with SBS, uses shadow copies to quickly replicate its database of e-mail and calendar items for all the users on the network. This reduces the load on the server and makes the backup process much less error prone.

Some users have expressed concerns that backups are very difficult to configure. The Backup application in Windows Server 2003 can be filled with confusing terminology, and if you don't have a normal tape drive—the type of drive historically used to make backups of servers—sometimes the Backup application can be intimidating. With SBS, you get the Backup Configuration Wizard, which makes it a trivial task to construct a backup scheme and regular schedule that will keep the data on your server safe.

Simple and Effective Security

Although the words "Microsoft" and "security" aren't usually uttered in the same sentence without some derogatory connotation, the company has lately made great strides to improve the integrity of its products. SBS is no exception—within all facets of the applications and consoles included with the product are wizards that help you create a secure computing environment from the ground up. It also helps that the core of SBS, Windows Server 2003, is the most secure version of Windows yet and has the benefit of being developed during the famous coding hiatus of 2002, when all of Microsoft took a one-month reprieve from writing new code and went through old code looking for security problems and obstacles. It's quite a bit better than its predecessors, and SBS certainly benefits from its presence.

Of course, firewalls have an increased prominence in today's networked environment, and SBS Premium Edition comes with Microsoft's Internet Security and Acceleration Server, an enterprise-class firewall that many Fortune 500 companies use. With ISA Server, you can safely and securely publish content residing on your SBS machine to Internet clients without worrying about external browsers creeping into your network. ISA also keeps transmissions between your internal machines and other Internet hosts secure, and performs intrusion detection and stateful packet inspection services. (Of course, all of these terms will be covered in depth later in the book.)

Don't feel left out, however, if you don't spend the money for SBS Premium Edition. Microsoft has constructed a packet filtering scheme using the built-in Routing and Remote Access service that keeps your network secure. It's not as extensible, customizable, and easy to administer as an ISA-based firewall, but the company decided that budget concerns shouldn't be a deciding factor in whether your network is secure or not.

Increased Reliability

The most welcome feature of SBS 2003 is the introduction of Windows Server 2003, which has the benefit of being a fourth-generation Windows server product. As such, there are quite a few improvements to the robustness and integrity of the product. Reboots are far less common. Security updates can be automated. Applications that fail don't bring down the entire system. If your small business network is currently running one of the consumer versions of Windows—Windows 95, Windows 98, and Windows Me are some—then you'll likely be amazed at how resilient Windows Server 2003 is to most types of problematic applications.

Part of being more stable is also offering monitoring utilities to keep abreast of the health of a machine, and SBS with Windows Server 2003 provides an excellent set of monitoring tools. You can receive e-mails each morning outlining events that happened on your server, its current vital signs (CPU usage, free memory, hard disk space analysis, and other similar metrics), and problematic entries into the Security and Application event logs. With these features, half the battle of troubleshooting is already fought when you go to fix a problem.

Improvements to Remote Connectivity

Microsoft took customer feedback that indicated that small business owners are mobile and integrated enhancements to their users' ability to access information from outside of the office. And it's true: businesspeople associated with concerns of all sizes are traveling more as a result of the globalization trend, and increasingly, time is spent outside of the office while the need to access data contained within the office increases as well. How does one cope?

Well, this is done in two ways:

- The new Remote Web Workplace (RWW), a portal for users connecting to your internal network from outside the office, offers a gateway to any SharePoint sites within your organization, any computer within the office, and other tools within the office network. Figure 1-1 shows a sample image of the RWW.

- Virtual private networking (VPN) technologies have improved with the inclusion of Windows Server 2003, allowing remote users to connect via most any recent client connected to the Internet and browse file shares, send e-mail, and access internal web sites just as if they were sitting in their own office in your building, connected directly to the office network. As the book goes on, you will see more about what Remote Web Workplace can offer as opposed to what VPNs can do for you.

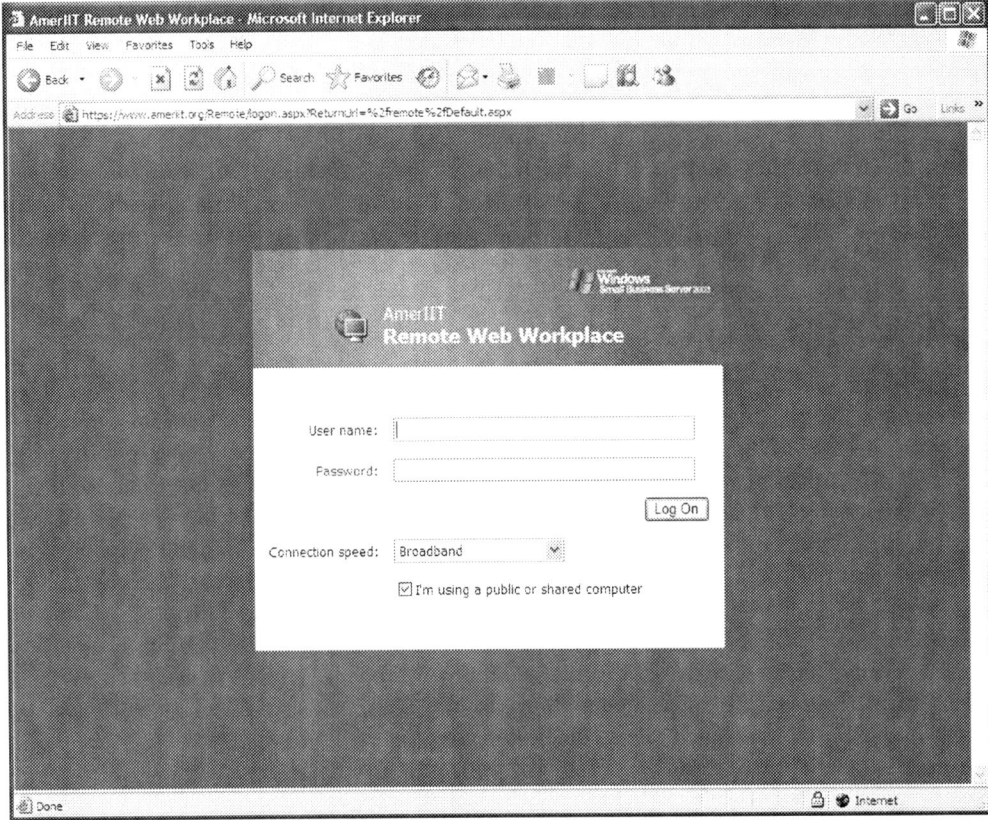

Figure 1-1. *A sample of the Remote Web Workplace*

Create a Larger Collaborative Environment

As smaller businesses move into the technology age, collaboration among team members becomes ever more important, and implementing a technology that simplifies that process was high on the list of architectural improvements Microsoft wanted to make when creating SBS 2003. To that end, SBS 2003 now includes a preconfigured internal web site based on Windows SharePoint Services, which allows coworkers to share and display information, including document libraries, announcements, events, and links. Figure 1-2 shows a sample image of the SharePoint site.

Also, your office users working remotely can share information almost as easily as within the office by using the Outlook Web Access (OWA) client, a mail program available over the Internet that mimics very closely the interface of the full Outlook 2003 client available within your office. Users away from their desks can still send e-mail to distribution lists, share calendars, and access and retrieve information stored in company public folders through OWA.

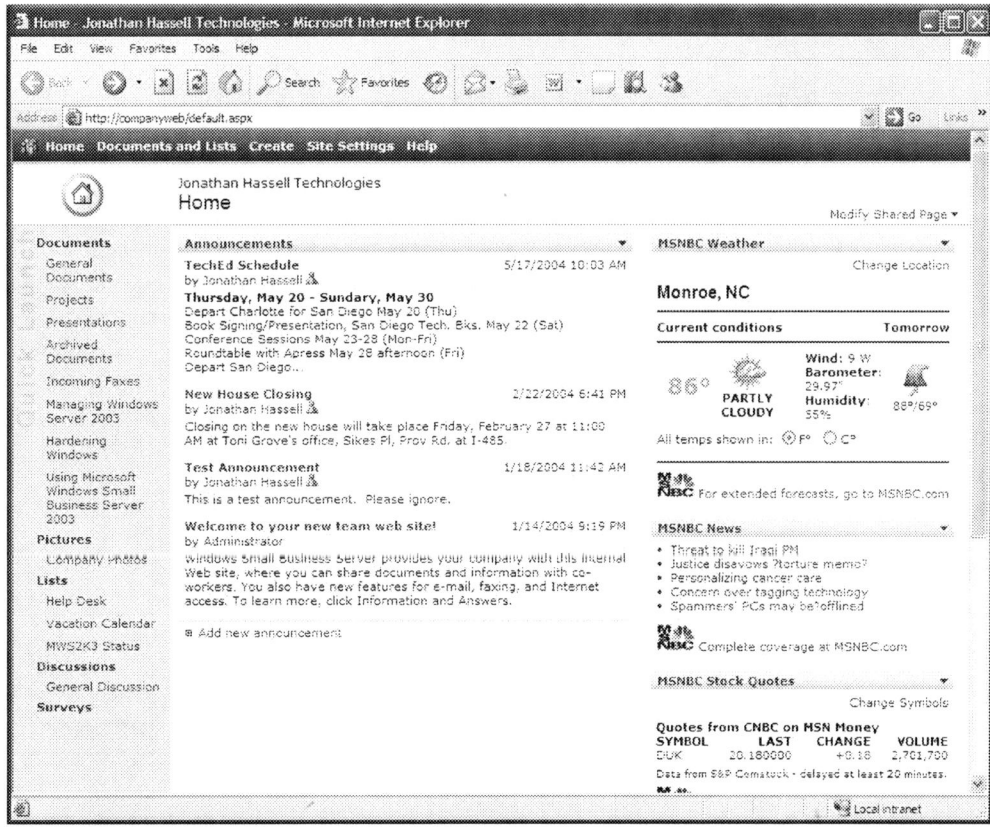

Figure 1-2. *A sample of an internal SharePoint site*

Better Support for Line-of-Business Applications

Many customers enjoy using state-of-the-art business applications, such as Great Plains Accounting, Microsoft's own CRM series, and other line-of-business (LOB) applications. SBS 2003 includes SQL Server 2000 with Service Pack 3, recently rated one of the top database applications in the industry, and one of the foundations of today's business software.

In addition, you can give up your Hotmail accounts for everyone and establish a real web presence by hosting your own e-mail and web site internally. This gives the mark of a professional establishment and convinces customers that you are, indeed, the real thing. SBS 2003 contains many wizards to make setting up, configuring, and administering your Internet applications very simple, and indeed value-added providers (VAPs) and consultants can monitor the health and welfare of your server remotely and, in most cases, fix any problems that occur from their offices as well—all without requiring a site visit.

Improved Configuration Process

A common complaint with users of previous versions of SBS and those with plain peer-to-peer networks was that network administration was a tough job. You needed a consultant to come in and perform the work, and you had to watch closely over the person's shoulder to learn how things were set up. Of course, you were rolled into purchasing lucrative service contracts so that the consultant could come check the health of your server every month or so, mainly because you lacked the confidence to do routine maintenance yourself. "Servers are like cars," you might have said. "You need a professional to do anything except use them."

SBS 2003 attempts to change a lot of that stigma. Microsoft has arranged with popular OEM distributors to package SBS 2003 preinstalled on server hardware; this means you can purchase a turnkey server solution for your business, unbox it, plug it in, and have everything on the server side up and running in about 20 minutes. You can also add and remove client licenses from your network online, removing the burdensome process of waiting for client access license codes to come in the mail. And, once everything is set up, you'll find the streamlined management consoles available on the server side of SBS 2003 to be quite easy to navigate. Plain-English labels like, "Add a new user" or "Set up e-mail and Internet access" in front of wizards that do the in-depth work for you make administering most daily operations on your new SBS network relatively pain free.

Improved Upgrade Path and Remove Encroachments

Previous versions of SBS didn't provide a very smooth upgrade path. SBS 2000, for instance, planned for a way out using the big BackOffice line of products, but Microsoft's subsequent total extinguishing of that suite left companies who outgrew SBS and were planning to move to BackOffice completely orphaned.

That is simply not true anymore: Microsoft has developed a migration pack that allows you to grow from SBS 2003 to any component included within the product—that is to say, the bigger, unrestricted version of any component included within SBS, like Exchange, SQL Server, or ISA. In addition, as your requirements grow and you need to expand the line of servers handling requests for your network, you can add Windows Server 2003 Standard Edition machines to your network to service file and printer sharing requests as well as to host web sites using Internet Information Services (IIS) and operate applications in Terminal Services mode.

Additionally, the Client Setup Wizard enables you to migrate profile settings (including desktop settings and data) from a peer-to-peer network (based on the Windows 2000 or Windows XP operating system) without disruptions to users.

Improvements for VAPs and Consultants

If you're a VAP or a consultant evaluating SBS for recommendation to clients, there are several key issues you should consider. For one, the market space for SBS 2003 has opened up considerably because of Microsoft's revised pricing strategy. Its studies have indicated that your potential customer base that could benefit from an installation of SBS has expanded by a factor of three. SBS is simple to sell at the $599 standard edition price point, and it's possible to find servers bundled with the standard edition in what amounts to a turnkey small business solution for less than $1,500. The product is ideal for first server adopters, especially since it used to be much more expensive than this to get started.

Second, you can deploy SBS 2003 at client sites much faster than with earlier versions. Why? For one, SBS has improved its out-of-the-box setup process, meaning once you plug in a server with SBS preinstalled, you can get to a usable OS and begin setting up client computers on the network in about 20 minutes. This was simply not possible with SBS 2000 or SBS 4.x. If you do a lot of installations of SBS, you can even develop your own preinstallation scripts and roll your own SBS image onto disks of new servers in less time than it takes to install a plain-vanilla, noncustomized version of Windows XP from scratch. And installing connectivity to client computers is easier now, too, with a web-based wizard you can run on any computer to join it to the domain and preload it with the necessary network client software and applications. Bringing it all together is the Health Monitor, which makes it a very simple process to keep tabs on the servers at all of your client sites via e-mail each day. You can see the Health Monitor in Figure 1-3.

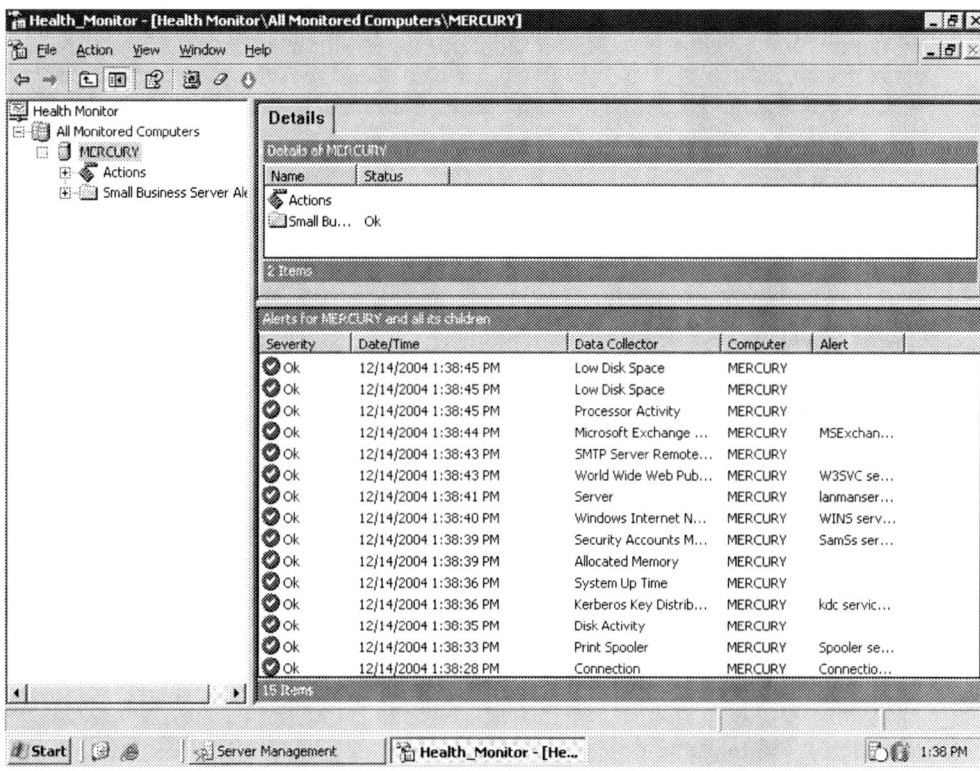

Figure 1-3. *A view of the Health Monitor*

Also, through the use of the Remote Web Workplace, you can customize an entire environment for mobile users or factory workers. Say that your assembly line workers in a small shop need e-mail access only: you as a consultant can create a custom RWW interface that only allows those workers to check e-mail. There are more places than ever with RWW, Windows SharePoint Services, and Outlook Web Access to customize and add value for your customer on top of what's already in the SBS box. The possibility also exists for extending the functionality of SQL Server in the premium edition or creating a custom business application using .NET Web Services in either edition.

Finally, there is a vast market of existing Windows NT–based networks that need to be upgraded in the next 12 to 18 months as the NT product nears the end of its supportability life. There are over two million Windows NT Server–based networks residing in small businesses worldwide. They could all use an upgrade to SBS 2003.

What Is Included?

Many users ask what is included with each edition of SBS 2003. SBS 2003 Standard Edition, one of the two flavors of SBS available on the market today, includes Windows Server 2003 for Small Business Server and the other components listed here:

- **Windows Server 2003**, the latest release of Windows on the server and the same software that Fortune 500 companies use to run their networks

- **Exchange Server 2003**, a leading enterprise groupware application that allows your entire organization to send and receive Internet e-mail, share calendars and contact lists, and collaborate with integration to other utilities and through Public Folders

- **Windows SharePoint Services**, a new feature allowing document management and team collaboration around an easy-to-use web site backed by a SQL-style database (note that this is not the full SQL Server product, but a lesser, more restricted version designed for small site hosting called the Microsoft Desktop Engine, or MSDE)

- **Internet Information Services 6.0**, the web server from Microsoft that has been improved and secured in its current release

- **Shared Fax Service**, which allows you to send faxes directly from any client computer on the network out through the server and monitor the status of faxes sent that way as well

- **Health Monitor**, a tool for on-site managers and consultants alike that checks on several key statistics on the server, like free disk space, processor utilization, and memory usage, and warns of upcoming problems that might otherwise not be avoided

- **Connector for POP3 Mailboxes**, a tool that integrates with Exchange to automatically download mail from existing mail accounts at third-party hosting provider sites and add them to Exchange mailboxes for a consistent user experience

SBS 2003 Premium Edition adds these components:

- **SQL Server 2000**, the premier enterprise database application that allows you to collect, archive, maintain, and analyze vast quantities of data

- **ISA Server 2000**, an enterprise-class firewall that provides more than adequate protection against "gremlins" on the Internet

- **FrontPage 2003**, a much cleaner and more revised version of the popular Microsoft web page authoring program

Pricing Points

A further question might be, "What is included for what price?" Since pricing depends largely on the channels in which you find the product available for sale, I'll simply briefly outline Microsoft's list price strategy for the product and trust that you can query your resellers and providers directly for more accurate pricing information for your situation.

Microsoft has priced the standard edition at $599 and the premium edition at $1,499. To step up from standard to premium is simply the difference in price between the two editions—only $900. You can also upgrade from SBS 2000 to SBS 2003 Premium Edition for only $599, which is an incredible value based on historical pricing data and what you receive for the money in the new edition. (As my technical reviewer, Jim Kelly, points out, Exchange Server alone can cost $1,500 for just ten users in the full retail packaging.) Transition packs, the utilities that let you migrate from the "SBS-ized" version of a particular component to the unrestricted, standalone version of the product, have prices set by individual resellers.

Client access licenses, or CALs, range from packs of 5 to 20, with prices from $489 to $1,929. CALs are available on a per-device (for each computer, PDA, or other machine accessing the SBS server box itself) or a per-user (each person using any device) basis. Five CALs are included by default in any purchase of SBS.

System Requirements

Microsoft always has its minimum system requirements that it posts on the box tops of its products and on its web pages at its site, but Microsoft is almost always very liberal with them. More stringent requirements for its products are almost always found to result in better performance and stability. To that end, I present here my recommended requirements for systems running each edition of SBS 2003.

- Any machine with a 1 GHz processor or faster. SBS will support dual CPUs and take advantage of them, and if you have the budget to spring for a server with two processors, I recommend it.

- At least 640 MB of RAM. SBS 2003 only supports up to 4 GB of RAM, but most servers aren't bought with that amount in the first place.

- At least 10 GB of available hard disk space. While Microsoft says you only need 4 GB, you tend to accumulate a lot of files when storing everything on the network.

- A DVD-ROM drive in the server. This will save you a lot of time installing SBS, since it comes on one DVD versus five to six regular CDs.

- A video card and monitor in the server that supports a resolution of at least 800×600. This will make initial setup not even just easier, but also possible. It's effectively not an option to try and scroll around in the setup wizard at a lower resolution.

- Two or more network interface cards: one for connection to your internal network and one for an Internet connection. Even if you have no intention of using a second adapter, go ahead and purchase one now: that way you don't have to take the server offline should you ever expand your connectivity and require the use of the second card.

You might also want to invest in a fax modem for use with the Shared Fax Service and a network printer for use over the network, but those certainly aren't required to get started with SBS.

SBS does have some limitations, however, from the regular enterprise versions of the products included in its suite. For one, installation of all components included in SBS is limited to one physical machine. Second, the SBS 2003 machine must be the root of a new Active Directory domain. (We'll cover what this means in Chapter 3, but suffice it to say for now that this restricts a business from simply buying SBS to integrate it into its existing network.) And third, you can only connect up to 75 users or devices to the network. If you outgrow that limit, you'll need to purchase the transition pack and move from SBS versions of the products to the standalone versions.

Those Not Suited for SBS

As great a product as SBS is, and as good as it is for a lot of clients, there are a few groups for whom SBS isn't a good fit. Those include the following:

- Businesses in tough economic times with ten users or less. I've found that if a business with ten people or fewer under its wings will have to uncomfortably squeeze out budget money for SBS, it's probably not a worthwhile upgrade at that point. Such a business would do better using a peer-to-peer network using the functionality built directly into Microsoft client operating systems. If you're a consultant, there's still money in these client sites—it just probably wouldn't be best spent upgrading to SBS yet.

- Businesses already large in size—with 50 users or so. It's tough to discern the line at which small businesses can use SBS to its fullest potential and when they become too big to make the monetary outlay worth it. At 50 employees, a business is probably growing fast and would soon outgrow the capabilities of SBS. The standalone versions of the SBS suite components would serve these types of clients better. However, in a very niche market with a slow growing business, it may still be a worthwhile deployment.

- Businesses with extensive Internet presences. The needs of these types of organizations are typically beyond what SBS can adequately provide, as conducting e-business requires some reasonably heavy-duty business applications.

And SBS has some inherent weaknesses that are by-products of its design and marketing as well. For one, security analysts have real problems with the idea that all business applications—including those facing the Internet—are located on one server. This is usually a bad idea for most applications. However, I'd counter that SBS Premium Edition, which includes ISA Server, includes some unique technology that I'll cover more in depth in Chapter 7 that mitigates this risk. Another answer, if you were using the standard edition of SBS, is to use a separate hardware firewall to provide additional protection for the server.

Also, the CALs—which are required for using SBS 2003—are expensive. Although Microsoft has reduced the price of the base SBS 2003 unit itself, purchasing more CALs if you have more than five devices out of the box can be a daunting proposition. Since this isn't a technical requirement but a licensing decision by the company, I include it here as a weakness. While most businesses can absorb the cost of additional CALs as they expand without too much difficulty, some smaller businesses might be put off by it.

Frequently Asked Questions

With a major upgrade to IT infrastructure in any size of business or organization, there are bound to be predeployment questions. Based on my consulting experience and Microsoft's product team, I've tried to anticipate the most common questions you as a business owner—or you as a consultant—might have about SBS. I'll conclude this chapter with those questions, and corresponding helpful answers, which are outlined next.

Does SBS require Active Directory?

Yes. During the setup process, SBS 2003 will use an unattended script to automatically install Active Directory without prompting you for complicated setup information. This is absolutely required, as Active Directory serves as the foundation for a lot of functionality in SBS 2003.

Can I count upon SBS for reliability and integrity?

In this version, certainly. This release marks the fourth version of SBS, so Microsoft has had quite a bit of time and experience in making improvements and corrections to their product. At the root of it all is Windows Server 2003 which, in my experience (and I wrote a couple of books on it too!), is the most stable release of Windows to date, including any client versions of Windows.

Will all of my applications run on SBS 2003?

SBS uses the application compatibility features of Windows Server 2003 to enable much greater and broader support of legacy applications. Chances are your applications will work if they ran on any prior version of Windows.

Do I have to use Windows XP and deploy it at the same time as I install SBS 2003?

Certainly not. While with Windows XP on the client side you'll enjoy many great new features, upgrades don't have to happen at once, and SBS 2003 includes enough improvements on its own that you will immediately see an increase in productivity, even with your current client computer OS.

Will SBS 2003 support my hardware devices?

Most major hardware devices have already been certified by Microsoft for use with Windows Server 2003 and will therefore work out of the box with no problems with SBS 2003. The surest place to check is on the Windows Hardware Compatibility List, which is available at http://www.microsoft.com/whdc/hcl/search.mspx.

If I outgrow SBS 2003, what are my options? Is there anywhere I can go?

SBS 2003 includes the full versions of all the application software in the suite. You can add member servers to the network to fulfill higher traffic and more demand, and as your business grows, you can always migrate to the standalone versions of the products using the aforementioned transition packs.

How secure is SBS 2003?

Very secure. If you purchase the premium edition, you get the benefit of the enterprise-class ISA Server firewall. And no matter which edition you prefer, you gain the security enhancements included and integrated into Windows Server 2003.

CHAPTER 2

■ ■ ■

Installing SBS 2003

BEGINNER SBS ADMINISTRATOR ■ **ADVANCED SBS ADMINISTRATOR** ■ **EXPERIENCED CONSULTANT**

It used to be that installing a suite of back-end applications took days of time, thousands of dollars, and tens of consultants to make sure that all the correct dials were turned and switches were toggled. How times have changed, and for the better, too.

With SBS 2003, the installation process is streamlined, so that all components of the suite are installed with a single wizard that has a consistent, easy-to-understand interface. In fact, with a fast machine, you can be completely up and running with SBS 2003—in a basic form, mind you—in less than an hour. For a more detailed install, or on a slower machine, you're looking at three hours, which is still a significant improvement over the days gone by.

In this chapter, I'll show you some considerations to think of before you break the shrinkwrap of the SBS 2003 package, and then, once you've made your server machine ready, I'll walk you through the process. You might notice this chapter is fairly short compared to others—that's because the process really isn't complex.

Let's begin.

Some Installation Considerations

There are a few items to consider to ensure that the setup process for SBS 2003 can be as smooth and uneventful as possible. For one, look at the server machine on which you're planning to install SBS 2003. If you have purchased a new server with SBS 2003 preinstalled, then a lot of this chapter will not apply to you. Specifically, you'll be interested in taking a look at the section entitled "Installing the SBS Core Products." The reason for this is that one of the major advantages of purchasing SBS 2003 preinstalled on a new server machine is your initial setup time is reduced from an average of three hours to approximately 30 minutes (and sometimes as low as15). If you are a consultant billing time, this is a winning situation for your clients— although it might not be the best situation for you.

If you are purchasing a server without SBS 2003 preinstalled, then you should consider where the components that will be included with your hardware are listed on the Windows Server 2003 Hardware Compatibility List (HCL), which can be found at http://www.microsoft.com/whdc/hcl/default.mspx. This list contains all devices that have been tested against Windows Server 2003 and are known to run successfully. (Since SBS 2003 is based on Windows Server 2003, you can accurately use the WS2003 HCL for this purpose— there isn't an SBS-specific HCL.)

Along those same lines, you may be wondering what an appropriate caliber of machine would be to run the server components of the SBS 2003 suite. Tables 2-1 and 2-2 present the Microsoft lists of minimum and recommended specifications for the SBS server machine.

Table 2-1. *System Requirements for Standard Edition*

Requirement	Minimum	Recommended
CPU	300 MHz	550 MHz or faster
RAM	256 MB	384 MB or higher, with a 4 GB maximum
Hard disk	4 GB available space	More than 4 GB of available space
Drive	CD-ROM	CD-ROM or DVD-ROM
Display	VGA	Display capable of 800×600 or higher resolutions
Network card	Ethernet	Two Ethernet cards

Table 2-2. *System Requirements for Premium Edition*

Requirement	Minimum	Recommended
CPU	300 MHz	550 MHz or faster
RAM	256 MB	512 MB or higher, with a 4 GB maximum
Hard disk	5 GB available space	More than 5 GB of available space
Drive	CD-ROM	CD-ROM or DVD-ROM
Display	VGA	Display capable of 800×600 or higher resolutions
Network card	Ethernet	Two Ethernet cards

You may also want to investigate having a dedicated external fax modem for your server to take advantage of the SBS faxing service.

You also will want to note any driver issues that may crop up. If your SBS server machine has a SCSI card or a RAID card that you know isn't yet supported by Windows Server 2003 out of the box, you will need to acquire a Windows driver for that card and have it available on a floppy disk. Then, in the character-based setup phase of the Windows Server 2003 installation process, you will be prompted to press F6 to indicate that you have supplemental drivers to install. This process is only necessary at this point for new drivers of storage-type devices. You can install drivers through the more friendly Windows GUI later in the process for all other types of cards and devices.

Finally, double-check the BIOS version of the server machine. On most of the popular brands of servers on the market today, the BIOS version is printed on the screen when you first turn the machine on. Check with your manufacturer to make sure that there isn't an updated version of the BIOS available. If there is, follow the instructions that came with your server to update the BIOS to the latest version—this can often cure some problems that seem very random and difficult to troubleshoot later, and it's best to start the SBS installation process with a machine as up-to-date as possible.

Installing Windows Server 2003

It's a fairly effortless procedure to install the first part of SBS, Windows Server 2003, onto new systems. Here are the steps:

1. Turn the system power on and insert the first SBS CD into your optical drive. If you receive a prompt to select from what location to boot, choose the option to boot off the CD. The system will boot a minimal, text-only version of Windows Server 2003 into main memory and begin the initial installation procedure.

2. The Welcome to Windows Setup screen will appear. Press Enter to continue.

3. Read the terms of the license agreement. If you accept (which, of course, you have to do in order to continue installation), hit F8 to continue.

4. A screen listing your current disk partitions will appear. You can simply move around the menu and select an existing partition on which to install by pressing the arrow keys and then Enter to confirm your selection. You can also delete partitions (be sure you have backed up first!) by selecting the partition and pressing the D key. Lastly, you can create a new partition by selecting the Unpartitioned space selection in the menu and then pressing the C key. Figure 2-1 shows the disk partitioning screen.

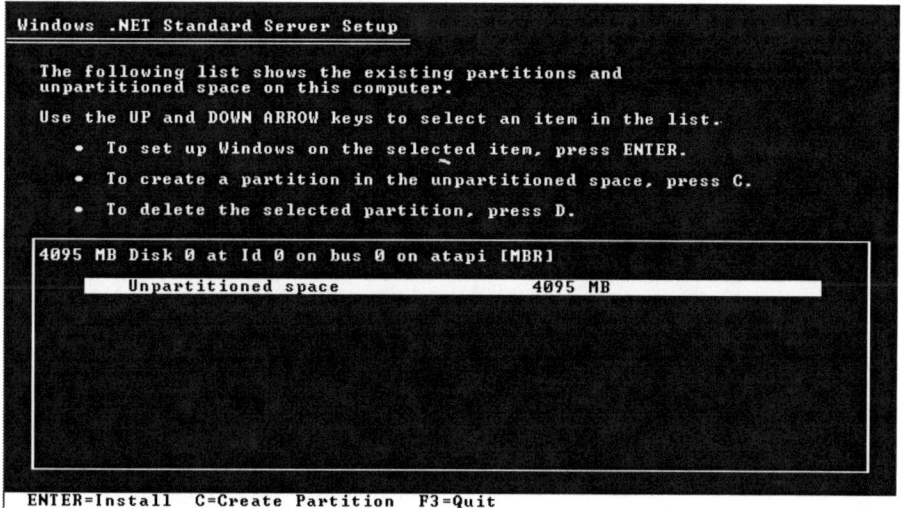

Figure 2-1. *The disk partitioning screen*

5. You'll now be prompted to choose a file system. Select the file system with which you want the partition formatted and press Enter to start the format. The formatting process can take up to one hour to complete, depending on the size and speed of your drive. Now's a good time to catch up on your e-mail backlog or take a coffee break.

6. Once the format is complete, you'll see a screen asking you to enter the location where you want to store the actual Windows Server 2003 system files. I recommend accepting the default location, \WINDOWS. If you select a different location, some legacy applications that rely on a default operating system root location might break. Press Enter to confirm the location and begin the file copy process, which could take up to ten minutes.

7. Once the copy is complete, the system will reboot, and the next portion of the installation will commence in graphical mode. The process starts with the Regional Settings screen, which pops up soon after the reboot. On this screen, you can change the language, locale, and keyboard settings depending on your geographical location. Click Next to continue.

8. Enter your name and organization. Click Next to continue.

9. Enter the appropriate product key, as listed on the back of the SBS 2003 CD case. Click Next to continue.

10. Choose your licensing mode, as explained earlier in the chapter. Figure 2-2 shows the options you are presented. Click Next when you're finished.

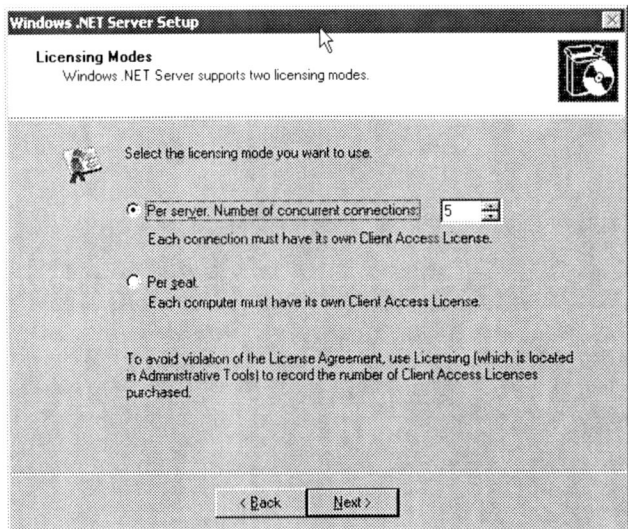

Figure 2-2. *Choosing the Windows Server 2003 licensing mode*

11. Choose a unique name for this server (using alphanumeric characters), which can be up to 15 characters long. This will end up being the name of your SBS server, so don't necessarily take the computer name that the Setup program automatically generates for you. Change it to something meaningful, and when you're done, click Next to continue.

12. Enter a password for the administrator account. Windows will alert you if you choose what it considers to be an insecure password. You'll need to enter your password twice for verification. Once you're finished, click Next.

13. Adjust the time zone and server time and date on the next screen. Click Next to continue.

14. If Windows detects a modem, it will present the Dialing Locations screen. Here, input your area code and any dialing-related configurations (including a prefix digit for an outside line or a required area code). Click Next to continue.

15. Finally, files are copied and settings are finalized. This step can take an additional 20 minutes, enough time for perhaps another coffee break.

Your installation will be complete once the system restarts. It's important that you immediately visit Microsoft Windows Update, at `http://www.windowsupdate.com`, to apply the latest security fixes and service packs before placing the machine into production use. (If you forget this step, SBS will remind you when you begin completing the To-Do list, which is covered in the next chapter.) Otherwise, constant security patch application could limit the availability of your production machine because of the need for constant reboots. It's best to do this ahead of time.

Installing the SBS Core Products

The next phase of the SBS installation process begins with logging in to your server using the Administrator username and the password you just assigned to the account in the previous setup process. The SBS 2003 setup process will launch automatically.

First, the setup procedure does a short scan of your system to see if it meets the absolute rock-bottom requirements, and it reports the results of that scan to you in two forms: informational warnings and blocking messages. Warnings don't interfere with the setup process and simply alert you to things you need to address, whereas blocking messages indicate errors that will prevent setup from continuing. Some examples of blocking messages include the following: an insufficient amount of memory, no network adapters installed, and inadequate disk space. An example of a common warning message is one that appears telling you that you have just one network adapter installed—you don't get the integrated firewall features of SBS 2003 with just one card, whereas having two cards installed would allow that featureset to work.

The Company Information screen is next, as shown in Figure 2-3. Here is where you enter your business contact details—phone number, fax number, address, city, state/province, zip/postal code, and country region. This is used in many places in the final SBS installation. Click Next to continue.

The Internal Domain Information screen, shown in Figure 2-4, appears. Here, you can pick how your domain will be referred to in terms of DNS and, for older systems, NetBIOS. For the Full DNS name for internal domain field, pick a short name that is relevant to your business—in my case, this is HASSELLTECH—and then add .local to the end of it to satisfy the required DNS name format. In the NetBIOS domain name, I recommend simply using the name with .local appended to it. Finally, you can change the name of the SBS server on this screen, but it's your last opportunity to do so for a while.

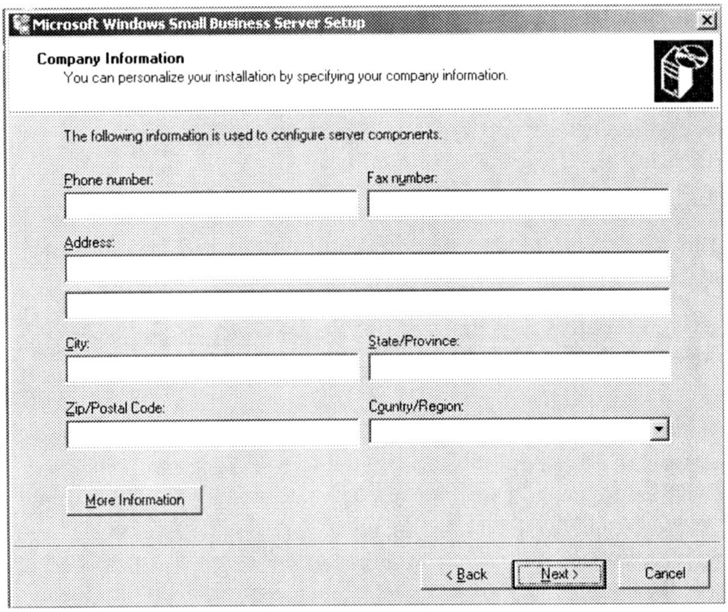

Figure 2-3. *The Company Information screen*

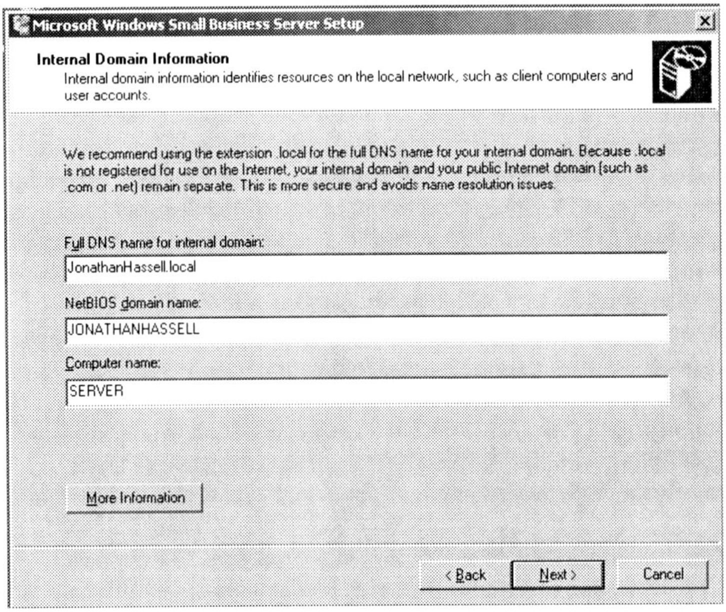

Figure 2-4. *The Internal Domain Information screen*

Why do you add the .local extension? Essentially, this is added because DNS is a public-facing service. When you have a public DNS domain name, like Microsoft.com, the information about the computers in that domain is published throughout the Internet. However, you can choose to use a set of private extensions (like .local or .priv or .int) that will keep the information on all of the computers in your DNS domain from propagating around the Internet. Not only is this a security benefit, but it also reduces the conflicts you might have hosting your web site at an ISP but hosting your mail on your SBS server using Microsoft Exchange. Just know that choosing .local here will not affect your ability to send and receive Internet e-mail using a common, public extension like .com, .net, or .org. It is only for Windows networking purposes and has very little to do with messaging. Click Next to continue.

The Local Network Adapter Information screen appears, as shown in Figure 2-5. Here, just pick the network card that you want to use for local network connectivity—not a connection to the Internet via your ISP. Click Next.

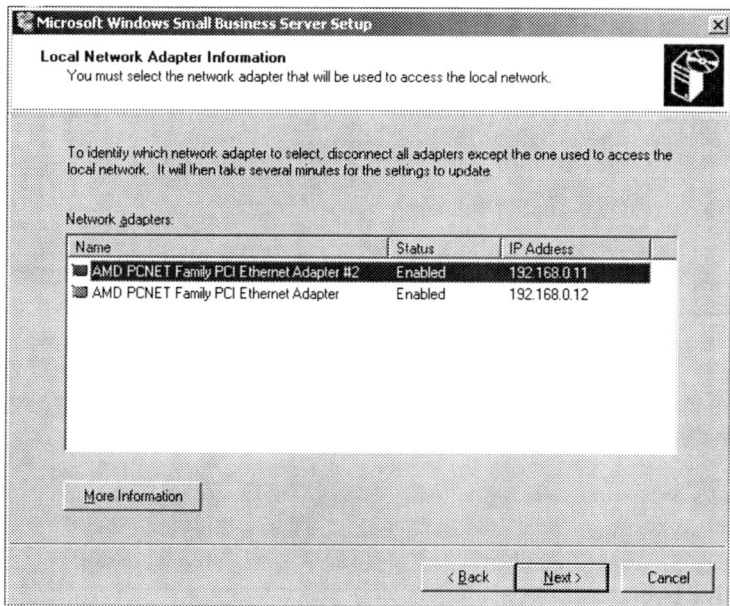

Figure 2-5. *The Local Network Adapter Information screen*

The Local Network Adapter Configuration screen appears (see Figure 2-6). You're asked to confirm the IP address and subnet mask assignments used in your SBS network. Unless you have a good reason to change these addresses, accept the defaults and click Next.

You're now asked if you'd like the setup program to log you (the administrator) on to the machine automatically during the first few reboots of the machine. As long as you are the one in control of the machine and it is not yet directly connected to the Internet, this feature can be a big timesaver and will allow you to take some coffee breaks and perhaps a lunch break while the process trundles along. Go ahead and enter the administrator password and then click Next.

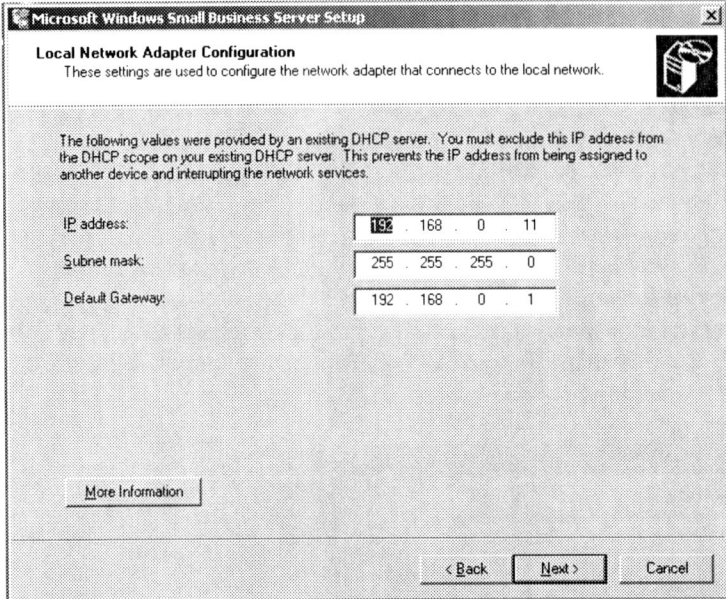

Figure 2-6. *The Local Network Adapter Configuration screen*

Finally, the Windows Configuration screen appears. This indicates that you've finished the first part of the actual SBS 2003 product installation (as opposed to just Windows Server 2003) and that the setup process is going to configure Windows for you. It could take a half hour to do this, and in my experience, that's a pretty good estimate. During this part of the process, the wizard installs Active Directory using the information you've provided and also configures the Indexing Service to allow your clients to search for files and folders and text contained therein.

Once this stage is completed, your server will reboot, and once it is back up, the Component Selection screen will appear, as shown in Figure 2-7. Ensure that under the Action column in the table, the selection reads Install. This will ensure you get a full installation of SBS 2003 on the first try. Click Next to continue.

▧**Note** If you have purchased the premium edition of SBS 2003, you won't be prompted to install those special products (SQL and ISA) until after the installation is complete. Right now, the wizard is focused only on the core components of SBS.

The Data Folders screen appears (see Figure 2-8). On this screen, you can tell the wizard where to store specific folders. You get the option of redirecting the location of the monitoring database, the folders for each user that store his own personal files, the folder containing applications to be deployed on client workstations, the folder where sent faxes are stored, and where the Exchange mailboxes and logs are stored. To change a folder's location, click the item and then click the Change Folder button. When you've arranged your folder structure how you desire it, click Next to continue.

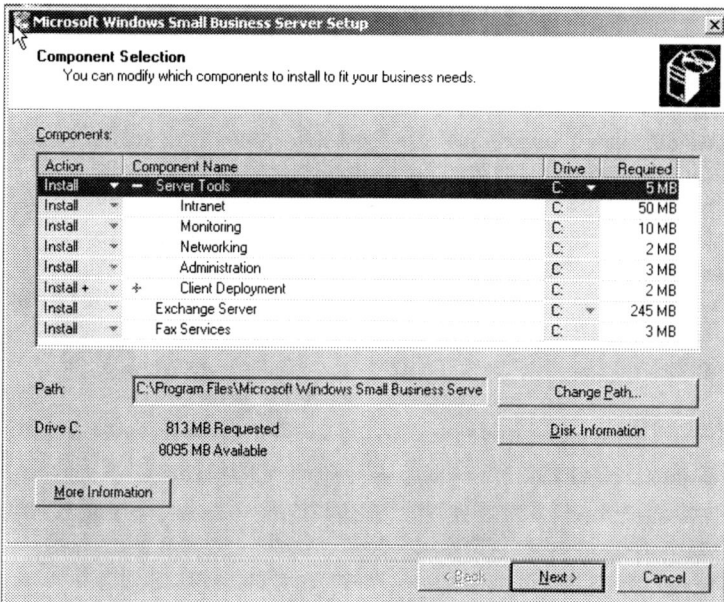

Figure 2-7. *The Component Selection screen*

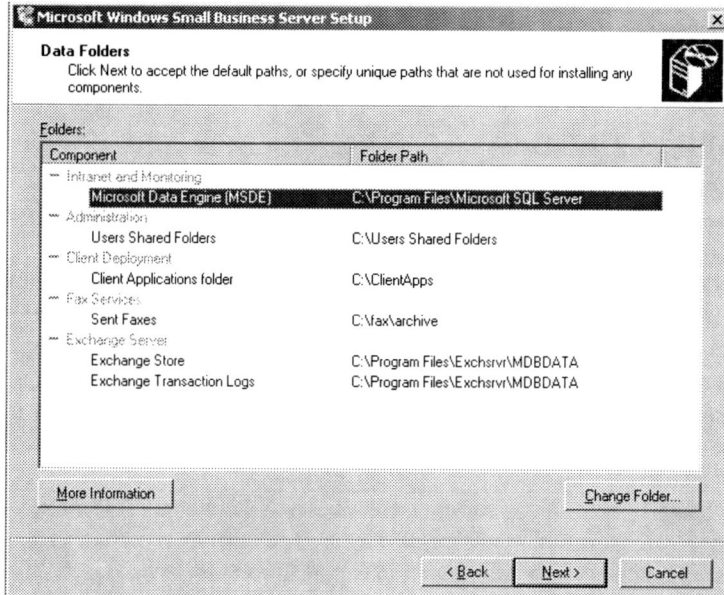

Figure 2-8. *The Data Folders screen*

Finally, the Component Summary screen will appear, which gives you the last chance to make changes to the products to install and their locations before you press the "big red button," as it were. Confirm your choices, and then click Next to get the wizard started installing the core components.

The next stage of the process takes a long time as the Fax Service, Microsoft Exchange, and several tools and applications are installed. You'll be prompted to change CDs along the way. Disc 2 is perhaps the longest disc, as Exchange modifies the structure of your Active Directory and takes it own sweet time doing it as well. Late in the process, you'll also be prompted to insert the Microsoft Office Outlook 2003 CD, which is Disc 4 in your package.

After 1 to 2 hours, depending on the speed of your server machine, the process will finish and the Finishing Your Installation screen will appear. Click Finish, and the process is complete. Next comes the configuration.

Note You may be presented with a screen called Components Messages that lists some errors that were encountered during the installation process. The items listed had problems—usually a file copy problem or disk space error or something similar—and thus were not successfully installed. Most often, simply repeating the installation process will cure these problems, which are minor in nature. Click Next to acknowledge the messages.

Setup will notify you that it needs a final reboot of your server machines. Click Yes, remove the fourth disc from the CD-ROM reader on your machine, and wait for the reboot to finish. SBS is now installed on the machine.

A Word About Product Activation

In retail and OEM copies of SBS 2003, there is a feature known as activation, which is an antipiracy measure instituted by Microsoft. In essence, when you install Windows with a specific license key on a computer, a hash is created using the key and several attributes of hardware on the computer, including the Media Access Control (MAC) address of the network card. (The exact way this hash is created is, of course, secret.) This hash can't uniquely identify a computer, but it identifies a specific installation of Windows. This hash is sent to Microsoft during the activation procedure. The theory is that if you later try to use the same product key for an installation on different hardware (for example, another computer), the hash created would be different, and activation would fail because it's likely you are trying to use more than one copy of Windows when you're only licensed for a single installation.

By default, you have 30 days to activate the product upon initial installation. When this deadline is reached, the server will continue to run in the background (although without console access, meaning you can't log in to it from the server itself) until you reboot it.

The catch to activation is this: if you change enough hardware in the same system to change the hash, Windows will complain that you need to activate the software again. You may need to actually telephone a toll-free number to speak with a representative in this case to explain why your hardware changed. This service is available 24 hours a day, 7 days a week, but it's a pain.

Conclusion

In this short but sweet chapter, we've looked at some considerations and issues to address when you first pick out a server to run SBS 2003, and then we went through a detailed installation of SBS 2003 onto a new machine. In Chapter 3, I'll take you through configuring the SBS server step-by-step and how to get it up and running to serve your business.

Let's move on.

Initial Configuration

BEGINNER SBS ADMINISTRATOR ■ **ADVANCED SBS ADMINISTRATOR** ■ **EXPERIENCED CONSULTANT**

Now that your SBS server has been installed, it's waiting for you to tell it what to do and how to do it, like an obedient servant waiting for instructions from its master.

Before you can begin to use SBS, you must first set up its connection to the Internet, tell Exchange how to handle e-mail, add users and computers, set up monitoring and backup options, and connect client computers to the network. It sounds like a lot, but SBS provides simple wizards to help you through the process.

In this chapter, I'll show you all of these procedures and walk you through them step by step.

The Server Management Console

The Server Management Console is the central place to manage the SBS server and network. It consists of two nodes, the Standard and Advanced management portions, which I'll cover in the next sections.

The Standard Management Node

The Standard Management node, shown in Figure 3-1, is where most of the easiest and straightforward administration of your SBS server is completed. This node focuses on active tasks—things that you must do in order to properly set up your server—while its brother, the Advanced Management node, simply exposes the normal Windows application management utilities so you can play around.

Let's step through the list:

- **To Do List**: The central place to store all of the initial setup options and processes just after installing the SBS server software. Here, you do things like configure Internet access and Exchange e-mail and add users and computers to your network. I'll be covering all of the steps in the To Do list in detail later in this chapter.

- **Information Center**: This area connects you to the different resources available for finding more details on SBS features and any issues you might encounter. Links to information on Microsoft's web site abound, and you can also view help installed locally on your server and automatically start an online support request with Microsoft.

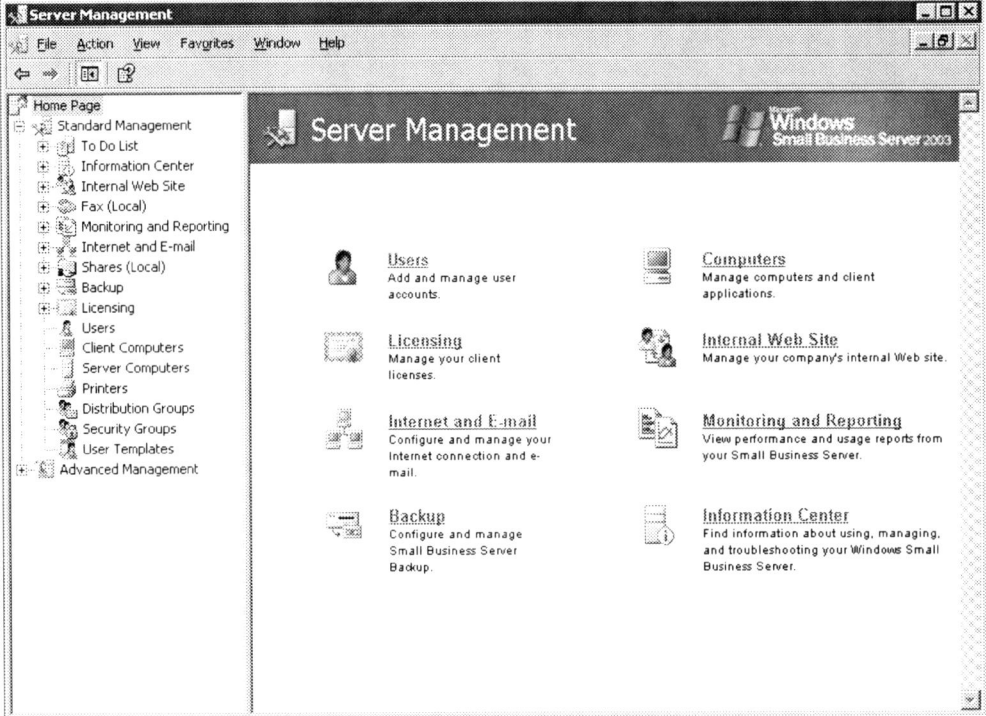

Figure 3-1. *The Server Management Console default view*

- **Internal Web Site**: This node exposes options to configure your Windows SharePoint Services web site. For more details on this node, consult Chapter 6, where you'll find an extensive discussion of the internal web site and instructions and advice on how to manage it.

- **Fax (Local)**: The location where you can manage the fax queue, configure cover pages and modem options for outbound faxing, and direct where inbound faxes are stored until your users retrieve them.

- **Monitoring and Reporting**: This area is Dashboard Central, where you can look at the performance, logs, and growth of your SBS server and the data stored thereon. I cover the reporting and monitoring features that SBS offers in depth in Chapter 10.

- **Internet and E-mail**: This area configures the routing, remote access, and basic Exchange features like outbound mail servers and the POP3 connectors. I cover most of the features available through this tab in Chapter 5, and I'll touch on some of the other features during the walkthrough of the To Do list in the section "Completing the To Do List" later in this chapter.

- **Shares (Local)**: Very simply, this node lists all of the folders shared out over the network on the SBS server. You can also use the View Connected Users feature in this node to look at who is currently logged on to your network, a useful feature if you need to take down the server for maintenance and must instruct all current users to log off.

- **Backup**: The Backup feature, controlled from this node, has been revamped to make it simpler to create a complete backup of your server, including all data and settings. I'll cover the features of this capability in Chapter 10.

- **Licensing**: Of course, licensing rears its ugly head again. It's a core component of SBS, but luckily you will only have to worry about it upon the initial installation of your SBS server and then only if you add computers to your network. The Licensing node shows you where your license situation currently stands, including how many licenses you have installed, the current "high water mark" for users, and the product ID.

- **Users**: This node shows the current users set up on your SBS network, with links to add more users and manage existing users (including options like group membership, permission to log on, Exchange mailbox properties, and so on). I'll cover user issues later in this chapter as we step through the To Do list.

- **Client Computers**: This node provides a link to view existing client computers on your network, set up new ones through the Setup Computer Wizard (SCW) that we'll see later in this chapter, provide and install applications for client computers, and add users to those computers.

- **Server Computers**: This node shows any servers on your network, including the SBS server itself. Recall from Chapter 1 that even though you are limited to one SBS server on your network, you can have any number of standalone, special-purpose servers (for instance, servers running your accounting software, or an additional file server). You can manage such computers from this node.

- **Printers**: From this node, you add and configure shared network printers and also manage a bit of the fax service functionality. There's more on printing in Chapter 4.

- **Distribution Groups**: These types of groups are very nifty for distributing information en masse to all employees in your business. By default, all users that you create on your SBS server are added to a distribution group named exactly what you entered in the Organization field during setup, minus the spaces. You can see other distribution groups on this node and add others as well.

- **Security Groups**: These types of groups simply contain members that have access to the same resource. However, note that in SBS 2003, by default you can send e-mail to security groups, making them both distribution AND security groups. Consult Chapter 4 for a detailed explanation of security groups and their purpose.

- **User Templates**: This is a fairly new feature of SBS that allows you to take a template user (an account whose ability to log in is disabled) and configure it exactly how you want it. Then, as you create new real users, you can base their configurations on the template user to automatically configure their accounts based on the template user's role. SBS comes with four by default, which are covered in detail a bit later in this chapter.

The Advanced Management Node

In the past, SBS users have been discouraged from being mechanics and diving under the hood of the product and configuring features and options using native tools. The management features of previous SBS releases have not been the most stable programs and mucking with configurations using other tools would leave them confused and unable to operate. However, Microsoft has devoted much effort in SBS 2003 to repairing the fragile nature of these tools so that while inexperienced administrators can continue to use the SBS wizards and setup tools, more experienced administrators and consultants can put their expertise to work and use native Windows Server 2003, Exchange, and ISA management consoles.

The Advanced Management node of the Server Management Console simply lets you view all of the standard management tools for the core components of SBS in one simple console. The view includes the following:

- Active Directory Users and Computers

- Group Policy Management

- Computer Management (Local)

- First Organization (Exchange)

- POP3 Connector Manager

- Terminal Services Configuration

- Internet Information Services

- Migrate Server Settings

One item of special interest is the last node, Migrate Server Settings. This is a wonderful tool that allows you to export server settings and later reimport them onto the same or a different server. I'll cover this tool in Chapter 10, but note for now that this is where the tool is located.

You'll see more of these native tools as we go through the remainder of the book and focus on each of the core applications in detail.

Completing the To Do List

The To Do list is most important when you finish the SBS setup process and first boot the server. You're prompted to do many things and to set a lot of options, but many of the actions you'll perform here will promulgate to the applications on the machine and make it much simpler to get up and running. The list comes complete with check boxes, which are stored with the list, so if you close it at the end of the day and reopen it the next, you remember which steps you have already completed. Figure 3-2 shows the To Do list.

It's also a very quick process to complete most of the items on the To Do list. Assuming that you have all hardware properly in place, your Internet connection has been installed and is ready for use, and your installation of the SBS server itself was clean and uneventful, you should allot approximately 90 minutes to fully complete the items on the To Do list. The most time-intensive tasks are creating user accounts and setting up client workstations.

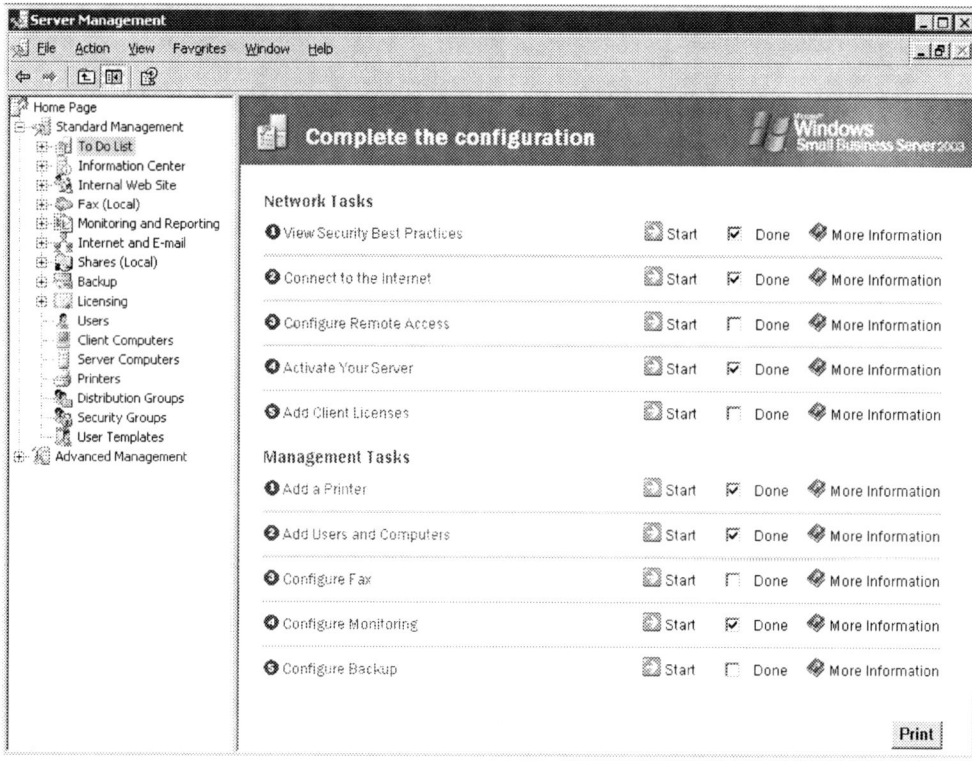

Figure 3-2. *The To Do list*

In this section, I will walk you through completing the items in the To Do list. But first, a warning:

■**Note** Always proceed through the To Do list in the order in which the items are presented to you. Most of the items have dependencies on features and configurations completed in earlier steps.

View Security Best Practices

Microsoft has placed a big emphasis on security of late, and in SBS there is no exception. The first step on the To Do list is to review a list of recommendations on secure configuration and behavior. The list is reproduced here, along with my commentary on what each item should signify to you:

- **Protecting your network from the Internet by using a firewall**: When you configure your Internet connection, the firewall configuration will automatically be created and deployed. You might also consider deploying a hardware firewall between your SBS server and your router or gateway to your Internet connection.

- **Configuring password policies**: User passwords are one of the weakest links to security on your network. When you begin adding users, SBS will prompt you to set a very restrictive password policy, which would require complex passwords with letters, numbers, and symbols and have a minimum length. I strongly suggest you heed the warning and set this policy: passwords are not the most secure way to authenticate users, and you want to make the process as trusted as possible and have the least possibility of cracking.

- **Configuring secure remote access to the network**: The hard work of this item is taken out of your hands when you run the Configure Remote Access Wizard, which is a part of the To Do list. The wizard will automatically lock down ports and set policies that require encryption, so you shouldn't have to worry about this step.

- **Renaming the administrator account**: This "best practice" as listed is dicey, in my opinion. A lot of software that runs on servers, including third-party backup and mail software, runs as the administrator account so it can access restricted places on your machine. By renaming your administrator account, you may break some of these services, and not all of them can be fixed—some use a hard-coded reference to the administrator account, and it is impossible to change that value to the new name of your account. Proceed with caution here, and if you decide to rename the administrator account, wait until you have fully completed all of the steps on the To Do list before proceeding.

- **Implementing an antivirus solution**: This is always a good idea. I've found the best solution so far, an SBS-specific antivirus program that scans files, folders, and even inbound and outbound Exchange e-mail, is from Trend Micro (`http://www.trendmicro.com`). However, keep in mind that Computer Associates, the manufacturer of the venerable eTrust Antivirus products, is coming out with an SBS-specific product later in 2005. Keep your eyes out for it.

- **Managing backups**: Part of the To Do list involves configuring the backup service, so you can consider this best practice followed.

- **Updating your software**: Before you even begin the To Do list, open a web browser on the SBS server machine and immediately visit Windows Update. (I prompted you to do this at the conclusion of Chapter 2.) *Do this now.* Download all of the updates available. Better yet, consider configuring Automatic Updates to automatically download fixes and patches from Microsoft and install them overnight—one less thing for you to remember, and one more thing to make your server more secure.

- **Running security tools**: There are tons of good books out there on Windows security and the tools available to evaluate the integrity of your systems. Start with Chapter 7 of this book, and then check out *Securing Windows Server 2003* from O'Reilly and *Hardening Windows*, by yours truly, from Apress as well. However, make sure you wait to run these tools until after you finish all of the items on the To Do list.

- **Granting access permissions**: This is covered in detail in Chapter 4, so consult there in this book for the complete story on how to assign permissions on files and folders to users. This isn't a step that is required of you to complete the To Do list.

- **Educating users**: This is one of the most important but least followed best practices. A maxim of computer security is that your users will almost always be inconvenienced by increased security. Whether it's that they need to remember more and longer passwords, or if they need to use multiple accounts to access resources securely, it will seem to them that they are always jumping through hoops for no apparent reason. An important step to integrating security into your network is to provide your users with that reasoning: tell them why the "hoop jumping" is necessary, show them the risks that exist, and educate them on how you are helping to mitigate those risks. It won't necessarily make their lives easier, but it will at a minimum coax them to accept more stringent security procedures as a part of their daily professional life.

- **Not using your Windows Small Business Server as a workstation**: It's important to think of your SBS server as a dedicated machine that is ONLY for providing network services. If you install client-oriented software on the server machine, you open up the potential not only for software compatibility problems that can take hours to troubleshoot, but for security problems as well—it requires you to keep on top of that many more products and their associated security vulnerabilities.

- **Physically securing the server**: Always keep your server behind a locked door and make sure you know everyone who has a key really has a significant purpose for getting in the room. If your location doesn't easily allow for a separate server room, at least keep the keyboard for your server machine locked, put the machine in an inconspicuous place, and don't draw attention to it.

- **Limiting user disk space**: By default, SBS and Windows assign disk quotas to your users, so this step is completed when you create users through the Add Users and Computers Wizard in the To Do list. Note that manually creating users through the Active Directory Users and Computers interface does not automatically set this quota; you'll need to do so manually, and the procedure for this is covered in Chapter 4.

- **Keeping up-to-date on security information**: Head over to `http://www.microsoft.com/security` after you finish the To Do list and subscribe to all of the security notifications available there.

- **Auditing failed logon events and account lockouts**: See Chapter 7 for more information on this.

- **Using monitoring tools**: Chapter 10 is devoted to monitoring and reporting tools, and you configure these tools initially as a part of the To Do list.

Connect to the Internet

Microsoft has done a lot of work to make connecting your SBS server to the Internet and setting up Exchange a very simple task. In SBS 2003, you'll see a streamlined Configure E-mail and Internet Connection Wizard (CEICW) that takes care of what once was a huge task that required hours of consultant time in just about 15 minutes, if you know the right answers.

Let's step through the wizard and see how it works.

1. Click Connect to the Internet in the To Do list.

2. The welcome screen will appear. Click Next to move on.

3. The Connection Type screen appears, as shown in Figure 3-3. Select whether your Internet connection is based on broadband or dial-up. I'll assume you have a broadband connection, as dial-up is increasingly rare.

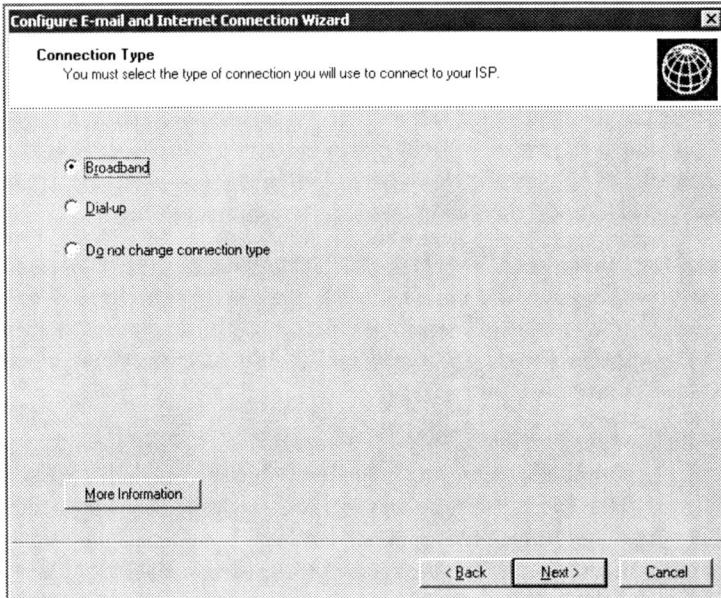

Figure 3-3. *The Connection Type screen*

4. The Broadband Connection screen appears, as shown in Figure 3-4. Here, tell SBS how your server connects to the router—is it through a hardware router that actually has an address on your local network, a direct connection to your server machine itself, or a connection that requires the use of a username and password in order for it to work? Select the appropriate option, and click Next. (My network uses a local router device, so I'll choose that option.)

5. The Router Connection screen appears, which you can see in Figure 3-5. Here, specify the DNS servers your connection should use—this information should be provided by your ISP. Also, enter the local address of the router device that connects your network to the Internet. More than likely, this address will begin with 10.0.x.x, 172.16.x.x, or 192.168.x.x. Finally, check the box if you do not have two local network adapters in your server machine and thus use the same connection to access resources on your local network and remote sites on the Internet. Click Next when you're done.

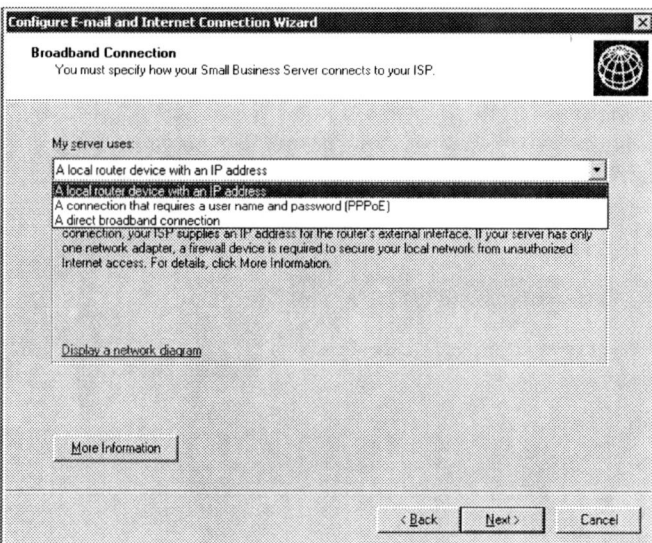

Figure 3-4. *The Broadband Connection screen*

Note When you select the option I mentioned on the previous page, you'll be presented with a warning that tells you that without two network adapters, SBS is not able to set up a firewall that will protect your server. If your router device does not include a firewall feature, you'll need to deploy a firewall in between your SBS server and the router. Fortunately, if you purchase a UPnP-compliant firewall device, Windows can configure it automatically for you. Click OK to acknowledge the warning.

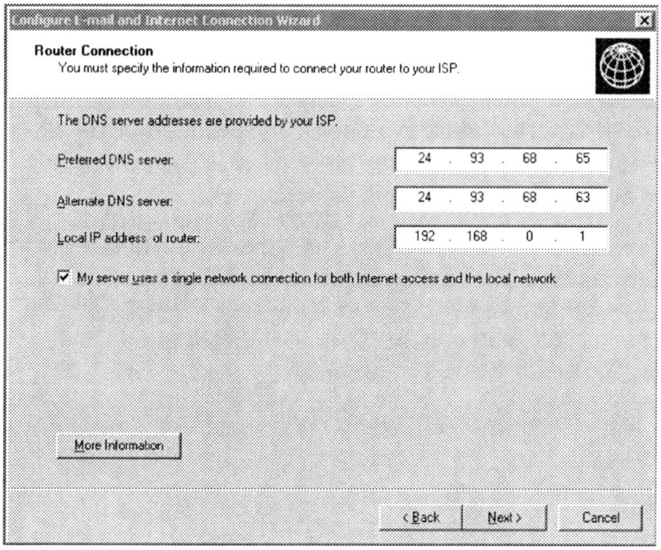

Figure 3-5. *The Router Connection screen*

6. The Web Services Configuration screen appears, which you can see in Figure 3-6. On this screen, you can specify which web sites hosted on your SBS server should be available to the public. You can choose from webmail, the Remote Web Workplace (see Chapter 9), performance and usage reports, e-mail from mobile phone, the full Outlook client from remote locations, your Windows SharePoint Services site, or the business web site that you may set up. Check or uncheck the appropriate boxes, and then click Next.

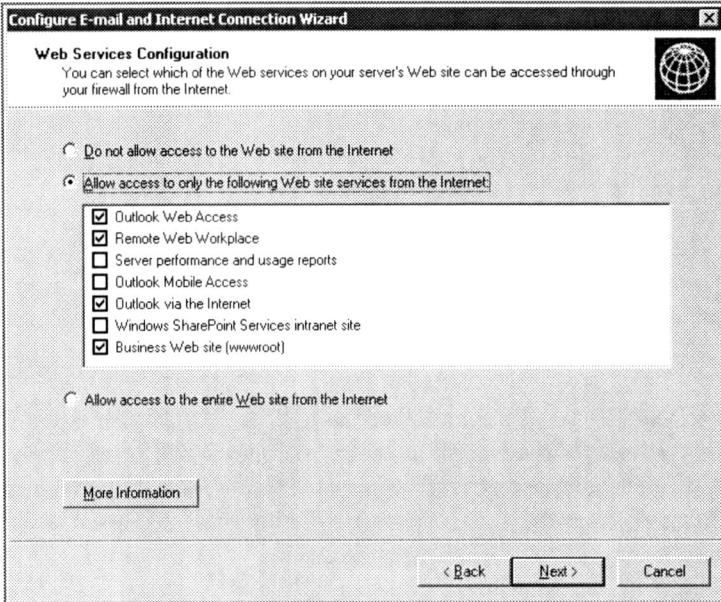

Figure 3-6. *The Web Services Configuration screen*

7. The Web Server Certificate screen appears, as seen in Figure 3-7. This will allow the identity of your server to be verified when clients connect to it over the Internet using SSL-encrypted HTTP. You'll need to select the first option and then enter your full Internet domain name with the server name (for instance, Sbsserver.yourbusiness.com) to generate the certificate correctly. Enter the name, and then click Next.

8. The Internet E-mail screen appears, as shown in Figure 3-8. Choose here whether to let Exchange handle your e-mail (enable it to allow Exchange to send and receive e-mail on behalf of your organization; disable it to leave it up to the client workstation to do so). I recommend enabling this setting, as you unlock a world of features and resources that you'll see in Chapter 6. Click Next to continue.

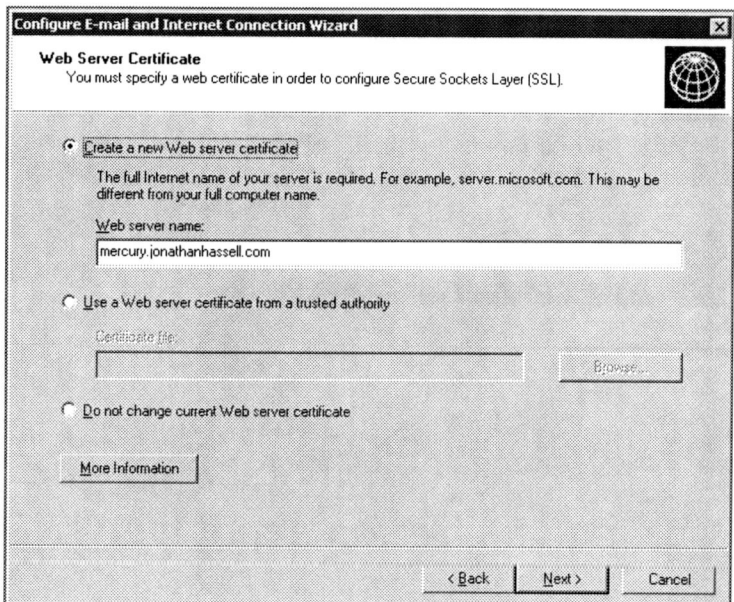

Figure 3-7. *The Web Server Certificate screen*

Figure 3-8. *The Internet E-mail screen*

9. The E-mail Delivery Method screen appears, as shown in Figure 3-9. On this screen, choose whether Exchange should personally deliver mail to your recipients or if e-mail should be forwarded first to your ISP for delivery. Either method will work; however, if you do not have a dedicated, "business"-level connection from your ISP, I recommend setting forwarding e-mail to your ISP's outbound SMTP server. They should provide you with this server name. Once you've selected the appropriate option, click Next to continue.

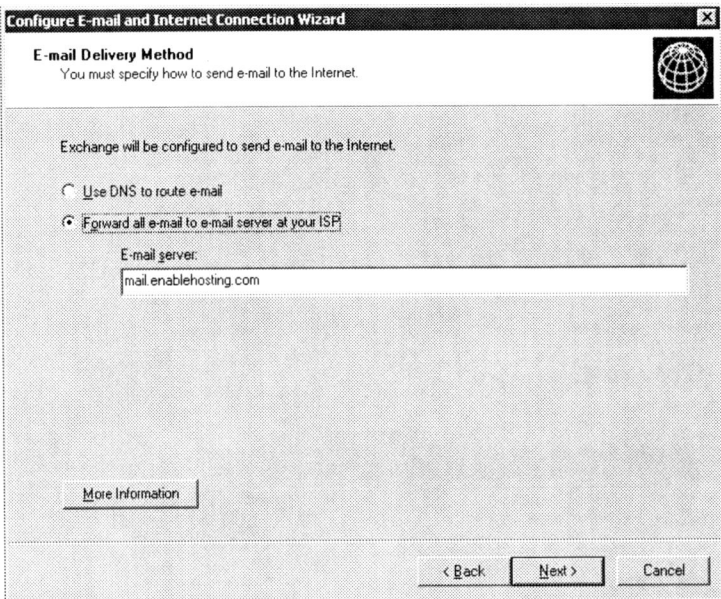

Figure 3-9. *E-mail Delivery Method screen*

10. The E-mail Retrieval Method screen appears, which you can see in Figure 3-10. If you plan on allowing e-mail to be sent directly to your server (and thus, directly to Exchange), select the Use Exchange option and click the first radio button. However, if your ISP receives your e-mail and queues it into one big batch for your SBS server to retrieve (this requires a separate service for you to arrange called backup MX service), select the second radio button, the name of your ISP's inbound mail server, and which type of signal to send. Your ISP will provide the type of signal and the server name. If you have a normal hosting account with an ISP and want to continue to use POP3-style mailboxes and download those to the Exchange Server, then select the first check box entitled "Use the Microsoft Connector for POP3 Mailboxes." Click Next to continue. (I'll assume that e-mail is being sent to Exchange in one manner or another, as the POP3 Connector option is not in very wide use.)

11. The E-mail Domain Name screen appears. Enter the domain name you have registered that should appear on all outbound mail, and then click Next. This does not have to be the same domain name under which the server operates. For example, your server might be operating as longbusinessname.biz, but you might want your e-mail addresses to be based on shortbiz.com.

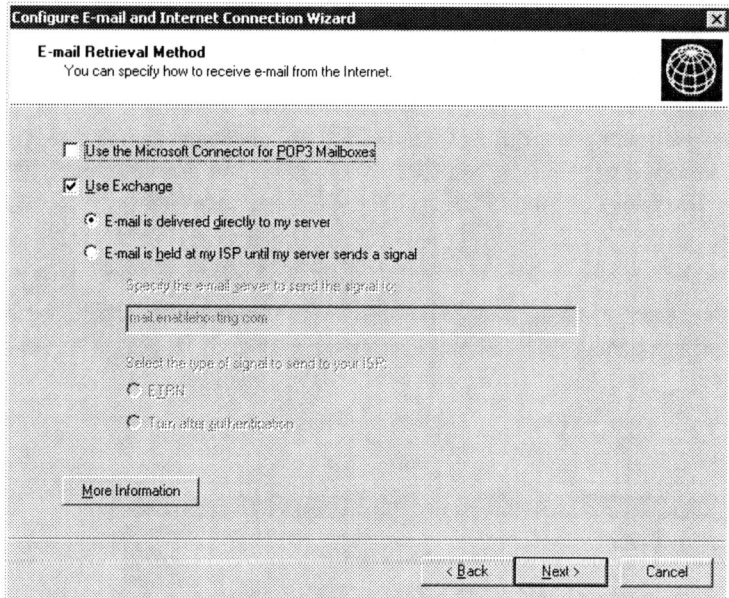

Figure 3-10. *The E-mail Retrieval Method screen*

12. The Mail Schedule screen appears, as shown in Figure 3-11. If you use the POP3 Connector or if you send a trigger signal to your ISP to allow inbound e-mail to be delivered to Exchange, you can choose to schedule for these operations. This can be as frequently as every 15 minutes. Select the appropriate option, and then click Next.

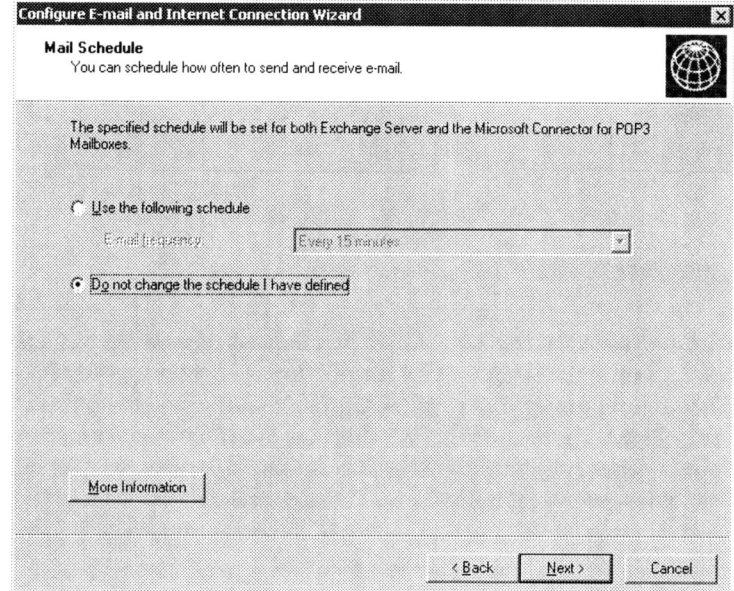

Figure 3-11. *The Mail Schedule screen*

13. The Remove E-mail Attachments screen appears, seen in Figure 3-12. Here, choose the types of e-mail attachments that will be scrubbed by Exchange before they ever hit your users' e-mail inboxes. A complete list of the attachments blocked by default is in Chapter 6. You can also choose to save the scrubbed attachments in a secured folder on the server itself, so if any legitimate files with these extensions are removed, they aren't permanently deleted. If you regularly exchange files with an extension listed here, unclick its check box; otherwise, accept the list and click Next.

Note In the 18 months that I have been running SBS 2003 so far, I have not once (that's right—zero times) received a legitimate attachment with the default file extensions that are blocked. That's just a data point.

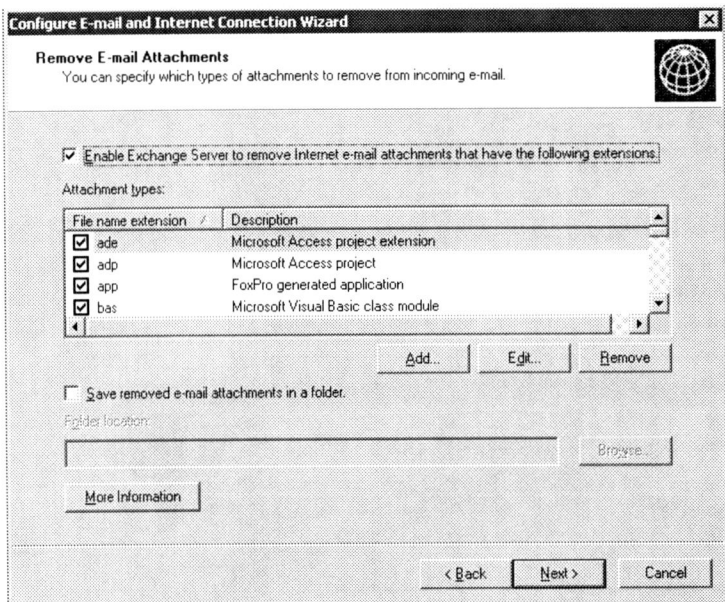

Figure 3-12. *The Remove E-mail Attachments screen*

14. Finally, you'll come to the conclusion of the wizard. Review the settings listed there, and then click the link at the bottom of the window to save the settings to a file—this way, if you have to run through the wizard again, you'll know the settings previously used. Then, click Finish and wait while the SBS server machine trundles and configures your Internet connection and Exchange the way you specified. This can take up to ten minutes, although five minutes is a pretty good expectation.

And now you've finished configuring your server for Internet access and e-mail.

Configure Remote Access

By configuring remote access to your server, you enable secure access from outside your local network to resources hosted on your SBS server—and potentially on other servers you might add to your network in the future. Let's get started configuring this functionality.

1. Click Configure Remote Access in the To Do list.

2. The welcome screen for the wizard will appear. Click Next to move on to the first step.

3. The Remote Access Method screen will appear, as shown in Figure 3-13. Here, you can specify the methods through which clients will connect to your server. I recommend enabling VPN access, as this is the most common and most compatible way of offering remote access. Click Next to continue.

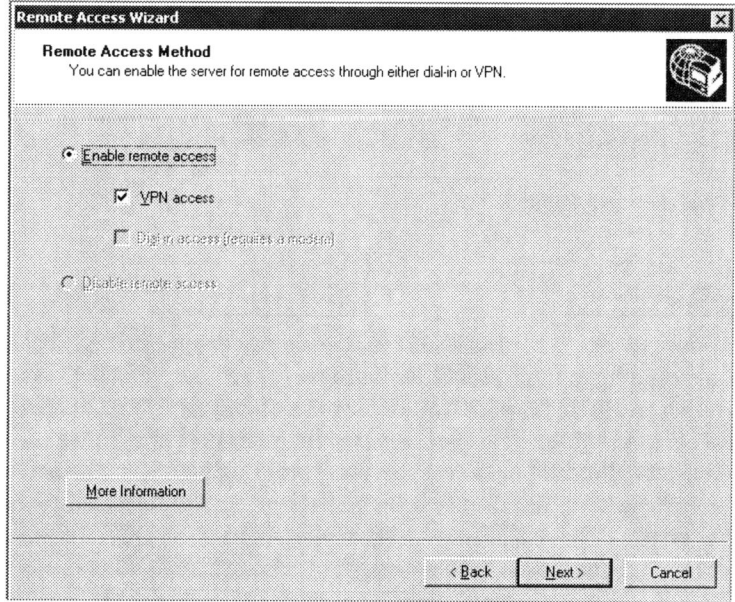

Figure 3-13. *The Remote Access Method screen*

4. The VPN Server Name screen will appear, as shown in Figure 3-14. Here, simply enter the full server and domain name as you entered during the CEICW. Click Next when you've entered the name.

5. The final screen of the wizard appears. Confirm your settings, and then click the link at the bottom of the window to save the results of the wizard to a file, much like you did at the end of the previous section. Then, click Finish. Your remote access settings will be deployed.

You now have configured remote access for your server—a much simpler task than configuring Internet access and e-mail handling.

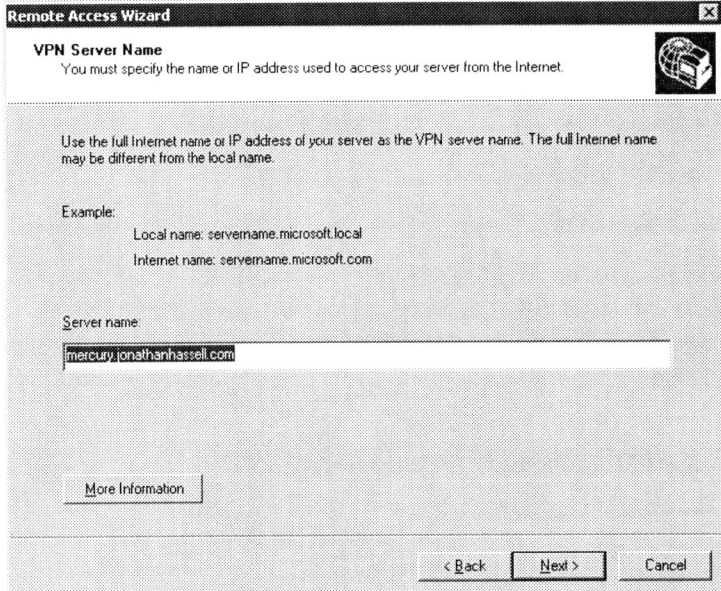

Figure 3-14. *The VPN Server Name screen*

Activate Your Server

Activation is a pesky but required part of any SBS installation. Microsoft, worried about the pirating and illegal distribution of its products, has introduced the concept of activation into most of its popular products. In this case, activation involves taking the CD keys you used to install the product, a couple of unique numbers generated from numeric addresses of your hardware, and sending it to Microsoft to store. (This is done during the first activation of a CD key.) Upon subsequent activations, the key generated during activation is compared with the key Microsoft has on file. If the two differ, it is assumed that the media is being used for an installation on different hardware, so activation will fail, since Microsoft thinks you're installing multiple copies of SBS when you're only licensed for one. However, if you upgrade your hardware and then need to reinstall for one reason or another, you might trip up the activation scheme. You'll need to call Microsoft to get them to activate the product. It's in reality not a big deal, but it's a pain.

To activate, simply click the Activate Your Server link in the To Do list. That's all there is to it.

Add Client Licenses

Adding licenses to your server is another very simple matter. Recall from Chapter 1 that all available SBS packages, no matter whether it's the standard or the premium edition, come bundled with five client access licenses (CALs). These are automatically added to your server during the setup process, so if you only require five licenses, you can tick this step off and move down the list to adding a printer.

However, if you require more than five licenses, you'll need to click the link the start the Add License Wizard. You'll need to first purchase the licenses, either from a reseller or

from Microsoft directly at the Microsoft Product Information Center, located at `http://
www.microsoft.com/windowsserver2003/sbs/howtobuy/default.mspx`. The licenses come with
codes, which you will input into the server to activate them. Click Next off the introductory
screen, and then accept the license agreement and click Next. You'll need to tell the wizard if
you are connected to the Internet directly or if you need a telephone connection to activate
the licenses. Click Next after you've made the appropriate choice.

At this point, you're prompted to enter the license codes, which look a lot like CD keys
that you use to install Microsoft software. Once you enter the key and click Add, the license
code will display in the bottom portion of the window, along with the number of licenses
associated with that code. Click Next once you've finished entering your product keys, and
then the licenses will be activated over the Internet. At that point, you're finished.

You can return to this wizard anytime and continue adding licenses until you reach the
maximum number—this is 75 licenses, as discussed in Chapter 1—and then you'll need to
look at upgrading to the individual core products.

Add a Printer

The Add a Printer process is relatively straightforward and involves telling Windows where
your printer is, what kind of printer it is, and how it will be shared over the network. In this
example, I'll assume you have an HP LaserJet printer that you want to share among all client
computers connected to the network.

1. Click Configure Remote Access in the To Do list.

2. The welcome screen for the wizard will appear. Click Next to move on to the first step.

3. The Local or Network Printer screen will appear. Choose whether the printer is local to
   the server (that is, if the printer is directly attached to a port on the server machine) or
   if it is somehow attached to the network. You can also choose to let setup try to detect
   the kind of printer you have, although I suggest leaving this box unchecked. Click Next
   to continue.

4. The Select a Printer Port screen appears. Choose the port in the top list. The most common port for printers is either the parallel port, known as LPT1:, or a USB port. Click
   Next to continue.

5. The Install Printer Software screen appears. Choose the make and model of your
   printer from the list. If it does not appear, insert the disk that came bundled with your
   printer package, and click the Have Disk button to choose the appropriate driver.
   Otherwise, click Next to continue.

6. The Name Your Printer screen appears. Enter a name for the printer, and select whether
   it will be the default printer for your server. The latter setting applies only to applications running on the server—that is, if you were browsing a page in Internet Explorer on
   the server itself and wanted to print the page, the default printer would come up first.
   It does not affect your client workstations' settings. Click Next to continue.

7. The Printer Sharing screen appears. Type a short name for the share that this printer
   will have. (See Chapter 4 for more information on printer sharing and how it works.)
   This name must be no longer than 15 characters. Click Next.

8. The Location and Comment page appears. This information will appear on your users' workstations if they try to find a printer using the Find facility on the Start menu. You can enter the physical location of the printer ("in the closet") and a comment ("relatively slow printer; try another for fast black-and-white printing") if it will help you. Click Next.

9. You'll then come to the final screen in the wizard. Confirm your settings, and then click Finish.

Your printer is now installed and ready for use both on your server machine itself and over the network. Now, let's add some user accounts and workstations to take advantage of the printer.

Add Users and Computers

Adding users and computers is probably the most in-depth task on the To Do list, if for no other reason than it can get quite repetitive to run through the wizard for all of your users. However, it's not difficult, and SBS makes it easy for you by providing four preconfigured templates that correspond to different levels of authorization and access:

- **User template**: Users under this template have limited abilities to access resources on the network, being restricted to network printers, shared folders, fax devices, e-mail, and the Internet. All other resources, including management abilities, are off limits.

- **Mobile user template**: This template builds on the user template and adds the permission to connect to the server using direct dial-in to the machine or through a VPN connection to the server.

- **Power user template**: This template builds on the two previous templates and adds the ability to manage users, groups, printers, shared folders, and faxes. Power users also get the ability to use Remote Desktop Connection to log onto the SBS server itself, but they cannot sit down at the server console and log on.

- **Administrator template**: Users in this template can do anything on your SBS server machine or network.

Note By default, user quotas for all templates but the administrator template are capped at 1024 MB (effectively, 1 GB) and a warning is sent at 900 MB alerting the user that he is close to reaching his disk space limit.

Let's get started.

1. Click Configure Remote Access in the To Do list.

2. The welcome screen for the wizard will appear. Click Next to move on to the first step.

3. The Template Selection screen appears, as seen in Figure 3-15. Choose the appropriate template as described previously, and then click Next.

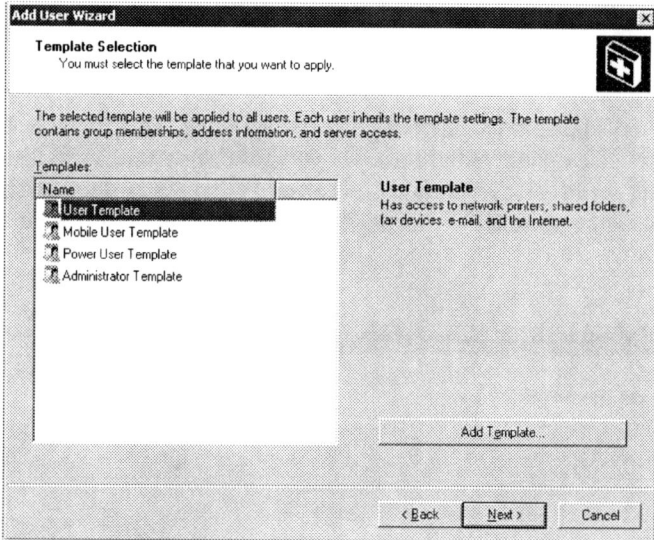

Figure 3-15. *The Template Selection screen*

4. The User Information screen appears. Click the Add button to add users who will fall under this template. A dialog box appears, as shown in Figure 3-16, where you enter the user's details, like first and last name, telephone numbers, e-mail alias, and the initial password for the account. When you're finished, click OK. You can continue adding all users who should be based on the template you selected in step 3. Once you've entered the user or users, click Next.

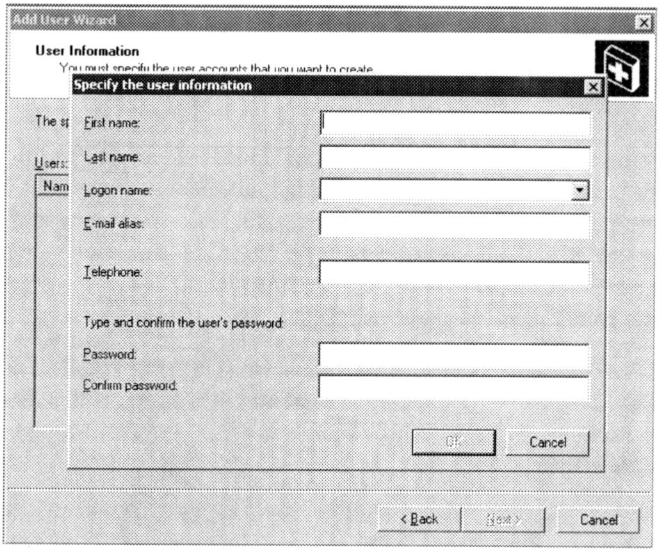

Figure 3-16. *Adding a user*

5. The Set Up Client Computers screen appears. Here, tell SBS if you intend to configure the client computer at this time, or if you'd like to bypass this. In this example, I'll continue adding computers, so select the first option and click Next.

6. The Client Computer Names screen appears, as shown in Figure 3-17. On this screen, you enter the names of the client computers that you'd like to set up. The names by default are based off the user's logon name. You can add other computers to the list by entering a name of the computer and clicking the Add button. When you're satisfied with the list, click Next.

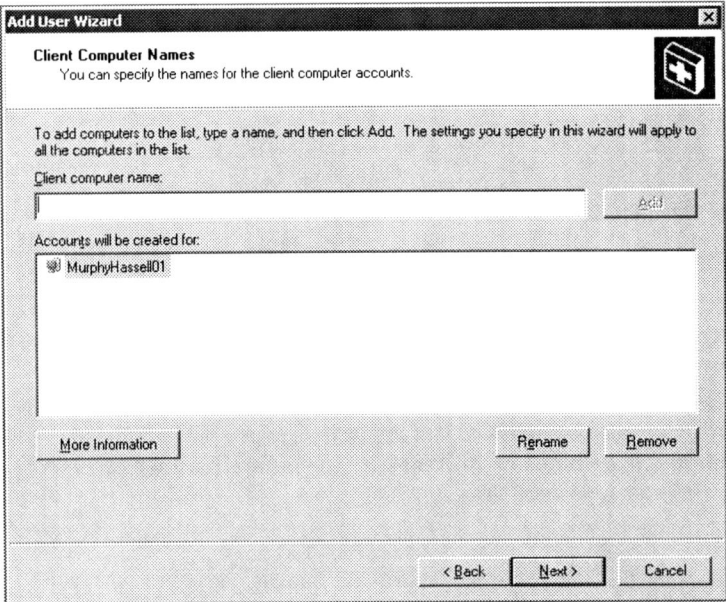

Figure 3-17. *The Client Computer Names screen*

7. The Client Applications screen appears, as shown in Figure 3-18. Select the applications that should be installed on the computer. By default, you can select from the latest version of Internet Explorer, Outlook, and the Shared Fax Client software. You can also select whether to let the user decide when she first logs on which software should be installed from this list or whether the account should be logged off once the software finishes installing. Click Next to continue.

8. The Mobile Client and Offline Use screen appears. Check whether to install Connection Manager, which is useful is you have a mobile computer like a laptop with a user based on the Mobile User template, or ActiveSync, which is essential software for users with PocketPC devices. Click Next.

9. You come to the final screen of the wizard. Confirm the settings as listed, and then click the link at the bottom of the window and save the settings as a file for future reference. Then, click Finish to complete the deployment.

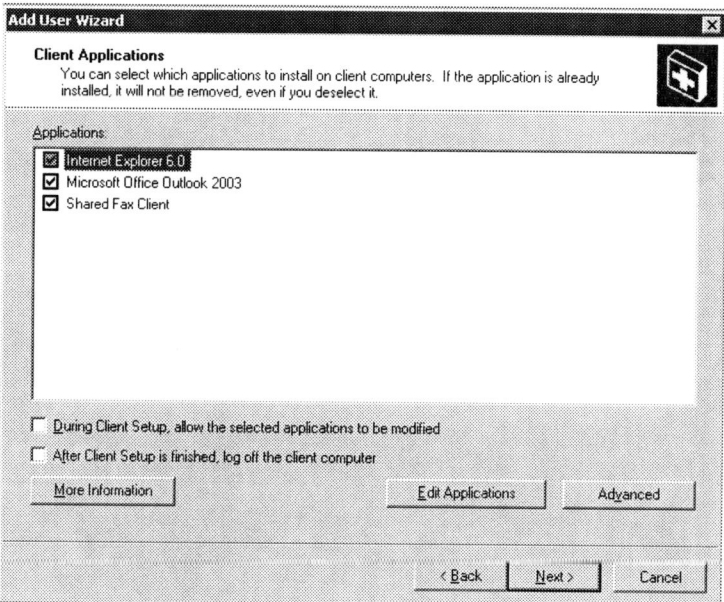

Figure 3-18. *The Client Applications screen*

Deploying the Client Computers

All that remains in this task is to actually physically connect the client computer to the network and then run a simple installation procedure from the client. At the client workstation, get it up and running and connected to the network. Then, from a web browser running on the client computer, surf to `http://sbsservername/ConnectComputer` and replace "sbsservername" with the computer name of your SBS server. The installation will commence, the computer will join the SBS network, and the necessary applications will be installed.

Conclusion

In this chapter, we've looked at the tools SBS provides to set up both the server and client machines, and we've stepped through the To Do list. At this point, your server is set up, your clients are connected to the network, and you are now in a position to delve into the core SBS components (Windows Server 2003, Exchange Server 2003, and so on) and learn about them in detail.

CHAPTER 4

Exploring Windows Server 2003

BEGINNER SBS ADMINISTRATOR ■ ADVANCED SBS ADMINISTRATOR ■ EXPERIENCED CONSULTANT

In the previous chapter, you learned the "SBS way" of administering your server: using the Management Console, the wizards contained therein, and the easy interface to get to the basic options for your server.

But there is more to SBS than meets the eye. As you learned in Chapter 1, SBS contains the industrial-strength Windows Server 2003 operating system, which has a ton of features that you can take advantage of in your business. In this chapter, I'll discuss some of these features and go beyond the simple interface of the Management Console.

Let's begin.

File and Print Services

One of the most common uses of Windows Server 2003 is to provide file and print services to a network of users and computers. While SBS 2003 provides a good interface for getting these services configured and operational, there may be instances in which you don't want to use the interface (for example, as a consultant you may want to customize the options for a file share, or you may be interested in configuring custom printing options for a new, expensive color printer). In this section, I'll step through file and print sharing.

Manually Creating a Share

Creating a share manually involves specifying a folder to share to other users, giving the share a name, and determining the users and groups that should have access to that folder. Only members of the Administrators, Server Operators, or Power Users groups can share folders by default, but you can also configure network-based Group Policy settings to restrict other users and groups from doing so as well. Shares created using Windows Server 2003 are by default configured to allow all users read-only access. This is a result of the new security consciousness at Microsoft; in previous releases, all users were allowed full control of a share by default, which made for some sticky situations on machines that were compromised.

Share permissions are different from file- and folder-level permissions, which are more granular. File- and folder-level permissions (also known as NTFS permissions) are covered later in this chapter.

There are a few ways to create a share, of which I'll profile two here: using the Share a Folder wizard, and using the Windows Explorer GUI.

To share a folder using a wizard:

1. Launch the Share a Folder wizard, which can be found on the Shares node of the Server Management console.

2. On the Folder Path page, select the folder for sharing. Click Browse to access a directory tree. Then, click Next.

3. The Name, Description, and Settings page appears. Enter the following data for the new shared folder:

   • In Share name (a required field), type the name you want to use for the shared resource. This should be short and descriptive, like "ACCTG" or "SCRATCHPAD," so that users can see quickly what a share's purpose is.

   • In Description (an optional field), type a description of the shared resource. Descriptions can assist you, as an administrator, in seeing the purpose of a share, and it can also clue your users in to the point of a share. Use something clear, like "Accounting documents for Q3 1999" or "Inactive Proposals."

   • In Offline setting, specify how you want to make the contents of the shared folder available to users when they are not connected to the network. Click the button to make further tuning adjustments. The three options are fairly self-explanatory: the first option gives the user control over which documents are available offline, the second makes all documents available, and the third prevents any documents from being used offline. Note that selecting the Optimized for performance box automatically caches documents so that users can run them locally, which is helpful for busy application servers since it lowers overall traffic to and from the server.

4. After you finish, click Next.

5. On the Permissions page, configure the permissions for the shared folder. Share permissions apply only to users who access the share from the network; users at the console will still be able to look at the contents of the share unless file-level NTFS permissions restrict them from doing so. "All users have read-only access" means that both administrators and normal users will only be able to read files from this share; no writing or modification is allowed. "Administrators have full access; other users have read-only access" means that members of the Administrators group retain full control over the share, including the ability to set new NTFS file permissions; everyone else only has read privileges. This is the best setting for a share that contains a program to be run over a network. "Administrators have full access; other users have read and write access" means that all users can read and write. Only members of the Administrators group retain the ability to change NTFS file permissions, however. Finally, "Use custom share and folder permissions" means that you can assign specific permissions and deny permissions to users and groups.

6. Click Finish when you're done.

The wizard completes by showing the Sharing was Successful page. You can share another folder immediately by clicking the "When I click Close, run the wizard again to share another folder" check box. Click Close to exit.

To share a folder using Windows Explorer:

1. Find the folder you want to share, and right-click it.

2. Select Sharing and Security from the context menu.

3. Fill in the form as presented.

4. In Share name (a required field), type the name you want to use for the shared resource. This should be short and descriptive.

5. In Description (an optional field), type a description of the shared resource. Descriptions can assist you, as an administrator, in seeing the purpose of a share, and it can also clue your users in to the point of a share.

6. In User Limit, enter the maximum number of users that can simultaneously connect to this share, or select Maximum allowed to permit as many connections as your OS license provisions.

7. Click the Permissions button to tune the restrictions users have on this share. On that screen, click Add to select the users to whom the permissions you assign will apply, and then click their names in the top pane and select the appropriate permissions using the check boxes in the bottom pane. Click OK when done.

8. Click the Offline Settings button to adjust the settings for how offline files are used for this share (see the descriptions earlier in step 6), and then click OK.

9. Click OK to finish sharing the folder.

Creating a Hidden Share

You may need to share a resource but not make it publicly known. For example, the Payroll department may need their own file share, but the rest of the company doesn't require access to it, and in the interests of confidentiality, you may want to hide it from public display. You can do this by typing $ as the last character of the shared resource name. Users can map a drive to this shared resource by naming it explicitly (including the $ sign appended to the end), but the share is hidden in Explorer, in My Computer on the remote computer, and in the net view command on the remote computer. Of course, you can also set permissions on hidden shares to further protect them, too.

Publishing Shares to Active Directory

By publishing the name and purpose of a share to Active Directory, you allow your users to use the Find command on their client desktops to find remote shares based on their identifier or description—handy for using a new piece of software that's simply being deployed on a network, or equally handy for retrieving an electronic PowerPoint presentation that might have been given earlier in the day. Note that you must use a domain administrator or enterprise administrator account to publish a share to Active Directory.

To publish:

1. Open Active Directory Users and Computers.

2. Right-click the appropriate organizational unit (OU).

3. Select Shared Folder from the New menu.

4. Enter a name and description of the share, and click Finish.

The share has now been introduced into the directory.

NTFS File and Folder Permissions

One of the most dreaded and tedious but most necessary tasks of system administration, file-and folder-level permissions are significant in protecting data from unauthorized use on your network. SBS 2003 does a pretty good job of hiding this complexity from you, but if you are at all interested in moving to the next level of system administration, one of the core elements of Windows that you'll need to understand is file and folder permissions.

If you have ever worked with UNIX permissions, you know how difficult they are to understand and set: complex CHMOD-based commands with numbers that represent bits of permission signatures—it's so easy to get lost in the confusion. Windows Server 2003, on the other hand, provides a remarkably robust and complete set of permissions, more so than any common UNIX or Linux variety available today. It's also true that no one would argue how much simpler setting permissions in Windows is than setting them in any other operating system. That's not to say, however, that Windows permissions are a cinch to grasp: there's quite a bit to them.

Standard and Special Permissions

Windows supports two different kinds of permissions: standard and special. Standard permissions are often sufficient to be applied to files and folders on a disk, whereas special permissions break standard permissions down into finer combinations and allow more control over who is allowed to do what functions to an object on a disk. Table 4-1 describes the standard permissions available in Windows.

Table 4-1. *Windows Server 2003 Standard Permissions*

Type	Description
Read (R)	Allows user or group to read the file.
Write (W)	Allows user or group to write to the contents of a file or folder and also create new files and folders.
Read & Execute (RX)	Allows user or group to read attributes of a file or folder, view its contents, and read files within a folder. Files inside folders with RX rights inherit the right onto themselves.
List Folder Contents (L)	Similar to RX, but files within a folder with L rights will not inherit RX rights. New files, however, automatically get RX permissions.
Modify (M)	Allows user or group to read, write, execute, and delete.
Full Control (F)	Similar to M, but also allows user or group to take ownership and change permissions. Users or groups can delete files and subfolders within a folder if F rights are applied to that folder.

There are a few key points to understanding how permissions work:

File permissions always take precedence over folder permissions. If users can execute a program in a folder, they can do so even if they don't have RX permissions on the folder in which that program resides. Similarly, users can read a file for which they explicitly have permission, even if that file is in a folder for which they have no permission, by simply knowing the location of that file. For example, you can hide a file listing employee Social Security numbers in a protected folder in Payroll to which user Mark has no folder permissions. However, if you explicitly give Mark R rights on that file, then by knowing the full path to the file, he can open the file from a command line or from the Run command on the Start menu.

Permissions are cumulative: they "add up" based on the overall permissions a user gets as a result of his total group memberships. Deny permissions ALWAYS trump Allow permissions. This even applies if a user is added to a group that is denied access to a file or folder that the user was previously allowed to access through his other memberships.

There are 14 default special permissions, shown in Table 4-2. The table also shows how these default special permissions correlate to the standard permissions discussed earlier.

Table 4-2. *Windows Server 2003 Special Permissions*

Special Permission	R	W	RX	L	M	F
Traverse Folder/Execute File			X	X	X	X
List Folder/Read Data	X		X	X	X	X
Read Attributes	X		X	X	X	X
Read Extended Attributes	X		X	X	X	X
Create Files/Write Data		X			X	X
Create Folders/Append Data		X			X	X
Write Attributes		X			X	X
Write Extended Attributes		X			X	X
Delete Subfolders and Files						X
Delete					X	X
Read Permissions	X		X	X	X	X
Change Permissions						X
Take Ownership						X

The default special permissions are further described in the following list:

- **Traverse Folder/Execute File**: Traverse Folder indicates the ability to access a folder nested within a tree even if parent folders in that tree deny a user access to the contents of those folders. Execute File indicates the ability to run a program.

- **List Folder/Read Data**: List Folder indicates the ability to see file and folder names within a folder, and Read Data indicates the ability to open and view a file.

- **Read Attributes**: Indicates the ability to view basic attributes of an object (read-only, system, archive, and hidden).

- **Read Extended Attributes**: Indicates the ability to view the extended attributes of an object—for example, summary, author, title, and so on for a Word document. These attributes will vary from program to program.

- **Create Files/Write Data**: Create Files indicates the ability to create new objects within a folder; Write Data lets a user overwrite an existing file. This does NOT allow the user to add data to existing objects in the folder.

- **Create Folders/Append Data**: Create Folders indicates the ability to nest folders. Append Data allows the user to add data to an existing file, but not delete data within that file, or delete the file itself.

- **Write Attributes**: Allows a change to the basic attributes for a file.

- **Write Extended Attributes**: Allows a change to the extended attributes of a file.

- **Delete Subfolders and Files**: Allows a user to delete the contents of a folder whether or not any individual file or folder within the folder in question explicitly grants or denies the Delete permission to a user.

- **Delete**: Allows you to delete a single file or folder, but not other files or folders within that folder.

- **Read Permissions**: Indicates the ability to view NTFS permissions on an object, but not to change them.

- **Change Permissions**: Indicates the ability to both view and change NTFS permissions on an object.

- **Take Ownership**: Grants permission to take ownership of a file or folder, which inherently allows the ability to change permissions on an object. This is granted to administrator-level users by default.

Setting Permissions

To set NTFS permissions on a file or folder:

1. Open My Computer or Explorer and navigate to the file or folder on which you want to set permissions.

2. Right-click the file or folder, and select Properties.

3. Navigate to the Security tab.

4. In the top pane, add the users and groups for whom you want to set permissions. Then click each item, and in the bottom pane, grant or disallow the appropriate permissions. Figure 4-1 shows the process of assigning write rights to user Lisa Johnson for a specific folder.

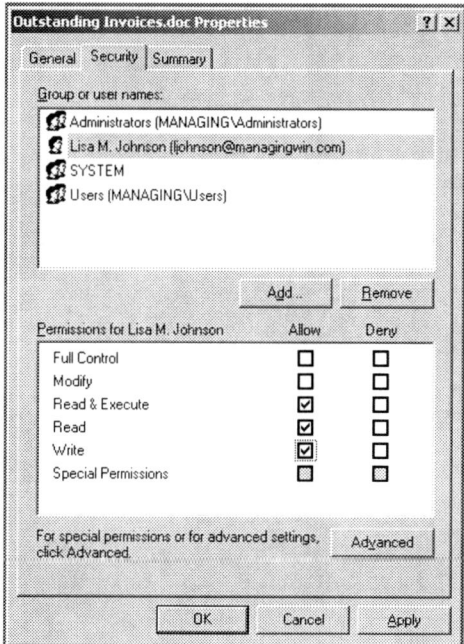

Figure 4-1. *Granting permissions on a folder to a user*

If a check box under Allow or Deny appears gray, this signifies two things: that the permissions indicated are inherited from a parent object (I discuss more about inheritance in the next section), or that there are further special permissions defined that cannot be logically displayed in the basic Security tab user interface. To review and modify these special permissions, simply click the Advanced button. On this screen, by using the Add button, you can create your own special permissions other than those installed by default with Windows Server 2003. You can also view how permissions will flow down a tree by configuring a permission to only affect the current folder, all files and subfolders, or some combination thereof.

Inheritance and Ownership

By default, permissions also migrate from the top-down in a process known as inheritance. This allows files and folders created within already existing folders to have a set of permissions automatically assigned to them. For example, if a folder has RX rights set, and you create another subfolder within that folder, the new subfolder will automatically receive RX rights. You can view the inheritance tree by clicking the Advanced button on the Security tab of any file or folder. This will bring up the screen shown in Figure 4-2, which clearly indicates the origin of rights inheritance in the Inherited From column.

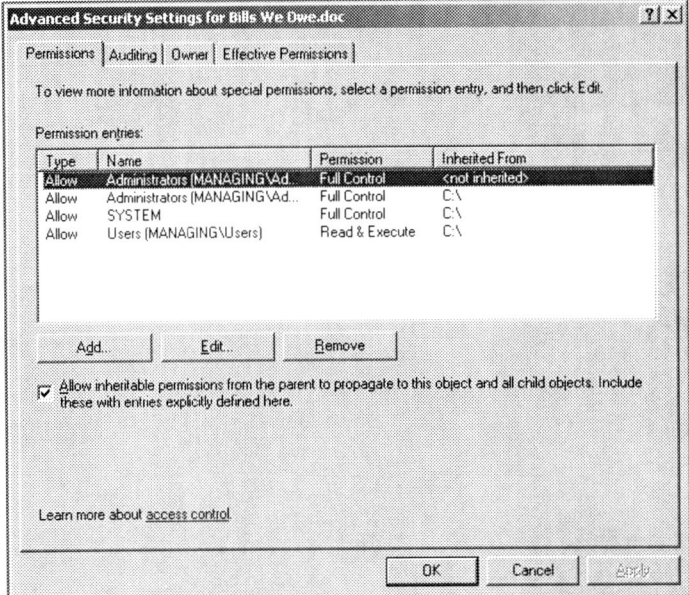

Figure 4-2. *Viewing the origin of permissions inheritance*

This process can be blocked by clearing the "Allow inheritable permissions from the parent to propagate to this object" check box on the screen shown in Figure 4-2. Any children of the folder for which you've stopped inheritance will receive their permission from that folder, and not from the top of the folder tree. Also, if you ever decide to revert to standard permissions inheritance on an object for which you've blocked the process, simply recheck the box. Custom permissions that you've defined will remain, and all other permissions will automatically trickle down as normal.

There is also a concept of ownership. The specified "owner" of a file or folder has full control over it and therefore retains the ability to change permissions on it, regardless of the effect of other permissions on that file. There also exists a standard permission called Take Ownership that an owner can assign to any other user or group; this allows that user or group to assume the role of owner and therefore assign permissions at will. The high-level administrator account on a system has the Take Ownership permission by default, allowing IT representatives to unlock data files for terminated or otherwise unavailable employees who might have set permissions to deny access to others.

To view the owner of a file, click the Owner tab on the Advanced Permissions dialog box. The current owner is enumerated in the first box. To change the owner—assuming you have sufficient permissions to do so—simply select a user from the white box at the bottom and click OK. Should the user to whom you want to transfer ownership not appear in the white box, click Add, and then search for the appropriate user. You can also elect to recursively change the owner on all objects beneath the current object in the file system hierarchy. This is useful in transferring ownership of data stored in a terminated employee's account. To do so, click the box for "Replace owner on subcontainers and objects" at the bottom of the screen. Click OK when you've finished.

Determining Effective Permissions

As a result of Microsoft's inclusion of Resultant Set of Policy, or RSoP, tools in Windows Server 2003, you can now use the Effective Permissions tab on the Advanced Security Settings screen to view what permissions a user or group from within Active Directory would have over any object. Windows examines inheritance, explicit, implicit, and default access control lists for an object, calculates the access that a given user would have, and then enumerates each right in detail on the tab. Figure 4-3 demonstrates this.

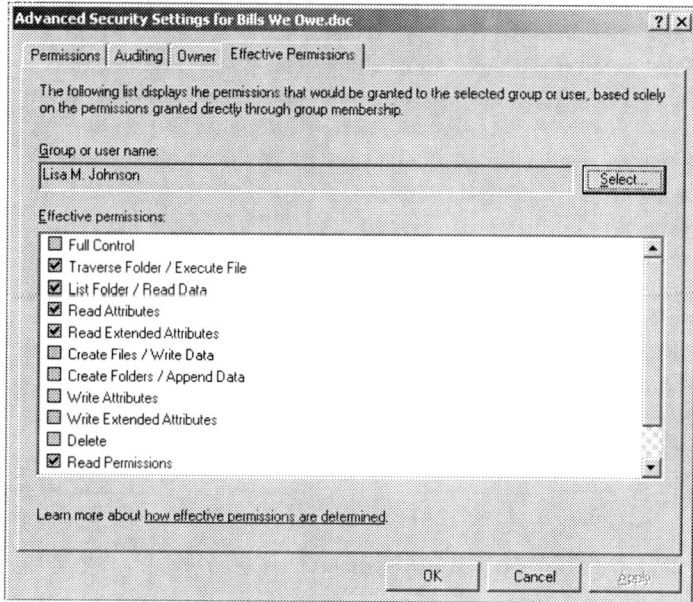

Figure 4-3. *The Effective Permissions tab*

There are two primary limitations of the Effective Permissions display: for one, it does not examine share permissions. It concerns itself only with NTFS file system–based ACLs, and therefore, only file system objects. And secondly, it only functions for users and groups in their default accounts—it will not display correct permissions if a user is logged in through a remote access connection or through Terminal Services, and it also might display partially inaccurate results for users coming in through the local Network service account. While these are reasonably significant limitations, using the Effective Permissions tool can save you hours of head scratching as to why a pesky "Access Denied" message continues to appear. It's also an excellent tool to test your knowledge of how permissions trickle down, and how Allow and Deny permissions override such inheritance at times.

Using Offline Files and Folders

Offline Files and Folders is a neat feature, offered for the first time in Windows 2000 Professional, that synchronizes files and folders when you connect and disconnect from the network. Similar to the Windows 95 Briefcase, except much more versatile and automated, Offline Files caches a copy of selected files and folders on a computer's hard drive. When that computer becomes disconnected from the network for any reason, Windows reads the cache on the machine and intercepts requests for files and folders inside the cache. The end user still can open, save, delete, and rename files on network shares, since Windows is fooling him into thinking everything is still on the network and not in the cache. Windows records all changes, and then, the next time an appropriate network connection is detected, the changes are uploaded to the network and the cache and the actual network file store are synchronized.

This has obvious advantages for mobile users. In fact, as I write this, I am sitting at a rest stop on Interstate 20 outside Augusta, Georgia, taking an extended break from a road trip. To open this file, I navigated through Windows Explorer to my regular network storage location for this book and its assorted files. I noticed no difference between being in my office and being in this car right now, at least as far as Windows' interface to the network is concerned. However, tomorrow, when I am back in my office, I will plug the Ethernet cable into my laptop, and Windows will synchronize any files I modified in that folder with the files on my servers in the office. Using this feature, I always have the latest file with me wherever I am, be it in the office or on the road, and I don't really have to consciously think about it. But there's also a plus side that you might not have considered: if you enable Offline Files on regular desktop machines, not just mobile laptops, you create a poor man's fault-tolerant network. That is, when the network connection disappears, Windows doesn't care if you are using a big mini-tower system or an ultra-thin notebook. So your desktop users can still safely and happily use network resources, even if the network has disappeared, and you as the administrator can rest assured in knowing whatever the users do will be safely updated on the network when it reappears. Now, of course, this is no substitute for a well-planned network with quality components, but in a pinch, it does well to avoid user panic and wasted help desk calls.

Enabling Offline Files

To make a share's contents available offline using Control Panel:

1. Open Control Panel, and double-click Computer Management.
2. In the left pane, expand Computer Management ➤ System Tools ➤ and Shared Folders, and select Shares.
3. In the right pane, right-click the share in question, and select Properties.
4. Navigate to the General tab, and click the Offline Settings button.
5. Select the appropriate settings, and then click OK when finished.

To make a share's contents available offline using Explorer:

1. Open Windows Explorer.
2. Right-click the shared folder in question, and select Sharing and Security.
3. Click the Offline Settings button.
4. Select the appropriate settings, and then click OK when finished.

In both of the preceding processes, the individual offline availability configuration set-tings are as follows: The first option gives the user control over which documents are available offline. The second option makes all documents available. The third option prevents any doc-uments from being used offline.

Be careful to note that offline access is allowed by default when creating a new share. If you have sensitive data stored on a share that is accessed by mobile computers frequently, that data essentially represents a real business intelligence risk. Consider disabling offline access for shares that contain potentially private corporate information not suitable for stor-age on computers that leave the corporate campus.

Also, beware of the false sense of security that Offline Files gives the user. If I were to have left for the airport without plugging my laptop into the network right before I left, I've certainly not gotten the latest version of any files I have modified since I last connected the laptop to the network, and potentially, I'm missing many more files that perhaps had been added since that time as well. A good rule of thumb, even though it's low tech, is to plug up the laptop right before you leave the office, and then disconnect the laptop, and reboot. This allows you both to synchronize for a final time and to verify that the utility is working correctly too. It's a lot better than arriving to a conference without the PowerPoint slides that derived a significant portion of your talk. (Not that I know from experience . . .)

Note that selecting the Optimized for Performance box in the Windows GUI automatically caches documents so that users can run them locally, which is helpful for busy application servers since it lowers overall traffic to and from the server.

Using Shadow Copies

Shadow copies are a new technology within Windows products that allows a server to take snapshots of documents on a disk to record their states at certain points in time. If users acci-dentally delete or otherwise overwrite a file, they can open a version that was saved by the server earlier in time, thereby eliminating the need to either re-create their work or contact the help desk to get them to restore the file from the most recent backup. When shadow copies are enabled on a disk, clients connecting to a share on that disk will be able to view and access previous point-in-time copies of either individual files or entire directories.

Further benefits lurk beneath the surface of this feature, however. The service behind shadow copies, called the Volume Shadow Copy service, is actually responsible for a newly developed application programming interface (API) that will allow server-based applications like Exchange, SQL, and backup programs to access the benefits of shadow copies. Perhaps the most famous example is a backup that skips open files, either because a user opens them or because they are locked by another process. In the past, this resulted in incomplete back-ups, either because the backup process halted in midstream due to this unrecoverable error, or because the process skipped the open file. If the open file is, say, your Exchange mail data-base, that's not necessarily a good thing. But now, with volume shadow copies, the backup application can simply use an API to take a snapshot of any open files and back up that snap-shot. Now you have an instant backup of a database at any point in time, with no interruption in availability to the user. This is a very nice feature.

But there are definitely ways to take advantage of shadow copies in the user realm as well. Part of the Volume Shadow Copy service is a piece of client software that can be pushed out to any computer in your domain through Group Policy. Once the user has this client, Windows adds a tab to the Properties sheet for any document. This is shown in Figure 4-4.

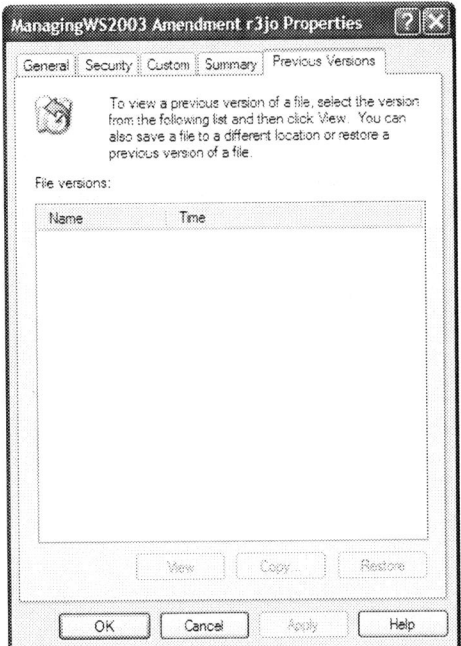

Figure 4-4. *The Previous Versions add-on for the Volume Shadow Copy service*

To restore a previous version of a file, all the user has to do is select the appropriate version and either copy it to a different location using the Copy button or restore it to its location at the time the snapshot was taken by using the Restore button. Note that viewing an executable file will run that file.

To reduce user confusion, when users access the Previous Versions link in the Explorer view (in Windows XP) of a particular share, they are only presented with a list of unique copies—that is to say, a list of versions that differ from each other, a condition that indicates the file or folder changed. In addition, shadow copies are read-only, in that users can copy, drag and drop, and perform any other function on them as usual except overwriting or deleting them.

Some restrictions on shadow copies from an administrator standpoint are noted as follows: local views of folders on a disk do not permit accessing shadow copies. For the Previous Versions link to appear in a folder's view, you must be accessing that folder from a network share. Also, the Windows XP clients that require the Previous Versions update can find it (on any Windows Server 2003 system) inside the \systemroot\system32 folder; its name is TWCLI32.MSI. It is installed by default on all Windows Server 2003 machines. It can also be pushed out, as discussed earlier, through a group policy object.

Enabling Shadow Copies

To enable shadow copies on the server:

1. Open Control Panel, and double-click Computer Management.

2. Expand Computer Management ➤ System Tools ➤ Shared Folders.

3. Right-click Shared Folders, select All Tasks, and click Configure Shadow Copies.

4. Select the disk on which to enable shadow copies, and click Enable.

Enabling shadow copies prompts the creation of a folder on the volume that you've enabled called System Volume Information, where the actual snapshots and log files of the operations are stored. By default, this folder is allocated 10 percent of the volume's total disk space, much like the Recycle Bin defaults in client versions of Windows.

When you first enable shadow copies, a current snapshot of the volume is taken so that Windows can store a picture of the "state" of files on the disk. This state data is used to determine if files have changed from the time at which the state information was recorded. For example, a secretary is performing rudimentary formatting functions on an Excel spreadsheet, and she leaves for the day. Overnight, the Windows Server 2003 machine on which the file share resides is configured to take a snapshot of all files—for this example, I will use 5:30 a.m. When this snapshot is taken, the state information for this Excel spreadsheet is copied into the System Volume Information folder. Now, when the secretary arrives at work and begins to work on the spreadsheet, she is using the same version as the one she saved the previous night; remember that this is also the one on which the snapshot is based. When she finishes with some formatting, she saves the spreadsheet before she attends the Tuesday morning meeting of all employees. The VSS service detects that the Excel file is one which already has state data, and it also realizes that it has changed, so it immediately makes available the 5:30 a.m. version of the file—the previous version—under the appropriate tab in the Properties sheet for the Excel file. So now, when the secretary comes back and realizes she removed an entire page from the workbook unintentionally while she was formatting the file, she can retrieve the version from the previous night, and likely save her job.

There are three very important items to note about how shadow copies might and (most notably) might not rescue you or your users from catastrophe:

Only one previous version of a file is kept, and that is the version of a file that consisted of the oldest modification since the most recent snapshot. Even if multiple changes are made to a file throughout the day, the only previous version available for rollback is the one that was made directly after the most recent snapshot. This can be somewhat counterintuitive to understand, but it's crucial that your users not rely on the Previous Versions feature as a crutch and learn to use it only when a major disaster strikes.

If you delete a file, you must create an empty file with the same name. This is quite obviously because you can't navigate to the Properties sheet of an object if said object doesn't exist. In most cases, the workaround is simply to create a new file with the same name and then access the Previous Versions tab—Windows will figure out what's going on. Obviously the limitation here is that you must remember the exact name of a file. That is a simple request when the file is called 2003 Employee Dinner.doc, but not when it's called 0226ch1de12jo.doc.

If you rename a file, you lose all access to previous versions of that file, even if some exist. VSS tracks exclusively by file name and state, so if the file name changes, VSS (at least at this stage) isn't smart enough to follow the rename.

Backing Up Your Machines

The oft-neglected process of backing up your machines and the critical data they contain is perhaps the most effective insurance policy you can take out for your business. It's like exercise: although nearly everyone knows that it's an excellent idea, and vital to health, not as many people actually follow through. Fortunately, Windows Server 2003 includes a backup utility in the box that performs this function at a basic level. This section will discuss how to use the GUI program, Backup.

Using Backup from the GUI

To back up the contents of your server to a file or to another removable media device using the GUI:

1. From the Start menu, select All Programs ➤ Accessories ➤ System Tools, and then click Backup. The wizard starts by default. Click the Advanced Mode link.

2. Navigate to the Backup tab, and then select New from the Job menu.

3. Click the box to the left of a file or folder to select the files and folders you want to back up.

4. In Backup destination, choose File (the default selection) if you want to back up to a file on disk. Choose another device if you want to back up to a tape or something similar.

5. In Backup media or file name, if you are backing up to a file, choose a location for the backup (.bkf) file. Otherwise, choose the tape you want to use.

6. Make sure you've configured this backup operation the way you want by selecting Options from the Tools menu and verifying the choices there.

7. Click the Start Backup button, and then make any changes to the Backup Job Information dialog box.

8. Click Advanced to configure options like compression and verification. Then click OK.

9. Click Start Backup.

There are some considerations if you specify either Removable Storage or Remote Storage. You should make a note to back up the contents of `systemroot\System32\Ntmsdata` and `systemroot\System32\Remotestorage` on a regular basis. If not, then it's possible (although somewhat unlikely) that Removable/Remote Storage data could be lost and unrestorable.

The Active Directory in Windows Server 2003

Active Directory was first introduced in Windows 2000 Server and really shook up the Windows administration world. With SBS, some of the features of Active Directory are less relevant than others (for example, the ability to replicate information to branch offices is disabled in SBS), but other capabilities, like Group Policy, are definitely very useful. In this section, I'll explore Active Directory with you, walk you through how it works, and show you how you can benefit from it.

Active Directory Objects and Concepts

Before diving in any further, let me introduce a few common terms with their definitions early on in the process; this way, the explanations later in the chapter will be a bit clearer.

- **Directory**: A directory is a single repository for information about users and resources within an organization. Active Directory is a type of directory that holds the properties and contact information for a variety of resources within a network, so that users and administrators alike can find them with ease.

- **Domain**: A domain is a collection of objects within the directory that forms a management boundary. There can be multiple domains within a forest (described later in this list), each with its own collection of objects and organizational units. Domains are named using the industry-standard DNS protocol, covered in detail in the previous chapter.

- **Domain controller**: Domain controllers hold the security information and directory object database for a particular domain and are responsible for authenticating objects within their sphere of control. Multiple domain controllers can be associated with a given domain, and each domain controller holds certain roles within the directory, although for all intents and purposes all domain controllers within a domain are "equal" in power. This is unlike the primary and backup labels assigned to domain controllers in Windows NT.

- **Forest**: A forest is the largest logical container within Active Directory and encompasses all domains within its purvey, all linked together via transitive trusts that are constructed automatically—this way, all domains in a particular forest automatically trust all other domains within the forest.

- **Organizational unit**: Organizational units are containers with objects (see the next entry) contained within them. Organizational units can be arranged in a hierarchical, tree-like fashion and designed in a structure that best fits your organization for security boundary delineation or ease of administration.

- **Object**: Within Active Directory, an object is anything that can be part of the directory—that is, an object can be a user, a group, a shared folder, a printer, a contact, an organizational unit even. Objects are unique physical "things" within your directory and can be managed directly.

- **Schema**: The schema in Active Directory is the actual structure of the database—the "fields," to use a not-quite applicable analogy. The different types of information stored in AD are referred to as *attributes*. AD's schema also supports a standard set of classes, or types of objects. Classes describe an object and the associated properties that are required to create an instance of the object. For example, user objects are "instances" of the user class; computer objects are "instances" of the computer class, and so on. Think of classes as guideline templates describing different types of objects.

- **Site**: Sites are collections of computers that are in distinct geographical locations—or at least connected via a permanent, adequate speed network link. Sites are generally used to determine how domain controllers are kept up to date; Active Directory will select its methodology for distributing those updates (a process called *replication*) based on how you configure a site to keep traffic over an expensive WAN link down to a minimum.

- **Tree**: A tree is simply a collection of domains that begins at a single root and branches out into peripheral, "child" domains. Trees can be linked together within forests as well, and trees also share an unbroken DNS namespace—that is, hasselltech.local and america.hasselltech.local are part of the same tree, but mycorp.com and hasselltech.local are not.

- **Trust**: A trust in terms of Active Directory is a secure method of communicating between domains, trees, and forests. Much like trusts worked in Windows NT, trusts allow users in one Active Directory domain to authenticate to other domain controllers within another, separate, distinct domain within the directory. Trusts can be one-way (A to B only, not B to A), transitive (A trusts B and B trusts C so A trusts C), or cross-linked (A to C and B to D).

Domains

When examining Active Directory for the first time, it's easiest to examine the domain first, since so much of the basis of AD is derived from the domain. It's adequate to boil down the function of domains into three basic areas: to consolidate lists of usernames and passwords for all machines within a domain and provide an infrastructure for using that consolidated list; to provide a method of subdividing objects within a domain for easier administration (into organizational units, as described earlier); and to offer a centralized, searchable list of resources within the domain so users and administrators can easily query that list to find objects that they need.

Domains, at a minimum, keep a list of all authorized users and their passwords on a machine or groups of machines called domain controllers. This list is stored in Active Directory. However, there are many other objects stored within the directory—which is actually a file on a domain controller's hard drive called NTDS.DIT—including sites, organizational units, groups of users, groups of computers, Group Policy objects, and contacts, just to name some.

Organizational Units

A domain can be an awfully big, comprehensive unit to manage, and most environments would benefit from some mechanism to separate that large, unitary domain into smaller, more manageable chunks. An organizational unit is AD's way of doing that. Organizational units, or OUs, act like folders on a regular client's operating system, containing every type of object that AD supports.

A particularly interesting feature of OUs is the ability to delegate administrative control over them to a subset of users in AD. Take, for instance, the third example in the previous list. Perhaps you, as the domain administrator, would like to designate one technically savvy person in each department as the official Password Change Administrator, to reduce your administrative load. You can delegate the authority to modify users' passwords to each of those users over only their respective OU, thereby both allowing them power but finely controlling it over certain areas of your AD infrastructure. This ability is called *delegation*.

Organizational units are designed to be containers in Active Directory, meaning that their point is to hold objects and to have contents. You can apply group policies to the objects within a specific OU, controlling users' desktops, locking them out of potentially dangerous system modification settings, and creating a consistent user experience across your domain.

Groups

The point of groups is to make assigning attributes to larger sets of users easier on administrators. Picture having 2,500 users in your directory. You create a new file share and need to give certain employees permissions to that file share—for example, all accounting users. Do you want to take a hard-copy list of all members of the accounting department and handpick the appropriate users from your list of 2,500? Of course not. Groups allow you to create an object called Accounting and insert all the appropriate users into that group. So, instead of selecting each individual user from a large list, you can pick the Accounting group, and all members of that group will have the same permissions on the file share.

There are four different scopes of groups within Windows Server 2003 and Active Directory, and each scope can nest groups differently. Let's outline the group scopes first, and then bear with me as I explain the concepts of each:

- **Machine local groups**: These types of groups contain objects that only pertain to the local computer (or more specifically, objects contained within the local computer's Security Account Manager—SAM—database). These types of groups can have as members global groups, domain local groups from their own domain, and universal or global groups from their own domain or any other domain that they trust.

- **Domain local groups**: These groups can be created only on a domain controller, so ordinary client computers or member servers of a domain cannot host domain local groups. Domain local groups can be put inside (a process called *nesting*) machine local groups within the same domain. They can contain global groups from a domain that trusts the current domain and other domain local groups from the same domain. As you will see later in the chapter, they are of limited utility.

- **Domain global groups**: These kinds of groups too can be created only on a domain controller, but global groups can be put into any local group of any machine that is a member of the current domain or a trusted domain. Global groups can now be nested in other global groups (a process called nesting), with the exception that all nested global groups must be from the same domain. Global groups are great tools that contain all the functionality of domain local groups and more, and they are the most common type of group used across a domain.

- **Universal groups**: This sort of group is a "do-it-all" type of group. New to Active Directory in Windows 2000 and Windows Server 2003, universal groups can contain global and universal groups, and those nested groups can be from any domain in your Active Directory forest.

Briefly, I'll also mention that there are two types of groups: a security group, which is used for the purposes of assigning or denying rights and permissions; and a distribution group, which is used for the sole purpose of sending e-mails. A security group, though, can also act as a distribution group.

Nesting

Nesting is a useful ability that has been around in limited form since Windows NT. By nesting groups you achieve the ability to quickly and painlessly assign permissions and rights to different users. For example, let's say you have a resource called COLORLASER, and you want all full-time employees to be able to access that resource. You don't have a group called FTEs that contains all of your full-timers throughout your organization, but your departmental administrators have set up a structure wherein full-time employees are put into groups and part-timers are in another. To quickly create your overall FTE group, you can take your different groups of users from each department (ACCTG_FTE, ADMIN_FTE, PRODUCTION_FTE, SALES_FTE, for example, and so on) and put them within a new group you create called ALL_FTE. Then, you can quickly assign access rights to COLORLASER by giving the ALL_FTE group permission to use the resource. You have "nested" the departmental groups within one big group.

Different scopes of groups, as you saw in the list of groups previously, support different methods of nesting. Table 4-3 shows the relationships between the types of groups there are and the respective abilities to nest.

Table 4-3. *Nesting by Group Type*

Type of Nesting	Machine Local	Domain Local	Domain Global	Universal
Within themselves	Yes	Yes (from the same domain)	Yes (from the same domain)	Yes
Within other types	None	Machine local	Machine local Domain local Universal	Machine local Domain local Domain global

A couple of important issues regarding backward compatibility with Windows NT 4 and Windows 2000 and the types of group capabilities available:

AD cannot support universal groups until you operate at least in Windows 2000 Native functional level, as NT 4 supports only one level of group nesting. Additionally, a group cannot have more than 5,000 members until your forest is operating in the Windows Server 2003 forest functional level.

Forests

Forests, in the simplest terms, are just groups of trees. All trees in a forest automatically trust each other. Think of a forest as an extended family, and individual domain trees as brothers. If you have five brothers in a family, each child of those brothers trusts their immediate brothers, and (usually!) each brother's family trusts the other brothers' families—cousins typically get along. Forests just refer to collections of domain trees that trust each other.

Shared Folders and Printers

As you saw earlier in this chapter, the concept of shared folders and printers within AD merely relates to a "pointer" residing within the directory, guiding users to the real location on a physical file system of a server for a particular shared directory, or the location of a print share on a print server. This process is known as *publishing a share* (or *publishing a printer*).

The point of publishing shares and printers in AD is to make them available for searching, either through AD Users and Computers for administrators or through Start/Search or Start/Find for client users. You can search for shared folder or printer names containing target keywords, and their locations will be populated within the results box.

Contacts

Contacts are simply objects in the directory that represent people and contain attributes with indicators as to how to contact them. Contacts do not represent users of any directory, nor do they convey any privileges to log on to the network or use any network or domain resources.

The point of the contacts object is to create within AD a phonebook of sorts with names of vital business contacts that may reside outside of your organization—partners, customers, vendors, and the like. Since AD as a directory can be queried by the LDAP protocol, which most groupware applications support, the contents of contacts objects can likely be accessed directly within that application.

Group Policy

Group Policy is one of the most useful administrative tools in Windows Server 2003, and it is made possible through the use of Active Directory. Group policies are simply common policy elements applied to certain containers within Active Directory.

Group policies consist of five distinct components: **Administrative templates** configure registry-based policies. **Folder redirection** alters the target location of various elements in the UI, such as My Documents, to other places on the network. **Scripts** execute when computers are first booted and shut down. They can also run during user logon and logoff. **Security settings** configure permissions, rights, and restrictions for computers, domains, and users. And finally, **software policies** assign application packages to users and computers.

The data for each of these components is stored in a group policy object (GPO). In domain-based group policies, GPOs are stored at various levels in Active Directory, but they're always associated with a domain. GPOs are affiliated with a variety of objects within Active Directory, including sites, domains, domain controllers, and organizational units, and they can also be linked to multiple sites, domains themselves, and OUs. For non-domain-based (i.e., local) group policies, you simply configure those settings on individual servers.

GPOs store their contents in two parts: as files as part of a group policy template (GPT), and as objects inside a specialized container in Active Directory called a group policy container (GPC). GPTs are stored in the C:\WINDOWS\SYSVOL directory on each domain controller and contain settings related to software installation policies and deployments, scripts, and permissions information for each GPO. The GPTs usually contain subfolders called Adm, USER, and MACHINE, to separate the data to be applied to different portions of computers' registries—the USER portion is applied to keys in HKEY_CURRENT_USER, and the MACHINE portion is applied to keys in HKEY_LOCAL_MACHINE. The GPCs simply contain information, such as version, status, or extensions for the policy itself, regarding the GPO's link to Active Directory containers. Each GPC is referred to by a string called a globally unique identifier, or GUID. Data stored in the GPC rarely needs to be modified and is used to indicate whether a specific policy object is enabled and to control the proper version of the GPT to apply.

Local computer policies are stored in the %SystemRoot%\System32\GroupPolicy directory, since they apply only to the computer on which they're stored and need not be replicated. Local policies are also more limited in scope and ability, as you'll see later in this chapter.

When you first set up an Active Directory domain, two default GPOs are created: one that is linked to the domain itself, and therefore affects all users and computers within the domain, and one that is linked to the domain controllers OU, which affects all domain controllers within a domain.

Group Policy Implementation

Now that you know the components of Group Policy, let's take a look at how they are actually implemented. Like NTFS permissions, group policies are cumulative and inherited—cumulative, in that the settings modified by a policy can build upon other policies and "amass" configuration changes, and inherited, in that objects below other objects in Active Directory can automatically have any group policies applied to their parent object be applied to themselves.

Group policy objects are associated with, or linked to, any number of objects, either within a directory or local to a specific machine. To implement a group policy on a specific type of object, follow this guide:

- **Local computer**: Use the Local Security Policy snap-in inside Control Panel ➤ Administrative Tools. Or, for a more complete look, use Start ➤ Run ➤ gpedit.msc.

- **A specific computer**: Load the Microsoft Management Console (MMC), and then select Add Snap-in from the File menu. Browse in the list and add the Group Policy Object Editor to the console. On the Select Group Policy Object screen, peruse the list to find the specific object you'd like.

- **Entire domain**: Launch Active Directory Users & Computers, and right-click the domain name; select Properties from the context menu. Navigate to the Group Policy tab, and create or edit a policy from there.

- **Organizational unit (OU) within Active Directory**: Launch Active Directory Users & Computers, and right-click the organizational unit's name; select Properties from the context menu. Navigate to the Group Policy tab, and create or edit a policy from there.

- **Active Directory site**: Launch Active Directory Sites & Services, and right-click the site's name; select Properties from the context menu. Navigate to the Group Policy tab, and create or edit a policy from there.

Group policies are applied by Windows in the following order:

- Local group policy objects

- Site-specific group policy objects, in an order which the site administrator configures

- Domain-specific group policy objects, again in an order which the domain administrator configures

- Organizational unit-specific group policy objects, from the child OU up through the ranks to the parent OU

The only exception to this rule is when you're using NT 4 system policies that are created and set with the NT System Policy Editor. Recall from NT administration days that the system policies are called NTCONFIG.POL, so if Windows finds that file present, it applies these policies before the local GPO. Of course, these policies can be overwritten by policies that come farther down in the application chain.

Here's an easy rule of thumb to remember: for domain-based group policies, the lowest-level Active Directory container has the last opportunity to override inherited policies. For example, a policy applied to a site will be overwritten by a policy applied to an organizational unit, and a local policy will be overwritten by an Active Directory object-based policy.

Creating and Editing Group Policy Objects

To look at how group policies are created and edited, launch Active Directory Users and Computers from the Start ➤ Administrative Tools menu, right-click your SBS domain name, and select Properties from the context menu. You can also launch tools to access Group Policy from the command line by running DSA.MSC for Active Directory Users and Computers or DSSITE.MSC for Active Directory Sites and Services.

Navigate to the Group Policy tab, and click the New button to create a new group policy object. Enter a name for the object, and then choose an action to perform with the object: **Add,** to link the policy with an object; **Edit,** to open the policy object for modification; **Options,** to disable the policy or set the policy to No Override; **Delete,** either to remove the link for the policy to the object, or to remove it from the directory entirely; or **Properties,** to limit the scope of the policy through ACL permissions and security groups.

Click the Edit button to edit the object. You're presented with a screen much like that shown in Figure 4-5.

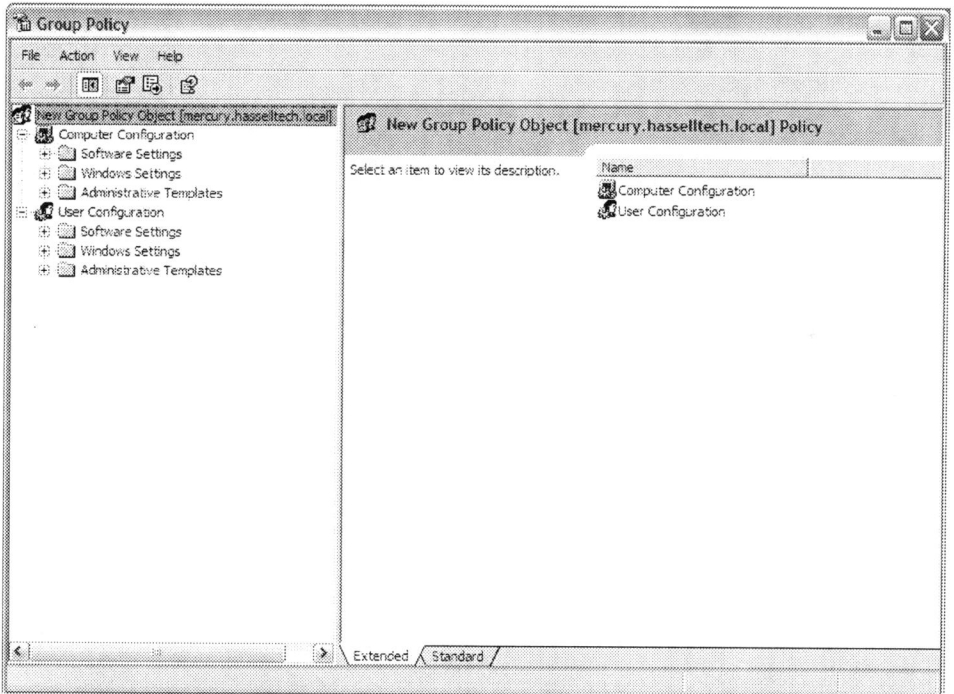

Figure 4-5. *The Group Policy Object Editor screen*

You'll note there are two branches to each GPO: Computer Configuration and User Configuration. Each contains the same subtrees: Software Settings, Windows Settings, and Administrative Templates. The Computer Configuration tree is used to customize machine-specific settings, which become effective when a computer first boots. These policies are applied across any users that log on to the system, independent of their own individual policies. Using computer policies, you can lock down a group of computers in a lab or kiosk situation while still maintaining an independent set of user policies. The User Configuration tree, you might suspect, contains user-specific settings that apply only to that user, no matter where she is on the network.

Disabling Portions of Policies

A group policy object has the potential to be large since it can contain numerous computer and user settings. If you don't intend to populate either computer or user settings, you can disable that portion of the group policy object. Doing this speeds up propagation time over the network and processing time on the computers that need to load the settings in the object. So if you have a group policy object that applies only to users, you can disable the computer configuration branch of the policy and significantly improve the performance of your network. To do so:

1. Open the Group Policy Object Editor.

2. Select the group policy object in question, right-click it, and select Properties from the context menu.

3. Navigate to the General tab, and uncheck either the Computer Configuration or User Configuration nodes of the policy.

4. Click OK.

The portion of the policy you selected previously is now disabled.

Refreshing Policies

Speaking of changes to policies, it can take some time for modifications to propagate across domain controllers within a domain and finally to the objects for which they're destined. Policies are refreshed on a client when the computer is turned on, a user logs on, an application requests a policy refresh, a user requests a policy refresh, or the interval between refreshes has elapsed (assuming this option is enabled, which indeed it is by default).

To enable the policy refresh interval:

1. Open the Group Policy Object Editor.

2. Edit the target GPO as described earlier.

3. In the Computer Configuration tree, navigate through Administrative Templates and System.

4. Click Group Policy.

5. In the right pane, double-click the setting "Group Policy Refresh Interval for Computers."

6. Select Enabled, and then enter an interval for the refresh. Be sure to make this a healthy interval; otherwise, you will degrade your network's performance with constant traffic updating policies across the domain. For smaller networks, 15 minutes should be an acceptable timeframe. Allow 30 to 45 minutes for larger networks.

7. Click OK.

You can also manually force a policy refresh from the command line on client computers with the GPUPDATE command. To refresh all parts of a policy, issue this command:

```
Gpupdate /force
```

To refresh just the Computer Configuration node of the policy:

```
Gpupdate /target:computer /force
```

To refresh just the User Configuration node of the policy:

```
Gpupdate /target:user /force
```

The Scope of Group Policy Objects

So how far do these GPOs go? What types of objects can GPOs affect? To deploy a group policy to a set of users, you "associate" a GPO to an object within Active Directory. By default, all objects within a container with an associated GPO have that GPO applied to them. If you have a large number of GPOs or Active Directory objects, it can be confusing to track the scope and application of GPOs. Luckily, you can find out to which containers a specific policy is applied by selecting the GPO, right-clicking it, and selecting Properties. On the Links tab, click Find Now, and all links will be detected and displayed.

Of course, in practice there are always exceptions to any rule; there will likely be some computers within a container that shouldn't have a policy applied to them. To limit the scope of a GPO, you can create security groups that contain the objects that are to be excluded from the policy application, and then not grant them the ability to read the group policy object, effectively removing them from the policy's effects. You can also play more tricks with groups and GPO ACLs to further limit the effects of policy application to objects. The following is a list of appropriate ACL permissions to grant to obtain the desired result:

If you'd like the policy to be applied to all members of a certain security group, add all the members to a group, add the group to the ACL for the object, and set the following permissions for the group: Apply Group Policy, Allow; Read, Allow. All members of the group will then have the policy applied, except if they are members of another group with either of the former permissions set to Deny.

If you'd like the policy to NOT be applied to all members of a certain security group, add all the members to a group, add the group to the ACL for the object, and set the following permissions for the group: Apply Group Policy, Deny; Read, Deny. All members of the group will then NOT have the policy applied, regardless of their existing memberships to other groups.

If group membership (at least in a specific group) shouldn't play a part in the application of this policy, then leave permissions alone.

To limit the scope of a GPO to certain groups of objects within Active Directory:

1. Create the groups of objects that don't need the policy to be applied to them.

2. Open the GPO you want to administer within the Group Policy Object Editor, right-click the GPO, and choose Properties from the context menu.

3. Click the Security tab.

4. Add the groups that do not need the policy applied.

Inheritance and Overriding

Policies applied to parent objects are automatically inherited by child objects, unless there are conflicts; if a child's directly applied policy conflicts with a general inherited policy from a parent, the child's policy will prevail, on the assumption that the administrator really wanted the result of the specifically applied policy and not one that is granted indirectly because of directory tree position. Policy settings that are currently disabled migrate to child objects in the disabled state as well, and policy settings that remain in the "not configured" state do not propagate at all. Additionally, if there are no conflicts, then two policies can coexist peacefully, no matter where the initial application occurred.

Also like permissions, group policy object inheritance can be blocked by using two options available within the user interface: No Override, which instructs child containers to not replace any setting placed higher on the tree than they are, and Block Policy Inheritance, which simply eliminates any inheritance of parent object policies by child objects. If both of these options are set, the No Override option always trumps the Block Policy Inheritance feature.

Explicit permissions, be they Allow or Deny permissions, will always trump inherited permissions, even if Deny permissions on an object are inherited from a parent. Explicitly granted access to an object cannot be overridden by an inherited denial.

To set a group policy object to not override parent group policy object settings, open the GPO for which you want to set the policy. Right-click the object, and select No Override from the pop-up context menu. This is shown in Figure 4-6.

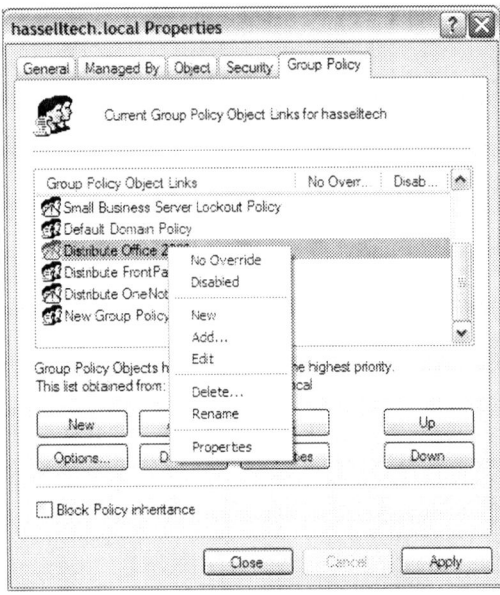

Figure 4-6. *Setting the No Override option on a group policy object*

Click Apply to apply the changes.

To block any inheritance of parent policy settings for the current administrative container, right-click the domain that the GPO resides in and select Properties. On the Group Policy tab, select the GPO for which you want to set the policy. Click the check box under Block Policy Inheritance to enable the setting. The resulting screen is shown in Figure 4-7.

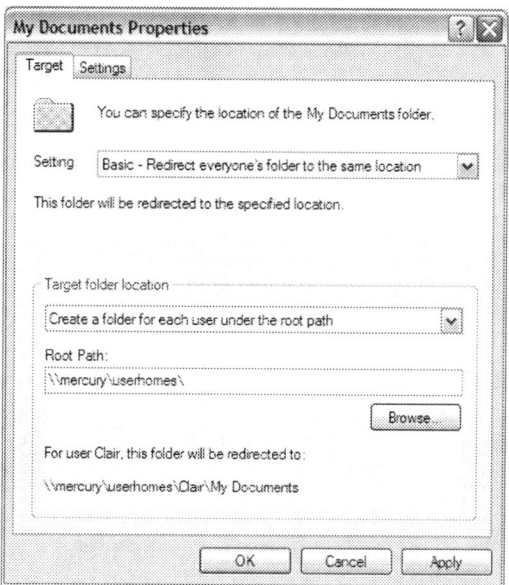

Figure 4-7. *Setting the Block Policy Inheritance option on a group policy object*

Click Apply to apply the changes.

If there are multiple GPOs assigned to an object, GPOs at the bottom of the list (on the Group Policy tab of an appropriate object) are applied first, and objects at the top are applied last. Therefore, GPOs that are higher in the list have the higher priorities.

Domain Group Policy

Domain-based group policies offer a much more flexible and configurable set of standards and settings for your organization than local group policies. In this section, I'll discuss the four most common methods of managing your IT assets centrally using domain group policy: configuring a security standard, installing software using the IntelliMirror technology found in Windows Server 2003, redirecting folders present in the user interface to network locations, and writing and launching scripts triggered by events, such as logons and logoffs.

Restricted Groups

The restricted groups option allows you to modify the current group configuration and membership on your client computers. When this policy is applied to workstations and servers, their individual group configurations are modified to match that configured inside the policy. The policy contains members and members of lists that overwrite any configuration on the target computers. For example, if you were to add the Administrator group to the policy but not add any users to the members of this group list, and then applied the policy, Windows would remove any users currently in those groups on the client computers. However, the other facet of the policy, groups of which the added group is currently a member, is only additive: if the list is empty, no modifications are made to the client computers. Only additions are processed and changed.

Only the groups listed inside the Details window of the Restricted Groups policy branch can be modified using the policy, but it's a great way to keep individual users from modifying powerful groups on their own systems.

To modify the restricted groups policy, do the following:

1. Inside the Group Policy Object Editor, right-click the Restricted Group branch and select Add Group from the context menu.

2. Click the Browse button, and select any group currently inside your directory. Click OK.

3. Now, right-click the newly added group, and select Security from the context menu.

4. Add the users who belong to this group to the Members of this group list, and add the groups within which this group is nested to the "This group is a member of" list. Use the Add button in both cases. Figure 4-8 shows this screen.

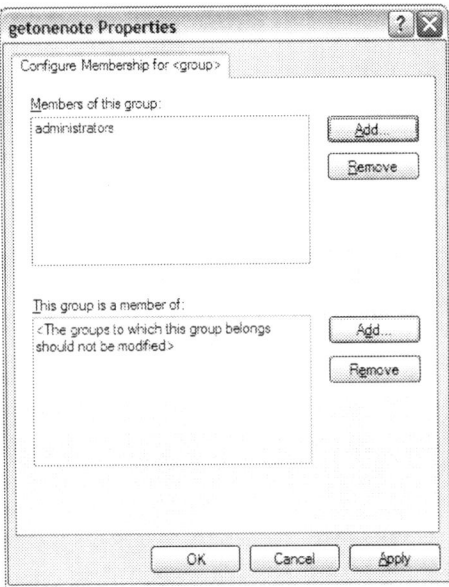

Figure 4-8. *The Restricted Groups list screen*

5. When you're finished, click OK to close out the boxes.

File System and Registry Policy

You can also use group policies to configure permissions on file system objects and registry keys. You can set entries on the ACLs of individual files, folders, and registry keys from a central location. If you make this change at the domain-wide level—one of the few changes that I would recommend and endorse at that level—then registries are protected against meddling users all over the enterprise, which is definitely a benefit.

To add a registry key to be protected to a group policy object:

1. Inside the Group Policy Object Editor, navigate through the Computer Configuration, Windows Settings, Security Settings, and Registry nodes. Right-click Registry, and select Add Key from the context menu.

2. You can add three registry keys at a time, and you can selectively apply permissions to each key. Figure 4-9 shows the screen.

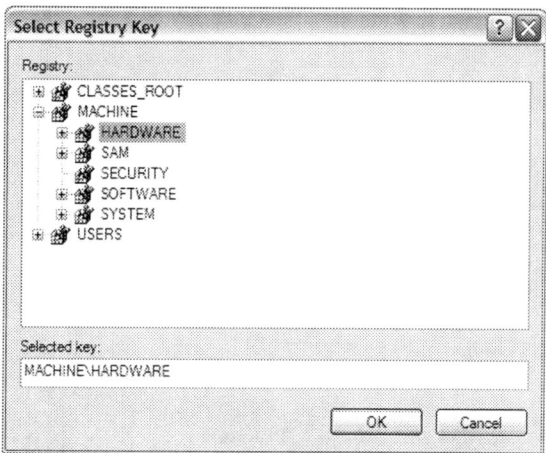

Figure 4-9. *The Registry Key ACL editor screen*

To add a file or folder to be protected to a group policy object, inside the Group Policy Object Editor, navigate through the Computer Configuration, Windows Settings, Security Settings, and File System nodes. Right-click File System, and select Add File from the context menu. You can explore the entire directory structure and selectively assign permissions to files and folders. Figure 4-10 shows the screen.

Once you've selected the objects in question, you'll be prompted for their permissions just like I discussed in Chapter 3. After you enter the appropriate permissions, you'll be prompted to configure the properties of inheritance for these new permissions. This is shown in Figure 4-11.

If you select the Configure option, you also will need to select how permissions are applied. If you choose to apply inheritable security to this file or folder and its subfolders, the new permissions are applied to all child objects that do not have a permission or ACL entry explicitly set. This preserves your custom permissions on a tree but also automatically overwrites permissions simply inherited by default. If you choose to replace existing security for this file or folder and its subfolders, you overwrite all permissions on any child folders, including those permissions explicitly set.

If you'd rather not have any of these methods used to apply permissions, simply choose the "Prevent the application of security policies to this file or folder and its subfolders" option. Doing so will make child files and folders immune to the permissions assigned by this new policy.

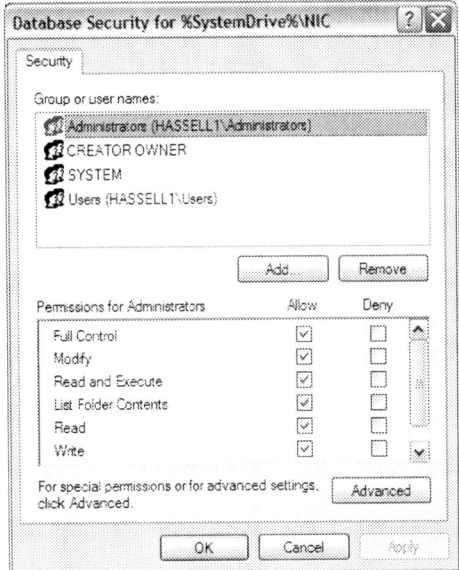

Figure 4-10. *The File System ACL editor screen*

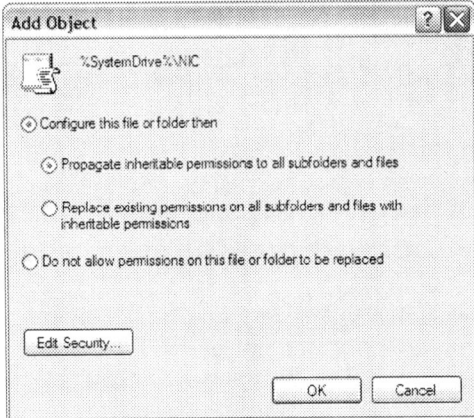

Figure 4-11. *Configuring inheritance on protected file system or registry objects*

IntelliMirror: Software Installation

In my personal opinion, software installation is one of the coolest and most useful features of Group Policy, and I know many administrators who agree with me. Using Microsoft's IntelliMirror technology introduced in Windows 2000, administrators using Group Policy can distribute software applications initially, using a push or pull method, and then upgrade, redeploy, or remove that software either wholesale or when certain conditions apply. Intelli-Mirror also offers intelligent application repair features, so that when critical files for an application deployed through IntelliMirror are corrupted or deleted, Windows takes over and fixes the problem so the application will start and function correctly. This is a big timesaver.

There are two ways to distribute and install applications in your organization. You can assign a software package, which places a shortcut on the user's Start menu and loads the advertisement for the package into the Registry of the computer. You can also publish an application, which simply places the program with the Add/Remove Programs applet in Control Panel. Users can elect to install the software at their own discretion and at a convenient time for them.

You can also distribute applications via the assign and publish functionality to a computer or a user. If you assign a package to a user, the application is installed on the local system the first time the user runs the software. The user-assigned applications follow a user around the network to each computer to ensure that he has all the applications he should on each computer. If you assign a package to a computer, the application is installed on that system when booted up, and the software is only installed on the computer defined in the policy. Applications don't necessarily follow a user around. If you use the publish functionality of IntelliMirror, you can only publish to a specific user, since computers can't choose how and where to install software. Published applications are also not quite as robust as assigned applications and the repair functionality of published applications is limited.

Software installation cannot be accomplished using local policies.

Packaging Software

The easiest way to publish and assign software is through the use of Microsoft Installer packages, or MSI files. Applications packaged in Installer format include a database of changes to make to files and registry keys, instructions on removing previous or outdated versions of software, and strategies to install on multiple versions of Windows within one single file. MSI files also allow intelligent repair functionality for use if installations become corrupted on individual computers, and their rollback function for removing or redeploying an application is useful as well. IntelliMirror and group policy–based software distribution is designed to work with applications that install using an MSI package.

But all is not lost if your software isn't offered in MSI format. First, you can use the ZAP file method. A ZAP file can be used when software isn't available with an MSI package to publish (but not assign) the application. A ZAP file is nothing more than a description of an application, its setup program, and any associated file extensions. A sample ZAP file for Adobe's Acrobat Reader 5.0 is shown here:

```
Line 1: [Application]
Line 2: FriendlyName = Adobe Acrobat Reader 5.0
Line 3: SetupCommand = \\deploy\adobe\rp505enu.exe
Line 4: DisplayVersion = 5.0
Line 5: Publisher = Adobe Corporation
Line 6: URL = http://www.adobe.com
Line 7:
Line 8: [Ext]
Line 9: PDF=
```

A few notes about the preceding ZAP file: the FriendlyName section shows the application name, which will appear in the Add/Remove Programs applet within Control Panel on the computers to which the package is published. It also contains the Setup directive, which tells Windows the network path to file to run in order to install the package. The other tags, while offering more information on the version, manufacturer, and Internet address of the manufacturer, are optional. The Ext section lists file extensions to be associated with the program, each followed by an equal sign.

There are a few caveats to the ZAP file method. First and foremost, since ZAP file installations can only be published, you lose the robustness and intelligent repair features of software applications assigned to computers and users. You also can't set an application deployed via a ZAP file to install automatically on first use. Second, a specific user must have appropriate permissions to run the package's installer executable and access the source files for the installation. Third, there is probably very little automation to the installation, so the process would likely require user intervention to answer prompts like the destination directory, installation options, and so forth, which is something we all try to avoid when possible. And finally, since the installer isn't granted sweeping administrative privileges during the setup process like an MSI installer is, there may be conflicts and problems to troubleshoot with a mass package deployment.

If a program you want to deploy uses the InstallShield installation software, you can run setup /r to automatically make a scripted installation file, called setup.iss. Copy the setup.iss file to whatever deployment share you have set up (more on that in a bit), and then modify the ZAP file to contain the following setup command:

```
setup /r /setup.iss
```

If the ZAP file method doesn't appeal to you, you can also use a repacking tool, such as Veritas WinInstall LE or InstallShield deployment tools. The tools will take a snapshot of your current system configuration, and then prompt you to install the software that you want to package. Once the installation is complete, these tools will take another snapshot, record what changed on the file system and registry, and then prompt you with a list of what it detected. You then go through the list, make sure that the changes listed were due to installing the software and not errant behavior on the part of Windows, then confirm the list. The software will create an MSI with the program's installer and a database of file system and registry changes.

Using this method, you gain the robustness and rollback features of using an MSI installer as opposed to ZAP files. However, the repackager tools can tend to be a bit flaky, and sometimes will have difficulty installing on multiple platforms. There's not a good way around that, other than obtaining an MSI directly from the software vendor, but it's somewhat of a middle ground between the inflexible ZAP files and a true MSI from the manufacturer.

If you still have a copy of a Windows 2000 distribution CD, you can find a limited version of WinInstall LE on that CD. However, Microsoft has removed, for whatever reason, this program from the Windows Server 2003 CD, so if you don't have the Windows 2000 CD, you are unfortunately out of luck.

An Example Deployment

In this section, I'll step through an actual software deployment using group policy, publishing an application for a user. Let's begin.

Copy the MSI file and necessary other files to a network share. This might require an administrative installation, if your software has one available. Consult the documentation and deployment instructions for more on this.

The network share should have these permissions:

- Authenticated Users should have Read.

- Domain Computers should have Read.

- Administrators should have Read, Change, and Full Control.

Create a new GPO and open it, or edit an existing GPO that you've created for the purposes of distributing this software, using the Group Policy Object Editor. Navigate through the User Configuration and Software Settings nodes in the left pane. Right-click Software Installation, and select Package from the New menu.

In the Find File window, use the Browse button to find the package you copied to the network share. You can select either an MSI file or a ZAP file in this step; if you select a ZAP file, ensure its related installer file is located in the same folder as the ZAP file itself.

If you are using a ZAP file, make sure the SetupCommand directive in the files points to the network path that contains the setup file and not the local path. Otherwise, Windows won't translate the path to the file correctly, and if the software package isn't present at the same local path on target systems, the installation will fail.

On the Deploy Software screen, select whether to publish the software or assign the software. (Skip the Advanced Publish and Assign option at this point, which allows you to use transform files to modify the installation process for an application. This is covered a bit in the next section.) For this example, I'll publish the software.

Click OK, and the software is added to the policy object and saved to the directory.

Of course, to assign an application to a user, you can simply follow the preceding steps, and select Assign instead of Publish. To assign an application to a computer, use the same process, but use Computer Configuration instead of User Configuration and select Assign instead of Publish.

Deployment Properties

You'll probably want to fine-tune the settings for deployment, and you can do this through the properties box for the software. Right-click the name of the package inside Group Policy Object Editor, and then select Properties. There are six tabs to the policy properties box, each of which is described next.

On the General tab, you can modify the name of the package that will be displayed in Add/Remove Programs. You can also view the version, publisher, language, and platform of the software. Figure 4-12 shows the General tab.

The Deployment tab lets you configure the deployment type and user interaction methods for the software. Under Deployment type, you can select whether to publish or assign this software. Under Deployment options, you can choose to "Auto-install this application by file extension activation," which prevents or allows application installation when a user attempts to open a file with an extension associated with the application. You can also elect to "Uninstall this application when it falls out of the scope of management," which dictates whether to remove the application when the user or computer leaves the scope of the current GPO. Additionally, you can choose "Do not display this package in the Add/Remove Programs control panel," which simply hides the application's availability. The application will still be installed when the user opens a file with the associated extension. Finally, under Installation user

interface options, you can choose whether to eliminate most user intervention by installing
the application using default values (with the Basic option) or to prompt the user for installation preferences and instructions (with the Maximum option). Figure 4-13 shows the
Deployment tab.

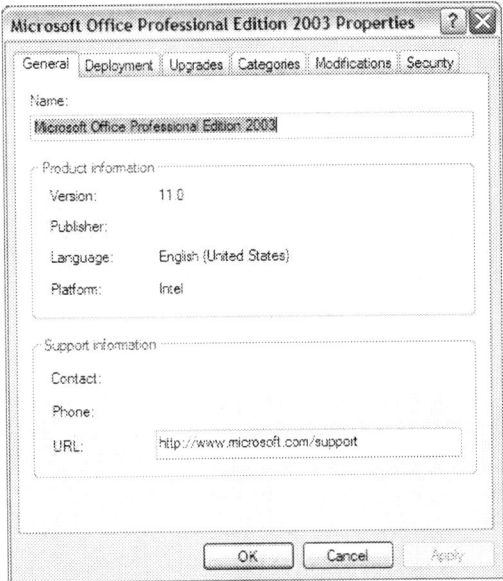

Figure 4-12. *The General tab*

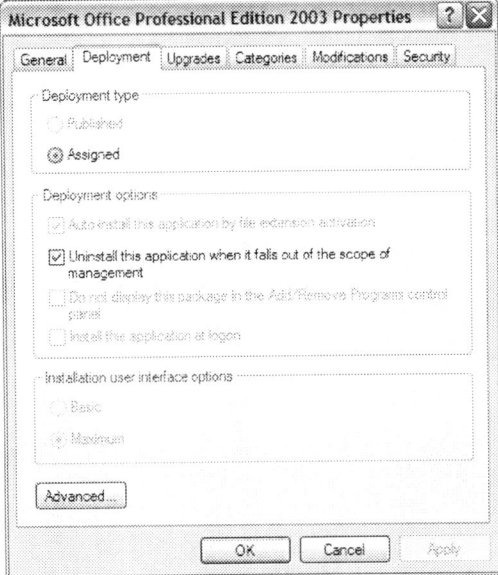

Figure 4-13. *The Deployment tab*

On the Upgrades tab, you can specify that this new package will upgrade an existing installed package. You can make that mandatory by checking the "Required upgrade for existing packages" check box. To add a package to be upgraded, click the Add button and find the package to upgrade within the current object; alternatively, browse through your Active Directory structure by clicking a specific GPO and choosing a different GPO and software package. You can then elect to uninstall the existing package and then install the new package, or to upgrade over the existing package. Figure 4-14 shows the Upgrades tab.

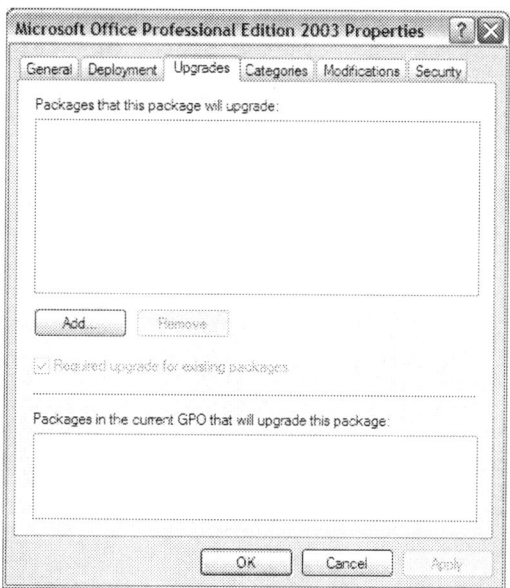

Figure 4-14. *The Upgrades tab*

On the Categories tab, you can create categories that will sort and filter the applications available through the Add/Remove Programs applet within Control Panel. Users can more easily find the published application that they'd like to install if they can click on the type of software they need, rather than wading through a list of 100 possible applications. To add categories, simply click the Add button and enter a new category name. Once you've added the category, you can then add packages under it. Choose a category from the Available categories pane and click Select to add the current package to it. Do this for each package you wish to categorize. Figure 4-15 shows the Categories tab.

On the Modifications tab, you can use a transform file (also called an MST file) to customize an MSI application's installation procedure; through the Modifications tab, you can use multiple MST files to ensure that various users, groups, and computers receive customized versions of a software package. To use a transform file for a particular GPO, click Add on this tab and browse on the file system for the MST file to apply. There are two caveats: you must have deployed an application using the "Advanced Publish or Assign" method, selected when creating the software installation GPO. Also, once an MST has been applied and the software has been deployed, modifications cannot be added or removed. Figure 4-16 shows the Modifications tab.

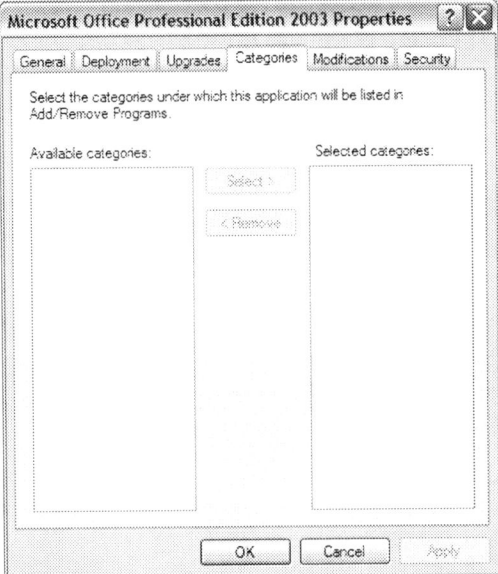

Figure 4-15. *The Categories tab*

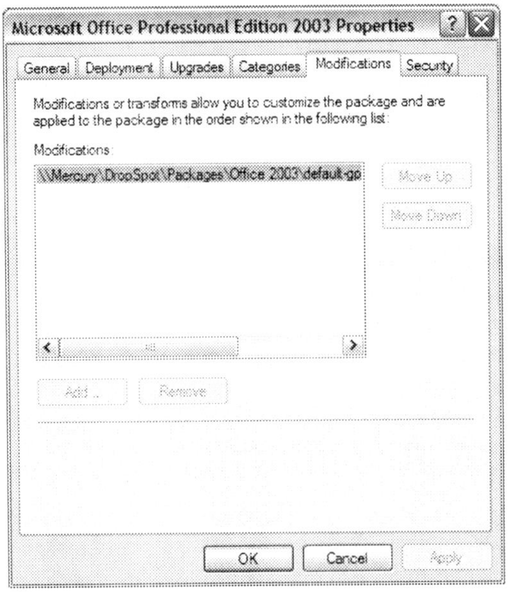

Figure 4-16. *The Modifications tab*

The Security tab, very similar to other ACLs on other objects within Windows Server 2003, allows you to specify permissions on a GPO for users, computers, and groups. You can use this tab in conjunction with the security group filtering strategy, discussed earlier in this chapter, to limit the scope of an applied GPO. For example, one policy assigning Office to computers might only apply to sales, but a policy publishing Windows administrative tools might only apply to administrators. If you want to assign applications to computers, you need to add the Domain Computers group here, unless you already have a security group containing the computers you want. Figure 4-17 shows the Security tab.

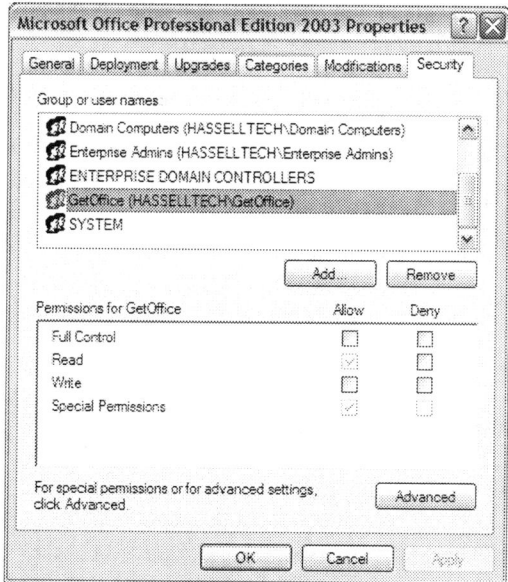

Figure 4-17. *The Security tab*

Remember the following security settings guidelines when deploying software via security group filtering:

If you'd like the policy to be applied to all members of a certain security group, add all the members to a group, add the group to the ACL for the object, and set the following permissions for the group: Apply Group Policy, Allow; Read, Allow. All members of the group will then have the policy applied, except if they are a member of another group with either of the former permissions set to Deny.

If you'd like the policy to NOT be applied to all members of a certain security group, add all the members to a group, add the group to the ACL for the object, and set the following permissions for the group: Apply Group Policy, Deny; Read, Deny. All members of the group will then NOT have the policy applied, regardless of their existing memberships to other groups.

If group membership (at least in a specific group) shouldn't play a part in the application of this policy, then leave permissions alone.

Look back earlier in the chapter to the section called "The Scope of Group Policy Objects" for a refresher on this.

You can also determine the order in which applications will be installed for a given file extension, a useful feature if your organization associates one file extension with multiple software packages. To do so, right-click the Software Installation node within the Group Policy Object Editor (in the left-hand pane) and select Properties. From there, navigate to the File Extensions tab. Select an extension from the drop-down list box, and then adjust the priority, from highest to lowest, of each application in the list box using the Up and Down buttons. If only one application in Group Policy is associated with an extension, this feature will be grayed out, since no priority needs to be established.

You can also configure other deployment options on this property sheet. There are three other tabs here:

- **General**: Here, you can configure the default action when adding new packages to this GPO—whether to assign them, publish them, or display a dialog box asking which action to take. You can set the default user interface options as well. Also, you can indicate the path that will serve as the default location for new packages added to this GPO.

- **Advanced**: On this tab, you can indicate that software packages should be uninstalled when they fall out of the scope of management. You can also allow 64-bit Windows client workstations to install 32-bit Windows applications, and also extend this capability to applications deployed via a ZAP file.

- **Categories**: The Categories tab was discussed a bit earlier in this section.

Redeploying and Removing Software

If you need to patch an existing software deployment that uses an MSI file, you can take advantage of the redeployment functionality of IntelliMirror. Simply copy the new MSI and associated files over the existing copies on the network share. Then, inside the GPO that contains the deployment configuration for the existing package, right-click the package in the details window inside the Group Policy Object Editor, and select Redeploy from the All Tasks menu. Click the Yes button to confirm your choice. The first time the application is started on client computers, regardless of whether the package was assigned or published, the new MSI will be installed.

Along the same lines, if you need to remove installed software, you can right-click the package inside Group Policy Object Editor and select Remove from the All Tasks menu. You'll be presented with the window shown in Figure 4-18.

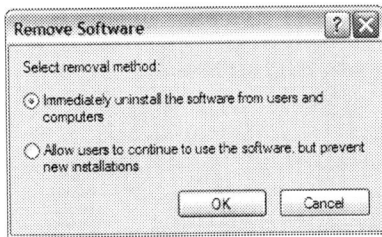

Figure 4-18. *The Remove Software dialog box*

You can choose to either forcibly remove the software immediately, which will uninstall the application no matter what, or to simply remove the software from the list of available software—this will allow current installations to continue to use the software, but will prevent new computers from obtaining the software through group policy.

Deploying Service Packs Using Group Policy

You can also distribute service packs for Windows 2000, XP, and Windows Server 2003 through the IntelliMirror software installation features of GPOs. Doing so can go a long way toward eliminating a tedious and time-consuming administrative task. You can assign the service pack to computers for mandatory deployment, or you can publish the service pack to users so they can choose to install it if their situation warrants it.

If you are assigning the service pack to computers, you can simply point a GPO to the UPDATE.MSI file included in the extracted portion of all current service packs from Microsoft. However, if you're publishing the service pack, you'll need to create a ZAP file and then point the software installation GPO to that ZAP file. Again, you can't publish MSI files.

To deploy a service pack using IntelliMirror:

1. Create a distribution share for the service pack, and extract its contents there. This process is described in Chapter 2, or you can consult the readme files within the service pack distribution file for information.

2. If you are publishing the service pack to users, create a ZAP file pointing to UPDATE.EXE inside the folder where the extracted service pack files are.

3. Create a new group policy object for the service pack. This isn't required—you can assign the service pack as part of default domain policy or any other level of policy— but it's best to keep software installations to their own GPOs so changes can be reversed easily.

4. In the GPO, navigate through Computer Configuration or User Configuration and then choose Software Installation.

5. Right-click Software installation, and choose Package from the New menu.

6. Find the network path to the service pack files, and select either UPDATE.MSI if you're assigning to computers or the UPDATE.ZAP file you created earlier if you're publishing to users.

7. Choose Assigned or Published in the Deploy Software dialog box.

8. Click OK.

The policy is now set, and the service pack will either be assigned or published, depending on your choices. Keep in mind that service packs are typically large files, so you should deploy them after considering the effect that process would have on both your network bandwidth and the time it would take to install locally on the client machines. Additionally, you should avoid automatically deploying service packs on your domain controllers. These machines are sensitive beasts that hold the keys to your Active Directory—manually install service packs on these machines one by one and test them to make sure there are no ill effects.

IntelliMirror: Folder Redirection

You can use the folder redirection functionality of group policy to change the target location of many folders within a particular user's Windows interface. For example, you can specify custom locations for the Application Data, Desktop, My Documents (and the My Pictures subfolder), and Start Menu folders. Using folder redirection circumvents the nasty problem of roaming profiles: severe network traffic hikes caused by copying large My Documents and Desktop folders to workstations around the network when users log on. You can also back up the share where the folders are redirected using a normal network backup procedure, automatically protecting the contents.

To access the folder redirection functionality, launch the Group Policy Object Editor for a particular GPO, and navigate through User Configuration ➤ Windows Settings ➤ Folder Redirection. In the right-hand pane, you'll see the four folders you can redirect. Right-click each to bring up the Properties window. Figure 4-19 shows this screen.

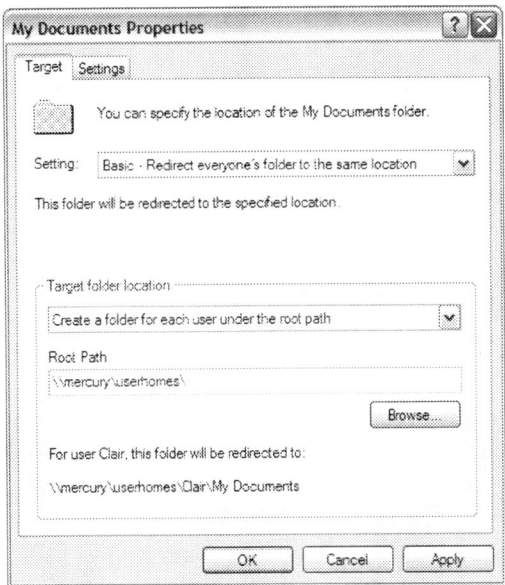

Figure 4-19. *The folder redirection interface*

On the Target tab, you can choose the type of redirection for this policy. For this example, choose the Basic method, which simply redirects all users' folders to the same location. Next, enter the target folder at the bottom of the screen under Root Path, and select the option to create a new folder for each user underneath the root path. Then, move to the Settings tab, and choose the following settings:

- **Grant the user exclusive rights to My Documents**: If this setting is enabled, the user to whom the folder belongs and the local computer have administrative and exclusive rights to the folder, to the exclusion of all other objects. If this setting is disabled, the current permissions on the folder are kept.

- **Move the contents of My Documents to the new location**: If this setting is enabled, everything in the current My Documents folder will be moved to the new, redirected location. If this option is disabled, nothing will be moved and the new My Documents folder will be empty.

- **Policy removal**: You can adjust the Windows default setting, which leaves the folder in the redirected location if the redirection policy itself is removed. You can also choose to move the folder back to its initial location.

- **My Pictures preferences**: The default action for the My Pictures subfolder is to follow the My Documents folder to wherever it rests.

Redirecting Folders Based on Group Membership

If you'd like to redirect some profile folders to different locations based on the different groups to which a user belongs, you can use the Advanced method of redirection inside the redirect policy properties page, on the Target tab. When you select Advanced from the drop-down setting box indicating the type of redirection, click the Add button. The Specify Group and Location box will appear, as shown in Figure 4-20.

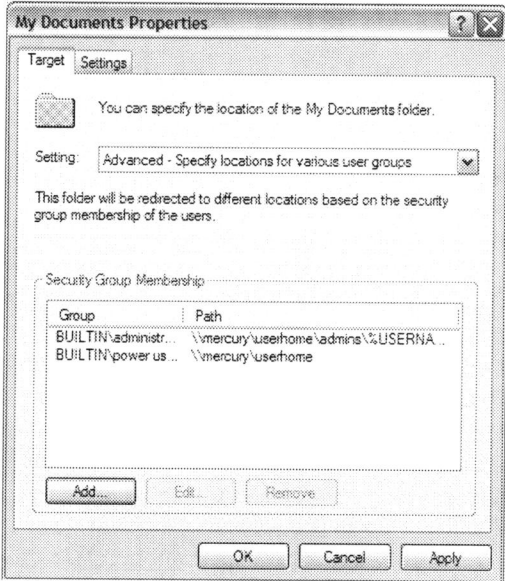

Figure 4-20. *Redirecting folders based on group membership*

Enter the name of a security group, and then enter the network path to the folders. Always use a UNC path, even if the folders are local, so that users taking advantage of roaming profiles will see the correct folders in an absolute path and not wrongly translate a local, relative path. Click OK when you're done, and then repeat the process for as many groups that you need.

If your users are creatures of habit, you can even turn on the Offline Files and Folders feature on the share where you've stored the redirected folders. This way, Windows will continue to display and use a customized environment even when the network is down and the share can't be reached.

Folder Redirection and Windows XP

As I pointed out earlier in the chapter, folder redirection policies are not updated in the background for obvious reasons—for one, how would you feel if suddenly your My Documents folder pointed itself somewhere else? Folder redirection policies are updated asynchronously, according to Microsoft, and only synchronous updates are allowed in the background.

Microsoft introduced a feature in Windows XP called fast logon optimization, which allows the user to see a logon box much faster than with Windows 2000 clients. This is done by using a set of cached credentials and not waiting for a network connection to boot. When a connection is found, group policies are applied in the expected fashion, but this too is asynchronous updating—of course, this means that folder redirection policies will again not be applied.

Fast logon optimization is designed to cause a normal reboot, without the optimization, if a GPO change is detected when the computer is logged on and connected to the domain within two reboots (for computer settings) or two logoffs (for user settings). However, you can turn off fast logon optimization to make an XP client mimic a Windows 2000 client by enabling the Computer Configuration ➤ Administrative Templates ➤ System ➤ Logon ➤ Always wait for the network at computer setting.

Removing a Redirection Policy

It can be a bit difficult to track what happens to redirected folders if you decide to remove a redirection policy. It really depends on the appropriate setting on the Settings tab of the redirected folder's policy properties sheet.

If you've selected to redirect the folder back to the local user profile when the policy is removed, and the option to move the contents of the local folder to a new location is enabled, the folder will return to its original location, and the contents of the folder are copied back to the original location but not deleted from the redirected location. If the option to move the contents of the folder to a new location is disabled, the folder will revert to its original location, but the contents of the folder are not copied or moved to the original location. This means that the user is unable to access the contents of the redirected folder from the special folder's UI within the shell, but using a UNC path, she can still access the redirected folder and retrieve its contents manually. If you've selected to leave the folder in the new location when the policy is removed, the folder and its contents will remain at the redirected location, and the user will have access to it, regardless of whether the option to move the contents of the folder to the new location is enabled or disabled.

Conclusion

I've covered a lot of material in this chapter: I looked at file and print services within Windows Server 2003, went over some basics of the Active Directory component of the operating system, and then walked through a detailed discussion of Group Policy and its feature set. In the next chapter, I'll look at Exchange Server 2003 in much the same fashion, going beyond the Management Console and digging into the power of the product.

CHAPTER 5

∎∎∎

Exploring Outlook 2003 and Exchange Server 2003

BEGINNER SBS ADMINISTRATOR ∎ **ADVANCED SBS ADMINISTRATOR** ∎ EXPERIENCED CONSULTANT

Continuing our discussion of the core applications that make up Small Business Server 2003, let's turn our attention to the messaging duo: Outlook 2003 on the client side, and Exchange Server 2003 on the server side. This combination of programs and server technology allows your business to take advantage of the same applications that large, worldwide businesses use to stay in touch with their customers, partners, and employees.

In this chapter, I'll first look at Outlook 2003, the client-side messaging application. I'll step through each of its modules, discuss some neat features, and then step through some advanced Outlook tasks. Then I'll move to Exchange 2003, which runs on the SBS server itself, and show its management features and discuss its limitations and SBS-specific features.

Let's begin.

Outlook 2003 in General

Microsoft's Office member Outlook has become a great e-mail application since its first release in 1997. It combines a robust e-mail client with a personal information manager, storing information on your appointments and other date-driven events, your contacts and address book entries, and a priority-based task list. Think of Outlook as one-stop shopping for your communication and information management needs.

SBS 2003 comes with Outlook and Exchange Server 2003, which are attached at the hip, so to speak. A lot of great Outlook functionality is available only when it's used in conjunction with Exchange Server (it used to be that there were actually separate modes for running Outlook—a standard mode for Internet mail only and a corporate mode for running against an Exchange Server). Large Fortune 500 corporations have standardized on Outlook and Exchange, so by deploying it as a part of SBS 2003, you are really getting an industrial-strength e-mail and PIM infrastructure.

In this section, I'll walk through the main areas of the product in case you're not used to this version of Outlook. This serves as good material for training your users on Outlook as well. I'll highlight some neat features as we go along, and then give you some pointers on how best to organize your mailbox.

Contacts

Outlook has a good contact manager, and it's one that can be extended to track all sorts of information, including birthdays, spouse names, notes on your last meeting, exchanged documents, and so on. The Contacts list will track all of the particulars for your people, including multiple addresses, multiple phone numbers, birthdays, spouse names, anniversary dates, web sites, and more. You can view your contacts as either a list of business cards or in "phone list" style, as shown in Figure 5-1. You can see this list by opening Outlook 2003 and then clicking the Contacts bar in the lower left of the screen.

Figure 5-1. *The Outlook phone list*

You can change the current view of your contacts by adjusting the selection in the bulleted list called Current View that you see in the upper left of the screen. To create a new contact, click the New button on the toolbar and enter the contact's information.

Allow me to highlight just one neat feature: Outlook will allow you to create multiple lists (these act effectively as address books), so you can sort different address books depending on the category of the contact, the priority of the contact, the nature of the relationship, or any other criteria that means something to you. For example, in Figure 5-1, you can see in the upper-left corner that I have a folder called Contacts in which I store my main addressee information, but I also have another list called Mail Blasts that I use to collect business names, addresses, and phone numbers in order to send marketing material for my consultancy. You might create lists for customers, personal names, and then potential leads, or you might choose to create different lists for the levels of service your company provides (i.e., small business, medium business, and then enterprise customers). It's very flexible.

E-Mail

Mail is the hub of Outlook and likely where you and your users will spend the most time in the program. The 2003 version of Outlook has been completely redesigned into a more vertical three-paned approach to reading mail, with your folder list in the leftmost column, the list of mail in the currently selected folder in the middle pane, and the currently selected e-mail message laid out as it would be on a printed page in the right pane. Studies have shown that up to 20% more of the message can be displayed when using this layout than with the standard, horizontally inclined message pane common among the other e-mail clients. That means less time scrolling.

The default view of the mailbox as I just described it is shown in Figure 5-2. You can access it by clicking the Mail bar in the lower-left corner of the Outlook screen.

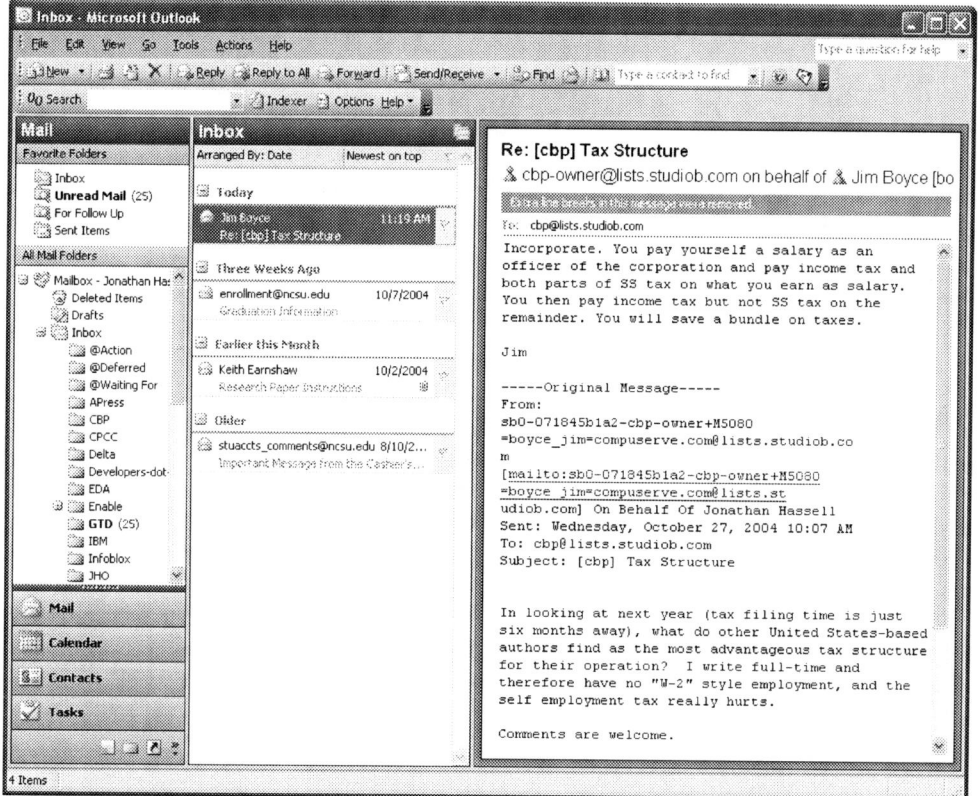

Figure 5-2. *The default e-mail view in Outlook 2003*

To create a new message, click the New button on the toolbar. To create new folders like you see in the left pane in Figure 5-2, simply right-click the existing folder inside of which you'd like to create a new folder and select New Folder from the pop-up context menu. Give the folder a name, and you're all set.

A cool feature of the mail portion of Outlook is the flagging feature. You can flag a message with a red, blue, yellow, green, orange, or purple flag, and use that color-coding scheme to identify the priority or nature of certain e-mail messages. For example, for e-mails from my publishers regarding text I need to edit or resubmit, I use the orange flag, but for e-mails from my web hosting customers that need a response from me, I use the purple flag. To set these flags, simply right-click the flag icon in the message list and choose the appropriate flag color.

What can you do with these flags? How would they help you? For me, I use them to catch up on e-mails during odd times—like waiting on an appointment, or when I am on hold during a conference call, or at the airport waiting for a plane. When I am somewhere where I can deal with e-mails quickly during some lag time, I can tell Outlook to only show me e-mails with colored flags on them by clicking the For Follow Up view option in the Favorite Folders box at the top-left corner of the Outlook window. This will show me only e-mails that I have tagged with a flag, and I can quickly respond to each e-mail. Once I'm done responding to those e-mails, I can right-click each flagged message and select Clear Flag, and the message disappears from that particular view. It's a great way to get a focused look at the e-mail I receive that needs my response, and an excellent way to stay on top of urgent e-mail in the sea of messages we all receive in this Internet age.

Note Outlook 2003 comes with its own built-in junk e-mail filter. Messages that Outlook thinks are spam will automatically be diverted to the Junk E-mail folder, which is visible in the folder list. Peruse this regularly, and tell Outlook which messages it has incorrectly characterized as junk by selecting the message and then clicking the Not Junk button on the toolbar. Also, keep the filter's intelligence on top of the latest techniques spammers use by visiting Office Update (http://officeupdate.microsoft.com) regularly.

Calendar

The Outlook calendar module is an adequate way for you and your company to track appointments, events, and recurring tasks that are driven by dates. There are several default views for the calendar, such as a monthly, weekly, work-weekly, or daily view. Figure 5-3 shows the monthly view for a typical Outlook calendar. You can access the calendar by clicking the Calendar bar in the lower-left portion of the Outlook window.

To create a new appointment, click the New button in the toolbar. You'll then be prompted for information on what type of appointment you're creating, the times, any relevant contacts, whether you'd like to be reminded of the event, and other options.

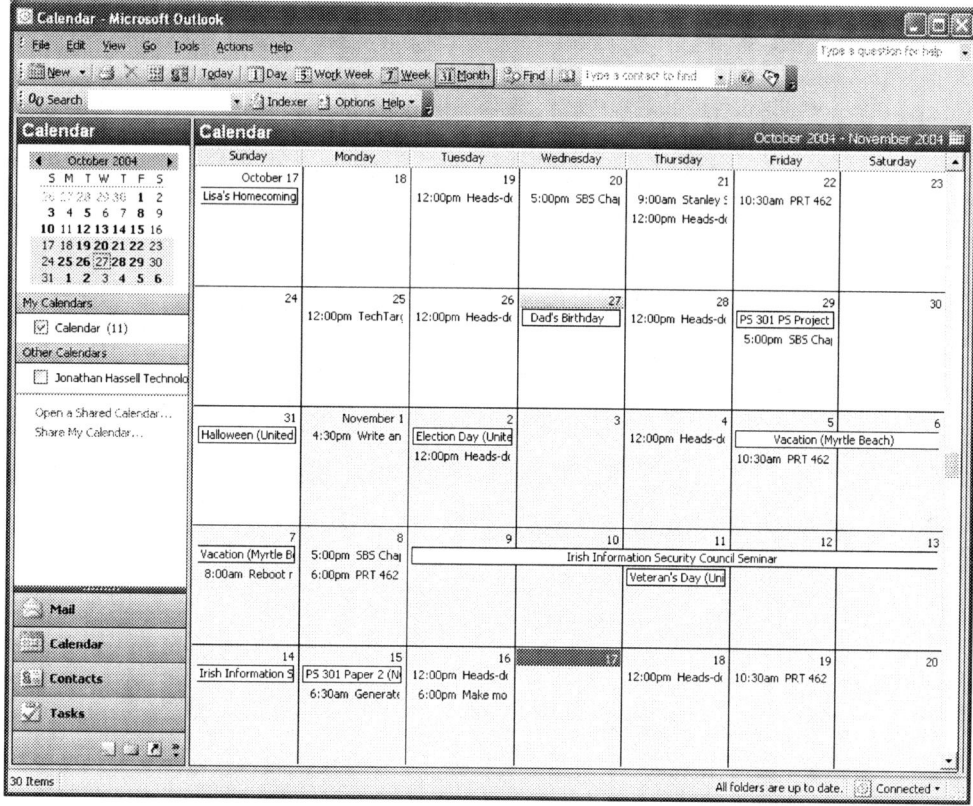

Figure 5-3. *The default monthly calendar view in Outlook 2003*

There are two cool features I'd like to outline in this section (not that there aren't others). For one, you can use color coding for your events for easy distinction. I tend to color code personal appointments and events, like doctor visits and vacations, using the green color, but for important client business I use the yellow color. It makes it very easy to prioritize your appointments so that you know what's absolutely critical for your business and what's possible to delay if a time crunch occurs. To color code an event, right-click the event, and from the Label menu, select the color and label that applies. Unlike with mail flags, you can assign custom label text to a certain color—the defaults are important, business, personal, vacation, must attend, travel required, needs preparation, birthday, anniversary, and phone call. You can change these as you see fit.

Note If you have a PocketPC and take advantage of color coding within Outlook, the coloring will transfer over to your handheld device when you synchronize with your host computer. A nice touch!

The other timesaving feature I use regularly is the ability to drag and drop mail messages into the calendar to prepopulate a lot of information I would normally have to enter myself into the new appointment form. For example, I might receive an e-mail from my editor informing me of a conference call date and time. I could try to memorize the details of the appointment, switch to the calendar, and then try to remember the details and type them in manually. Or, I could simply select the message from my editor and drag it over the Calendar bar in the lower-left corner of the Outlook window, and the form already has some information entered. This is shown in Figure 5-4.

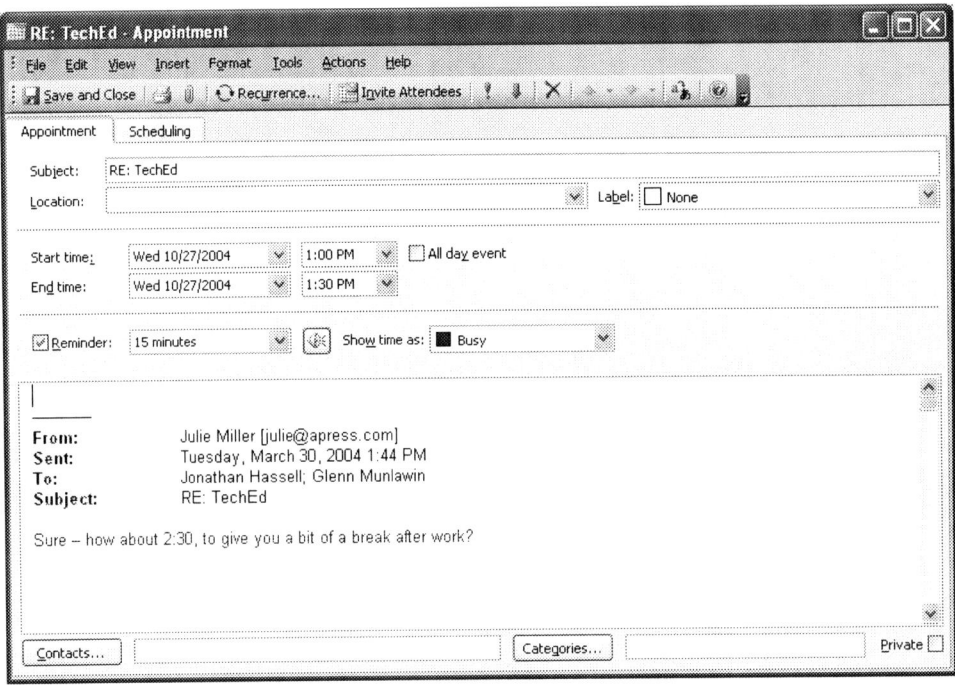

Figure 5-4. *Dragging an e-mail message into the calendar*

You can see that the subject of the appointment automatically assumes the subject of the e-mail message, and then the body of the e-mail message is automatically inserted into the notes section of the appointment. This way, when I'm reminded of the appointment, I can double-click it and see the relevant e-mail to remind myself of what I need to do to prepare for the appointment. I still need to manually enter the date and time of the appointment (by default the new appointment is set for the top of the next hour, according to your current time on your computer), but the message text is on the same screen, and I can simply scroll the find it.

Tasks

The Tasks view lets you enter in things you need to complete, track their progress, prioritize them, and assign tasks to other users within your SBS domain. To look at the default Tasks view, click the Tasks bar in the lower-left corner of the Outlook window. You'll see a screen much like that shown in Figure 5-5.

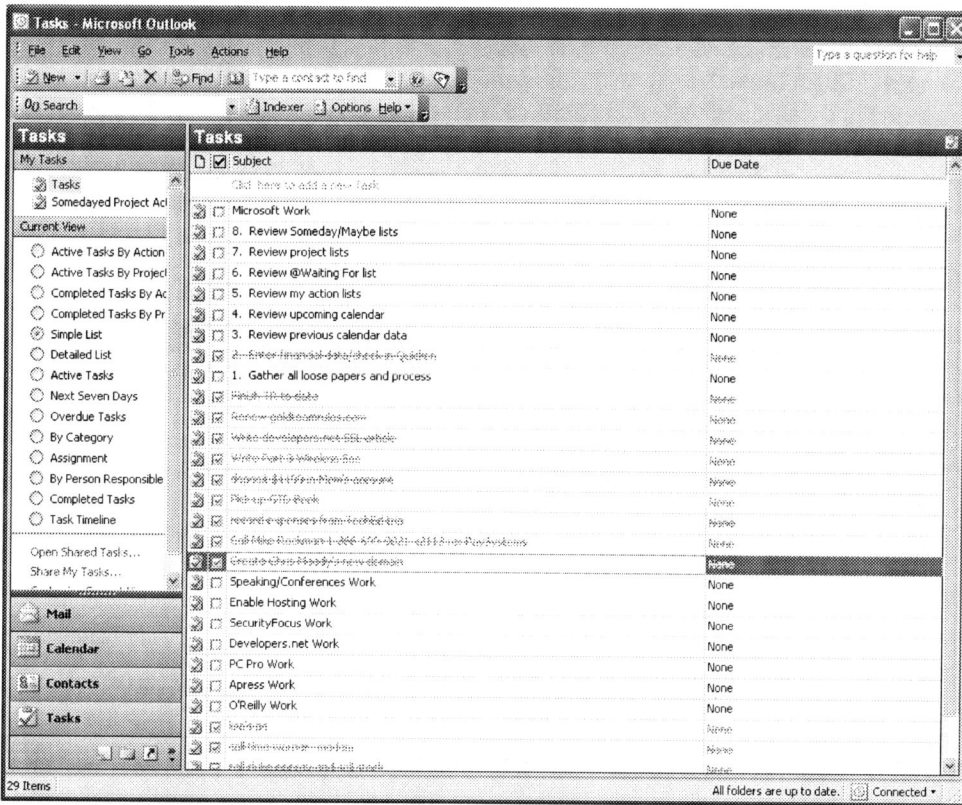

Figure 5-5. *The default Tasks view in Outlook 2003*

To create a new task, click the New button on the top toolbar. You'll be prompted to fill in a form containing the details of the task.

An interesting and useful feature about tasks is the ability to sort the tasks you have already entered into Outlook by view. Look back at Figure 5-5 and note on the left side of the window the box entitled Current View. You can select from any number of choices, which will then restrict the tasks listed in the right pane to only those that match those criteria. For example, if you only want to look at your active tasks, you can click Active Tasks by Action or Active Tasks by Project. However, if you are looking at what you have completed for a monthly status report for your manager, you can select Completed Tasks by Action or Completed Tasks by Project. You can look at critical tasks for the week ahead with the Next Seven Days view, or if you're a chronic procrastinator (you don't have to admit it here), you can select Overdue Tasks. There's really a view for almost any need.

Public Folders

Public folders are simply folders containing Outlook items that everyone can see. Your SBS users can access public folders inside Outlook in the full folder view or also through Outlook Web Access, something I'll cover in Chapter 8.

A public folder looks exactly like any other e-mail folder. The SBS installation wizard creates one by default, which is simply your company name. This public folder is mail enabled, which means that it has its own e-mail address and mail can be sent to it from any standard, Internet-based e-mail client. The default public folder stores copies of any e-mail sent to the "entire company" distribution list—an e-mail list I discussed in Chapter 3.

To get to the public folders interface within Outlook 2003, click the folder icon in the bottom left of the Outlook window to bring up the Folder List view, and then scroll down in the list in the left pane and click Public Folders. Expand it to see the default public folder view, as shown in Figure 5-6.

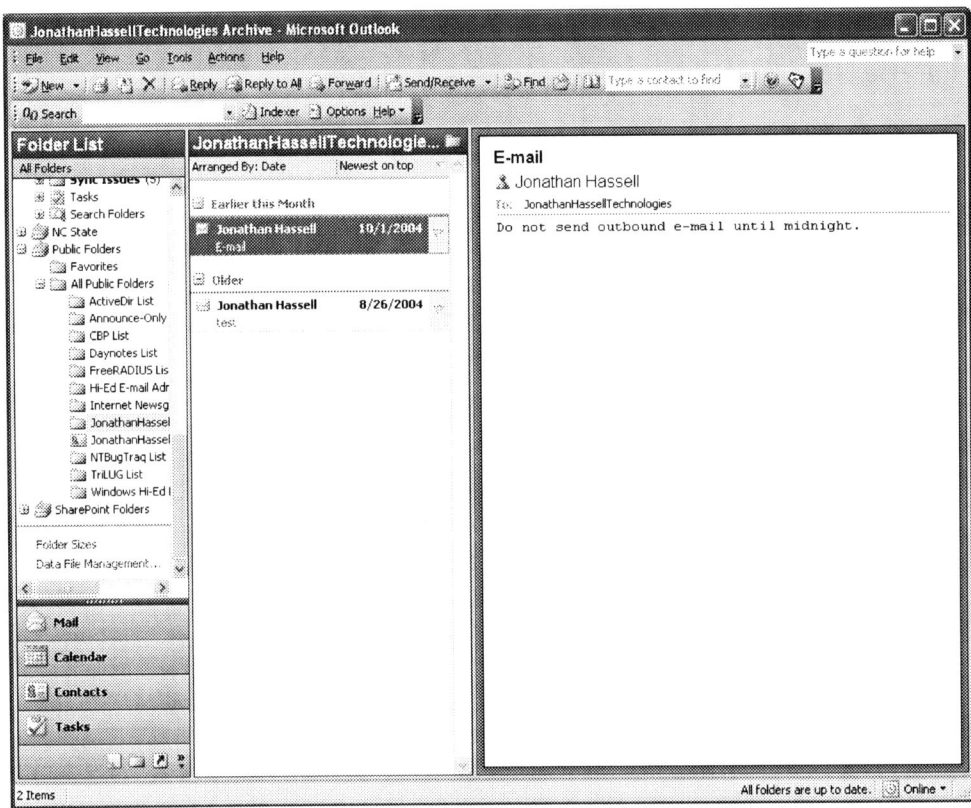

Figure 5-6. *The default public folders view in Outlook 2003*

You can create posts to this public folder by clicking the New button in the toolbar. All domain users will be able to read this.

Caution Don't run Outlook on the server. There are components of Outlook that are not exactly 100% compatible with some software running on the SBS server. Use Outlook on your client workstations only.

Advanced Outlook

In this section, I'll take a look at three ways you can use advanced Outlook features or plug-ins to help manage the flow of e-mail in your inbox.

▒**Note** I'm not devoting a whole section to this because the future of this tool is up in the air, but go get Lookout, a plug-in for Microsoft Outlook. It is a marvelous search plug-in that will allow you to find just about anything located in your mailbox. It can currently be found at `http://www.lookoutsoft.com/Lookout/download.html`, but that may change as Microsoft just bought the product from its original developers. Just double-click it to install and let it index your mailbox, and read the instructions at that site to learn more about how to use the tool.

Working in Cached Exchange Mode

Cached Exchange mode is one of the boons of working with Outlook 2003. Since Outlook is so wedded to the Exchange Server product in most business environments, previous versions of Outlook behaved quite strangely when that connection to the Exchange Server was broken. It could be that the Exchange machine was down for maintenance, or perhaps the user was on the road with a laptop without a permanent connection back to the server at the office. In these cases, especially with the really old versions of Outlook, it was so bad that you could hardly use your e-mail application when you were away from Exchange.

Outlook 2003 has helped to cure this situation with what it calls Cached Exchange mode. Essentially, Outlook works in the background to download a complete copy of your mailbox, which it stores locally on the hard drive of your client machine. Outlook works from this copy of your mailbox all the time, but it periodically checks in with the Exchange Server to see if you have new mail or other changes have been made to the real copy of your mailbox that resides on the server. It downloads these changes, if there are any, to your locally cached mailbox. In effect, you are working from a copy of your mailbox that is quite recent and continually updated as long as you have some sort of connection to your Exchange server.

The upshot of Cached Exchange mode is that you can load Outlook and work on it whenever, wherever you might need without worrying about whether you have a link to your Exchange server. So you can quite confidently use Outlook and respond to e-mail while on a plane, in an airport lounge, in traffic (I suppose it would have to be really bad traffic), or any other place you have significant downtime and a handy laptop. Your changes will be synchronized with the Exchange machine you call home the next time a link to it is available. Best of all, Outlook defaults to Cached Exchange mode when set up on your SBS client computers, so there's no extra work to take advantage of this feature.

Creating Rules to Handle Mail

Rules are great ways to handle a deluge of e-mail you may receive on a regular basis. For example, you might subscribe to several e-mail lists to monitor developments and discussions in your line of business. However, you might not need to see this e-mail as it comes in—you may want to wait until a convenient time on the weekend to scan through the messages you've received, and you don't want them filling up your Inbox folder during the workweek and distracting you. Rules are a great way to manage large amounts of mail from a single source.

I'll use one of my mailing lists as an example. The first step to creating a rule is determining a single, common characteristic of all mail to which you would like this rule applied. For me, it's that all e-mail I want to use this rule for comes from a single e-mail address: Getting_Things_Done@yahoogroups.com. I can use that as a basis for my rule.

Now, inside Outlook, do the following:

1. From the Tools menu, select Rules and Alerts.

2. The Rules and Alerts dialog box will appear. Click the New Rule button.

3. You can choose here to create a rule from a template or to start from a blank rule. Since our rule is common among Outlook users, it's listed under Stay Organized—it's called "Move messages from someone to a folder." Choose that and click Next.

4. Next, select the appropriate condition. The first option, "from people or distribution list," works just fine for us. Then, in the bottom box, click the link with the same name, and enter the e-mail address for which you'd like this rule to apply. Then, click Next.

5. Now, tell Outlook what to do with mail that matches those criteria. I want to move this mail to a separate folder under my Inbox folder, so I'll use the first option, "move it to the specified folder." In the bottom box, click the link and specify the folder to which that mail should be moved. When you're finished, click Next.

6. The next screen asks you if there are exceptions. Click Next.

7. Now, give the new rule you've created a name, and then choose whether to run that rule immediately on messages currently in your Inbox, and to enable the rule so it runs for all future mail received. Confirm the rule will do what you expect, and then click Finish.

Your mail rule has been created.

Recovering Deleted Items

Haven't we all inadvertently deleted an important e-mail message? Perhaps we don't even realize that the message we've deleted is important until we've already emptied the Deleted Items folder within Outlook, the default location where messages go when you hit the Delete key.

But with SBS 2003, all is not lost: there is a message recovery feature that is accessible from directly within Outlook that you should avail yourself of if the unfortunate deletion happens to you. By default, the SBS server (which runs Exchange, as you'll see later in this chapter) retains deleted messages for 30 days before completely purging them—this is known as the retention period. If your message was deleted within this month-long window, then you can recover it by performing the following procedure:

1. Select the Deleted Items folder within Outlook.

2. From the Tools menu, select Recover Deleted Items.

3. The Recover Deleted Items From window will appear. Select the e-mails you'd like to recover, and then click the Recover Selected Items button on the toolbar (the second from the left). The e-mail will be returned to the Deleted Items folder.

4. Close the window.

5. Move the message from the Deleted Items folder to wherever you would like it stored in your mailbox.

This is a lifesaver feature that could recover some weekends if you have a habit of being too quick with the Delete key on Friday afternoons.

Now, let's move our focus from the client workstation to the SBS server machine itself.

Exchange Server 2003 in General

Exchange Server 2003 is a powerful e-mail and groupware product. By e-mail, I'm speaking of the application's ability to send and receive electronic mail, both internally among users inside your company and externally, to users on the Internet using standard mail transfer protocols like SMTP. By groupware, I'm referring to the extended functionality of Exchange which allows users to share calendar data, collaborate within their e-mail applications and over the web, create distribution lists for easier team communication, and other types of facilitating features. Exchange also focuses on users' ability to send and receive e-mail on any device wherever they may be, and to that end, Exchange supports ActiveSync technology for your workers who use handheld devices, Outlook Mobile Access (OMA) to check e-mail on cellular telephones and other mobile gadgets, and other remote access tools.

Exchange has been lurking under the hood ever since you began the SBS installation process. During the initial installation of SBS, you encountered a long wait where Exchange actually took the Active Directory's list of columns (technically called the schema) and extended it, adding new fields for new, Exchange-specific information. These modifications to the schema allow you to store new kinds of contact information and other data about your users. You were also prompted to complete the Configure E-mail and Internet Connection Wizard (CEICW), which—as you'll recall—was where you specified your preferred settings for the server's built-in software firewall, the web server configuration, and how you wanted your mail services published to the outside world. We'll look at how each of these wizards affects your Exchange installation later in the chapter.

How Exchange Is Exposed

The user interface offers Exchange administrators a few different ways to touch the Exchange product itself. Perhaps first and foremost is within Active Directory Users and Computers, where one can adjust the e-mail addresses, phone numbers, contact information, e-mail mailbox size, and more on the properties pages for each user.

To see an example, open the Server Management Console, expand Active Directory Users and Computers under Advanced Management, select a user, and then right-click that user and select Properties. Then focus on the Exchange-specific tabs—Exchange General, E-mail Addresses, Exchange Features, and Exchange Advanced.

Figure 5-7 shows the Exchange General tab for a user.

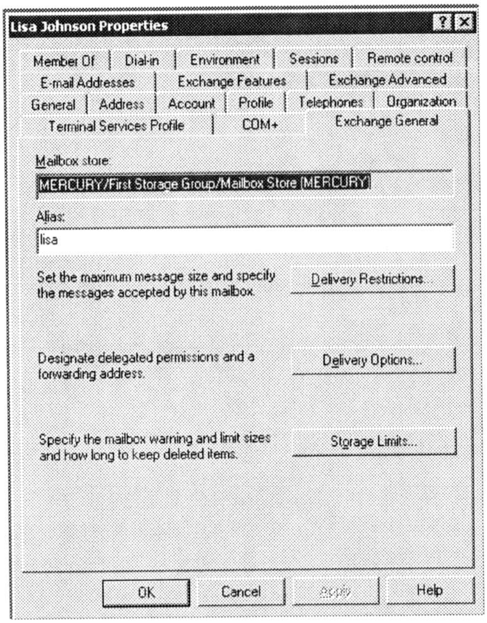

Figure 5-7. *The Exchange General tab*

On the Exchange General tab, you can see the store in which the user's mailbox is located, the alias for the mailbox, delivery restrictions and options, and storage limits.

Figure 5-8 shows the E-mail Addresses tab.

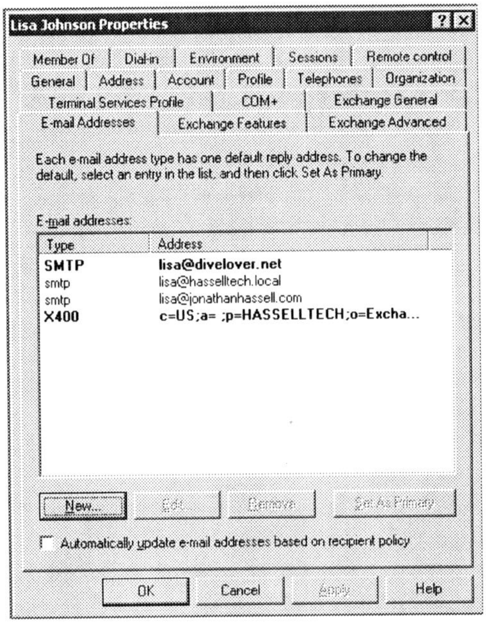

Figure 5-8. *The E-mail Addresses tab*

On the E-mail Addresses tab, you can see all of the different e-mail addresses currently configured for a user, as well as where you can add a new e-mail address for the user. Each of the preceding addresses represents a valid address for this user, which means that messages to both lisa@divelover.net and lisa@jonathanhassell.com would be delivered to Lisa Johnson's Exchange mailbox. Note the different types of address: they are specific to each protocol supported by Exchange. By far, the most common Internet e-mail protocol is SMTP, which specifies that e-mail addresses should be formatted in the format you're used to: name@company.tld.

Figure 5-9 shows the Exchange Features tab.

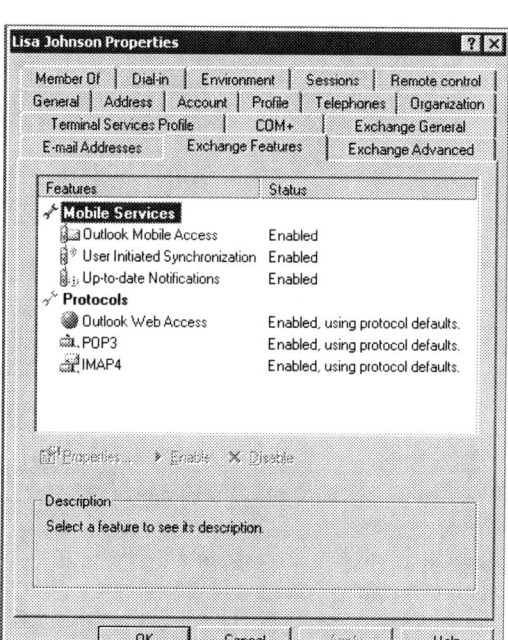

Figure 5-9. *The Exchange Features tab*

On the Exchange Features tab, you can see the different options and features for mobile users, including synchronization options, Outlook Mobile Access support, POP3 and IMAP support for other e-mail client software besides Outlook, and Outlook Web Access for user access to Exchange mailboxes through a web browser. I'll cover these features in Chapter 8, which is all about remote access to your work environment.

Figure 5-10 shows the Exchange Advanced tab. On this tab, you can see the display name for a user, whether this user is present on address lists available to the company, any custom attributes applied to the user, and the specific permissions on the user's mailbox in Exchange.

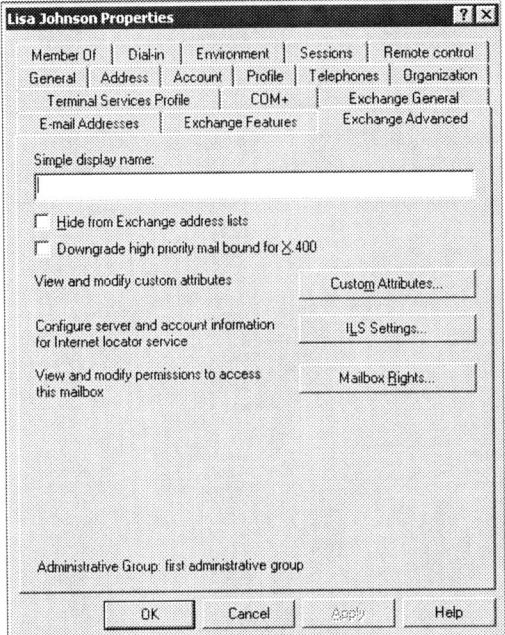

Figure 5-10. *The Exchange Advanced tab*

Why is all of this information present in Active Directory Users and Computers? This lies in the fact that Exchange and Active Directory are very closely married, so much so that Exchange depends on AD for its directory information. In previous versions of Exchange, the mail directory was created, stored, and managed only within Exchange itself, but in the latest versions of Exchange users lists are maintained only within Active Directory. Exchange simply hooks into AD when it needs information on users and the IT structure of your business— for example, to verify usernames and passwords, to replicate information about your users among multiple machines, and to store Exchange-specific data in a single, easily accessible place.

Next, let's take a look at the Exchange System Manager, a place in the UI where the internals of Exchange's operations itself can be seen. In the Server Management Console, expand the Advanced Management option, and then click the Exchange icon and expand it. You'll see a screen much like that in Figure 5-11.

Within Exchange System Manager, you can adjust several different, high-level options for Exchange. For example, you can configure policies for recipients (which are simply how e-mail addresses for new users are constructed and formatted), settings for the mailbox stores (groups of mailboxes that all are managed by the same set of rules like mailbox size, disk location, and other factors), mail connectors (pieces of software that allow mail to traverse between your Exchange server and other mail servers), and public folders (collaborative folders accessible by default to all Exchange users in your domain). Luckily, unless you are planning a very sophisticated Exchange extension, you probably will not have to worry too much about visiting the advanced parts of Exchange System Manager. We will, however, revisit it later in this book.

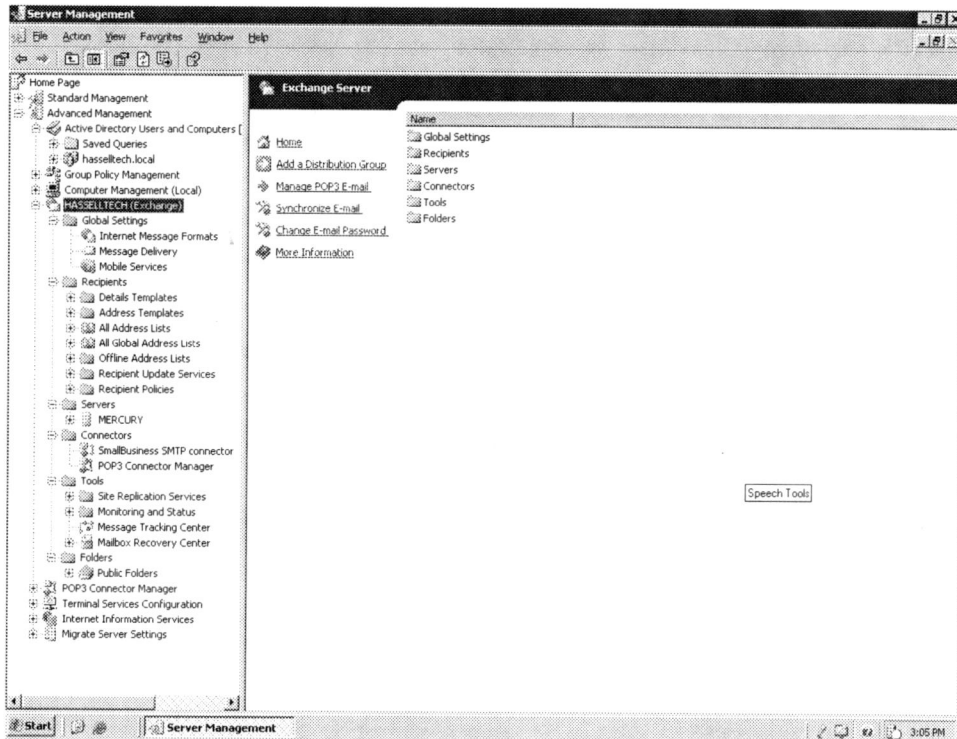

Figure 5-11. *The Exchange System Manager screen*

SBS-Specific Exchange Features

In this section, I'll take a look at three specific features that are only available with the flavor of Exchange Server 2003 included in SBS.

POP3 Connector

Throughout previous versions of SBS, the POP3 connector has been a welcome but some-times troublesome component of the product. The POP3 connector helps those organizations that can't put their SBS server directly on the Internet, for any number of reasons. Sometimes a particular ISP will not lease you a static IP address, or perhaps your office can only get a dial-up connection, which is not full time and therefore unsuitable for receiving Internet e-mail.

What does a small business do in this situation? Chances are that if you have a web site, an ISP is hosting it and provides with your hosting plan a set of standard POP3 mailboxes through which you can receive e-mail. The POP3 connector maps these POP3 accounts at your ISP with the Exchange mailboxes that are stored on your SBS server. It then downloads mail from the POP3 accounts at your ISP and routes that mail to the individual Exchange mailboxes, so your users connect only to the Exchange server and their mail has already been downloaded.

Microsoft did some heavy revision work to the POP3 connector in SBS 2003, and it is much easier to configure the connector initially and make changes to its setup as your SBS server grows. You can configure it directly from the Server Management Console on the SBS machine itself. Under Standard Management, click the Internet and E-mail link, and then select Manage POP3 E-mail. Finally, click Open POP3 Connector Manager. The screen you see in Figure 5-12 will appear.

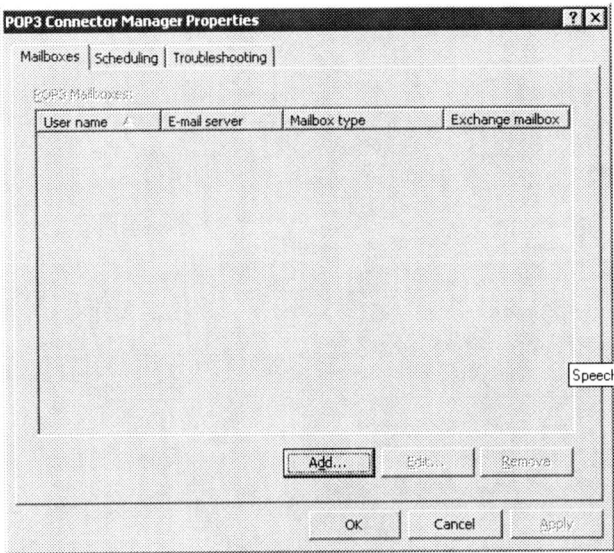

Figure 5-12. *The POP3 Connector Manager screen*

If you have POP3 mail accounts at an ISP and want the mail in those accounts downloaded to local Exchange mailboxes on your SBS server, do the following:

1. On the POP3 Connector Manager screen, click the Add button.

2. The POP3 Mailbox screen appears. Enter your ISP's e-mail server name, the port number its POP3 service runs on (110 is common and the default), and the username and password for the account at your ISP.

3. Next, select the mailbox on the Exchange server to which mail from the ISP should be downloaded. You can choose a name from the drop-down list box.

4. Click OK.

The account is now mapped and the mail will download.

By default, the POP3 connector will download mail once per hour. To customize this schedule, click the Scheduling tab. You can choose to immediately retrieve the mail (the big red button, so to speak) by clicking Retrieve Now. Under the Schedule section, you can set the intervals at which the connector will download mail. You can set it from as often as every 15 minutes to as few times as once per week. You can also create a custom schedule by clicking the Define Schedule button and highlighting the areas in which you'd like mail to be downloaded.

Attachment and Content Blocking

In this wave of Internet e-mail viruses and worms, it pays to have a solution where those sorts of nasty payloads in messages never reach your users' inboxes. (Remember—if you block viruses before they have a chance to fool your users into running them, then you've eliminated one vector of attack.) Microsoft chose to include in SBS functionality to by default remove attachments with file extensions proven over time to likely contain viruses. These file extensions are rarely used, particularly in a small business environment, for legitimate purposes and are almost certainly malware-containing objects that your users shouldn't see.

How does this work? It's primarily in the background, in fact. You might recall while running the Configure E-mail and Internet Connection Wizard as discussed in Chapter 3 that you chose to remove these types of attachments. That is actually the only place this functionality is revealed to you as the administrator. In the inner workings of Exchange, an *event sink*—a term for an action that is taken as a result of some given event, much like an e-mail rule in Outlook—runs when attachments are received, trapping the problematic ones and either killing them completely or sending them to another folder that you designated in the CEICW.

The following is a list of the attachments that are blocked by default:

Ade	Isp	Pif
Adp	Js	Prf
App	Jse	Prg
Bas	Ksh	Reg
Bat	Lnk	Scf
Chm	Mda	Scr
Cmd	Mdb	Sct
Com	Mde	Shb
Cpl	Mdt	Shs
Crt	Mdw	url
Csh	Mdz	vb
Exe	Msc	vbe
Fxp	Msi	vbs
Hlp	Msp	wsc
Hta	Mst	wsd
Inf	Ops	wsh
Ins	Pcd	xsl

If you wish to turn this functionality off, you will need to rerun the CEICW, keeping all other settings the same except for unchecking the box indicating you want these attachments removed.

Multiple Stores

To keep the freeloaders at bay, Microsoft restricted the version of Exchange in SBS in a couple of ways. The most significant limitation is the size of the Exchange store (the term for a group of Exchange mailboxes): you are only permitted to place 16 GB of data into a single Exchange store if you are running SBS. This might seem like a lot of space, but just in the past ten months I have received well over 1 GB of data in my Exchange mailbox. I am a heavy e-mail user, but these days e-mail use is growing, and you might run into this limitation more quickly than you would otherwise believe.

Of course, this might make you wary of being serious about using Exchange in your small business—after all, if you grow to depend on the features of the Outlook/Exchange combination, and then that capability is yanked out from under you by a store size limitation, that is certainly a problem. However, there is a workaround: use multiple Exchange mailbox stores, and group users into them. I would suggest creating three stores: one called Light, for light users of e-mail; one called Midsize, for users who send and receive e-mail more heavily; and one called Large, for users who have the largest mailboxes. This way, you have segregated store sizes and can get the most space out of each store.

To create a new mailbox store, you need to delve back into Exchange System Manager. Expand the System Manager node, and then expand the node corresponding to your domain. Then, under Servers, expand the node with your server name, and then right-click First Storage Group. From the context menu, select New, and then click Mailbox Store. Proceed from there—just give the store a name and accept the defaults, and you've then created a store.

This bit of "extension" only works for a little while, though: you are limited to four stores in the SBS version of Exchange. Once you have created the store, you need to assign mailboxes to it. Within your existing mailbox store, click the Mailboxes folder, and then choose a user's mailbox. Right-click the mailbox in the right pane and select Exchange Tasks from the pop-up context menu. Then, select Move Mailbox and click Next. The wizard will show the current location of the mailbox; you can select the new mailbox store in the drop-down list, and then click Next to complete the move.

Conclusion

In this chapter, we've explored some of the basic-to-intermediate features of Outlook 2003 and Exchange 2003. You've learned some tips and tricks about how to use Outlook most effectively, been introduced to Exchange management tools, and then you've learned about some SBS-specific features and limitations and how to make the most of them.

CHAPTER 6

∎∎∎

Windows SharePoint Services Techniques

BEGINNER SBS ADMINISTRATOR ▓ ADVANCED SBS ADMINISTRATOR ▓ EXPERIENCED CONSULTANT

Windows SharePoint Services is one of the best features of both editions of SBS 2003. Earlier in this book, I explored with you how SBS can be used in the small business environment to share documents, files, ideas, information, and other resources you may create or find. In this chapter, however, I would like to dig down to the meat of SharePoint and show you first how it works, and then explore some ways in which you can personalize, customize, and extend SharePoint on your SBS server to enhance your marketability, improve your productivity, and increase your access to company resources both in the office and on the road.

Let's get started!

Resources for Learning the Basics

There are so many fabulous resources available online about how to use SharePoint in a very basic manner that to replicate that information in this book would be a waste of both your time and our paper. Because of that, I've chosen to only highlight in this chapter how you can extend a general SharePoint installation in several different ways. Some pointers to the resources I've found thus far that have proved to be most valuable among my customers:

- The Microsoft Windows SharePoint Services site (`http://www.microsoft.com/ windowsserver2003/technologies/sharepoint/default.mspx`), which contains a wealth of technical information

- The book *Microsoft Windows SharePoint Services Inside Out*, by Jim Buyens (Microsoft Press, 2005)

Now, let's extend SharePoint!

Using Windows SharePoint Services with Access

One of the coolest features of SharePoint's much touted integration with the latest version of Microsoft Access is its ability to link with Access. A lot of small business software runs in Access, whether it's off-the-shelf, boxed software or a homegrown application, and it is wonderful to be able to link that data with a SharePoint site on your SBS server. Figure 6-1 shows what this integration looks like at a very basic level.

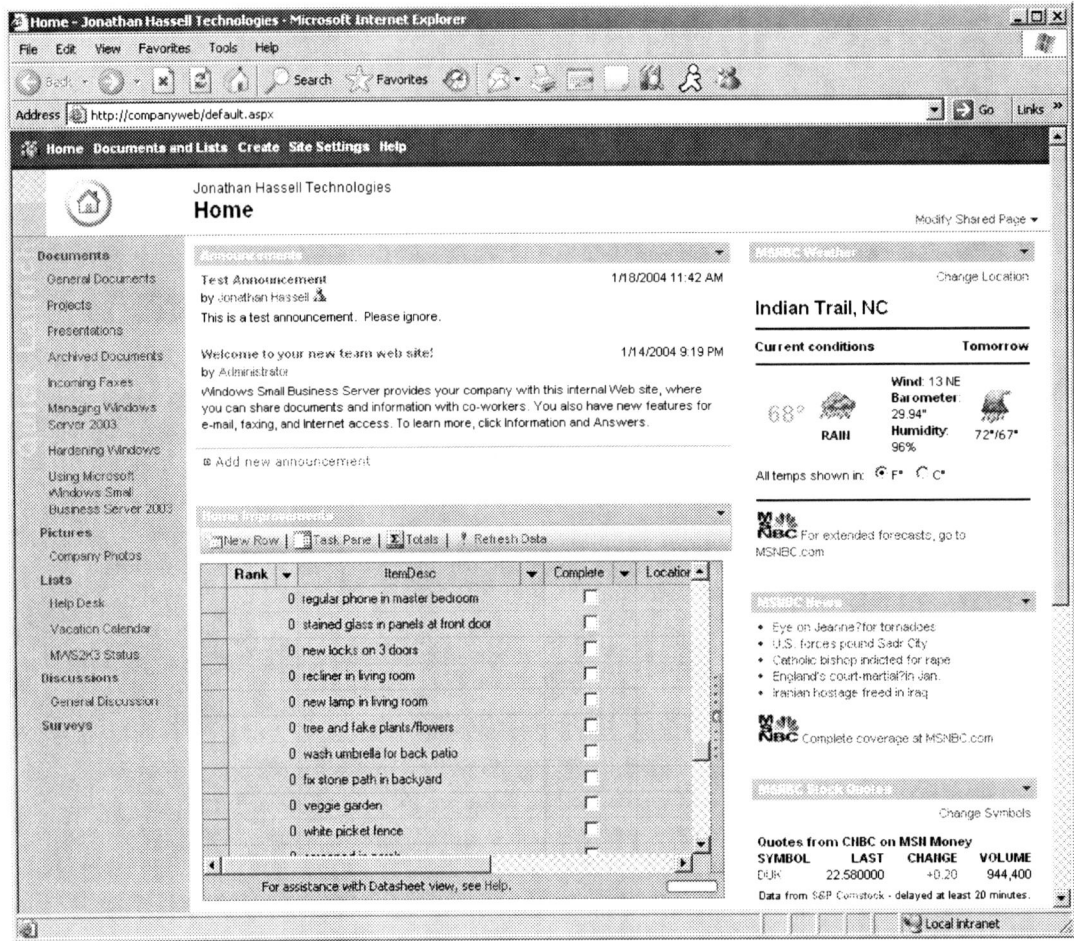

Figure 6-1. *Access tables integrated with Windows SharePoint Services*

I personally use this solution to track attendees to my Windows management and security seminars. When customers register for a seminar of mine, I keep track of the date of registration, their contact information, payment details, and attendee details within Access. Then, at the conference, I can use any PC at the check-in and registration desk, verifying registration information via tables linked from Access to WSS. It takes a lot less overhead to check people in over the web versus carrying a laptop with Access on it, and in a pinch, I can even use a PC provided by the hotel if something "undesirable" happens to my equipment. It's very convenient.

Using and linking data to and from Access happens in three different phases. Let's dig in and look at each.

Exporting Data

If you have some really basic data that doesn't change often, you can use the export feature within Access to dump a particular table to a SharePoint site for easy reference. This way, if you have pricing information for products or services, your representatives and employees don't have to load Access each time that they're on the phone with a customer—a definite timesaver.

So, to export a table from Access to SharePoint:

1. Open Access and load your database using the File ➤ Open menu.

2. Right-click a table in the database window and select Export.

3. Select Windows SharePoint Services in the Save As Type combo box.

4. The Export to Windows SharePoint Services Wizard will begin. Enter the URL of the SharePoint site where the exported data should reside. You can also enter a different name for the data, which will take the form of a SharePoint list, and a friendly description if you don't like the defaults. You see this in Figure 6-2.

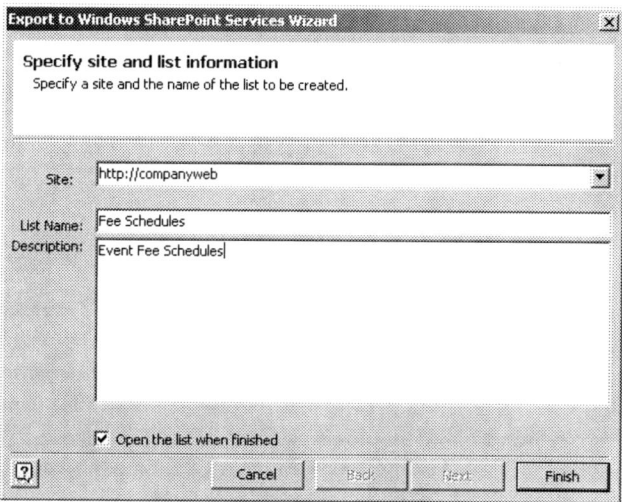

Figure 6-2. *Exporting to Windows SharePoint Services*

5. Click Finish to complete the process.

The exported list looks like that shown in Figure 6-3.

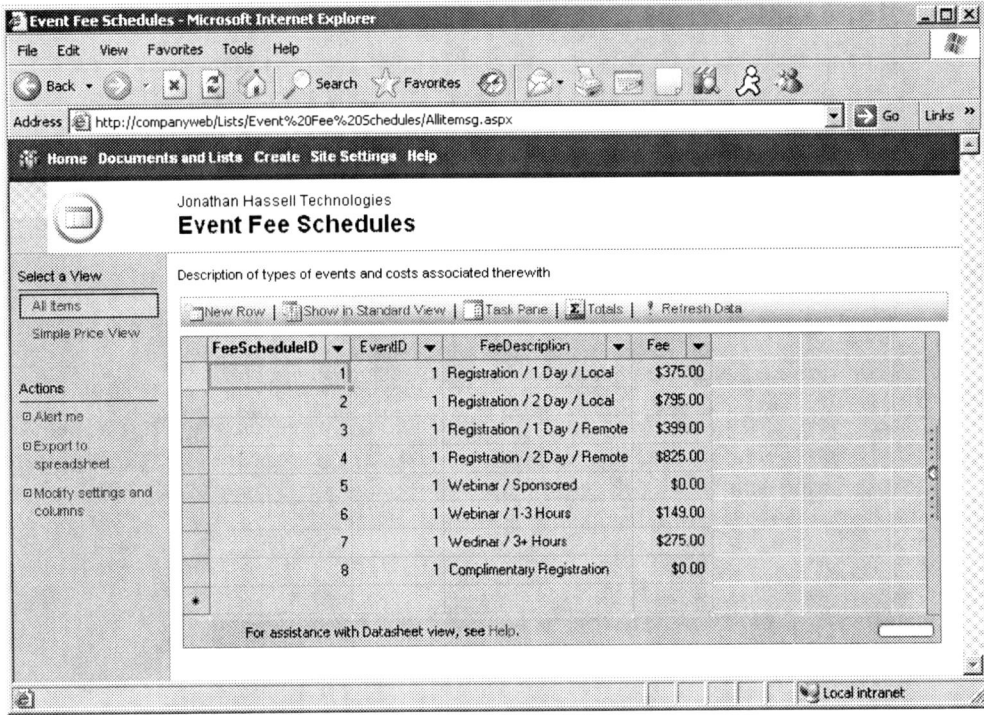

Figure 6-3. *Viewing the exported data in SharePoint*

Importing Data

Taking this a step further, let's try importing some information from SharePoint into Access. When you import SharePoint data to Access, Access does its best job at importing columns, trying to figure out their function and format—for instance, formatting currency columns with dollars and cents, etc. Since Access and SharePoint Services use a very similar database engine, it's fairly easy for Access to "inherit" the Required, Default value, Format, and Decimal Places settings from the SharePoint columns being imported. If you have maximum and minimum values set, Access will build a routine to enforce those upon import.

Let's begin the import of SharePoint items into Access:

1. Select File ➤ Get External Data ➤ Import.

2. Select Windows SharePoint Services in the Files of Type combo box, which launches the Import from Windows SharePoint Services Wizard.

3. Enter the URL of the SharePoint site containing the data to import and click Next.

4. On the next panel of the wizard, you can choose whether to import lists or views. A view represents a subset of a list, much like a Top 10 list is a subset of a larger list of rankings. You can select multiple lists to import by holding down the Ctrl key and clicking. You can see this screen in Figure 6-4.

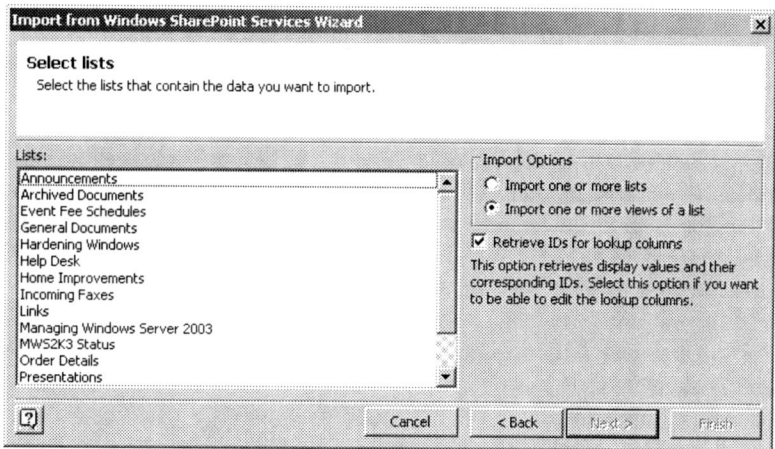

Figure 6-4. *Selecting lists to import*

5. Next, select the action you'd like to take with lookup columns. Lookup columns use numbers to identify the contents of other lists—for example, if you had two tables, one with product numbers and names and the other with product numbers and available inventory quantities, you could have a lookup column to the latter table to identify the product names. Those "lookup columns" can be a bit confusing in this dialog box, but the bottom line is if you uncheck this box, then the imported Access table will contain the actual names, rather than the numeric IDs. If you check the box, the numeric IDs will be imported.

6. The final pane of the wizard will confirm your choices. Click Finish to import the table or tables that you chose.

A sample imported table looks like the one in Figure 6-5.

ID	Edit	FeeScheduleID	EventID	FeeDescription	Fee
1	[...]	1	1	Registration / 1	$375.00
2	[...]	2	1	Registration / 2	$795.00
3	[...]	3	1	Registration / 1	$399.00
4	[...]	4	1	Registration / 2	$825.00
5	[...]	5	1	Webinar / Spon	$0.00
6	[...]	6	1	Webinar / 1-3 H	$149.00
7	[...]	7	1	Wedinar / 3+ Hc	$275.00
8	[...]	8	1	Complimentary	$0.00
(AutoNumber)					

Record: |◀| ◀ | 1 | ▶ |▶|| ▶*| of 8

Figure 6-5. *Imported data from SharePoint to Access*

Linking Data

Finally, you can link SharePoint data to Access, which is the most useful feature, since you can keep data stored in SharePoint but manipulate it using the advanced tools and features of Access. Access uses a stylized calendar icon to represent a list linked from SharePoint.

Now, you might be able to see where problems could occur if a user was working with the data within SharePoint and another user was working with the data in Access at the same time. Microsoft has foreseen this event and implements a "locking" procedure, in that if two users change the same record from within both Access and SharePoint, upon the second time that a change is made Windows will send up an error message. Within SharePoint, the error message is sent in the form of a web page and gives the user an opportunity to overwrite the changes made by the first user. If the second user is working inside Access, the second user gets a Write Conflict dialog box.

The main benefit of this arrangement is, as I mentioned before, the ability to work with database data once stored in Access without the need to have Access running on a local machine. My earlier example of a registration and check-in desk is a prime candidate to reap the benefits of linked data. Another example that might apply to you would be a field sales representative who works on simple PCs without licenses for Office. Sometimes small business, with limited technology budgets, might choose to go with cheaper laptop computers for mobile users and specify just Microsoft Word or open-source office software alternatives. You might be in this situation. Rather than hiring an expensive consultant to write a custom interface between your Access database and a web page for your mobile users, you can just use linked data and tables from Access and SharePoint.

To link tables:

1. Select File ➤ Get External Data ➤ Link Tables.

2. Select Windows SharePoint Services in the Files of Type combo box. This will launch the Link to Windows SharePoint Services Wizard.

3. Enter the URL of the SharePoint site containing the data to import and click Next.

4. On the next panel of the wizard, you can choose whether to import lists or views. You can use Ctrl-click to select multiple lists to import. You can see this screen in Figure 6-6.

5. You also need to select what to do about lookup columns. Remember: if you uncheck this box, then the imported Access table will contain actual names, rather than associated numeric ID numbers; if you check the box, the numeric IDs will be imported.

6. The final pane of the wizard will confirm your choices. Click Finish to import the table or tables that you chose.

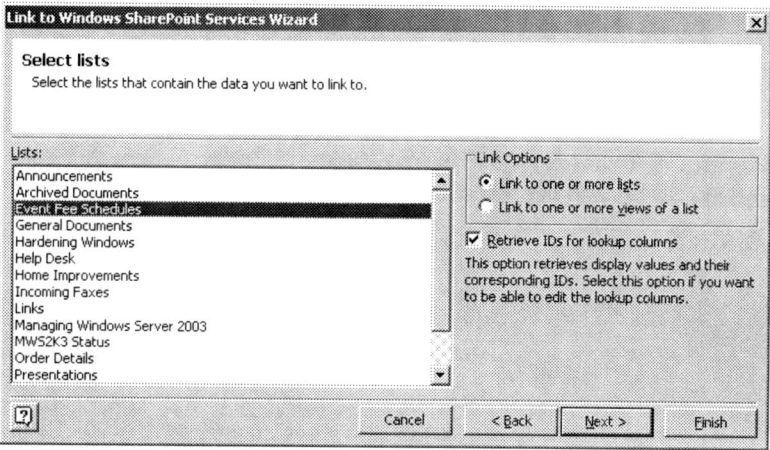

Figure 6-6. *Linking data to and from Access and SharePoint*

Views Within SharePoint

Views, as I've explained earlier in the chapter, are simply subsets of lists. They're just a "picture" of a list, displayed according to a certain set of criteria and preferences that you specify. Adjusting views can be beneficial for several reasons. For one, you can create a simple view of complex data for junior employees. You can also see trends and other important details from data by displaying it in other ways—we all have been there, done that after looking at the same set of numbers for hours. You then chart those numbers, see what you were missing before, and wonder how you could have been so dense. (Perhaps I shouldn't admit that.)

To continue along our earlier event management example, let's say I want my list view within Windows SharePoint Services to only contain the type of event and its associated price. There's no need for my salespeople to see the event ID, or the fee type ID, or any of the other data provided by the ancillary columns. To eliminate these columns from the display of the list, we need to create a custom view.

So let's get started. To create a custom view:

1. Go to the list within your WSS site.

2. In the left pane, click Modify Settings and Columns.

3. Scroll down to the bottom of the page, and locate the section called Views.

4. Click the Create a New View link.

5. The Create View page loads. From here, you can choose a standard view, which is simply a few columns with the data located in the correct places; a datasheet view, which more resembles a spreadsheet; and a calendar view, which is appropriate for date-driven data. Since we only need a simple view for our price list, select Standard View.

6. In the Name section, give the new view a descriptive name. I've chosen "Simple Price View." You can choose to make it the default.

7. In the Audience section, pick whether to make the view a personal view or a public view. Personal views are intended for your own personal use, but anyone with the correct URL can view it—there's no authentication involved. Public views are advertised for everyone's use on the site.

8. Select the columns you would like to see in this view in the Columns section. I have ticked off the FeeDescription and Fee fields for our simple view, which is shown in Figure 6-7.

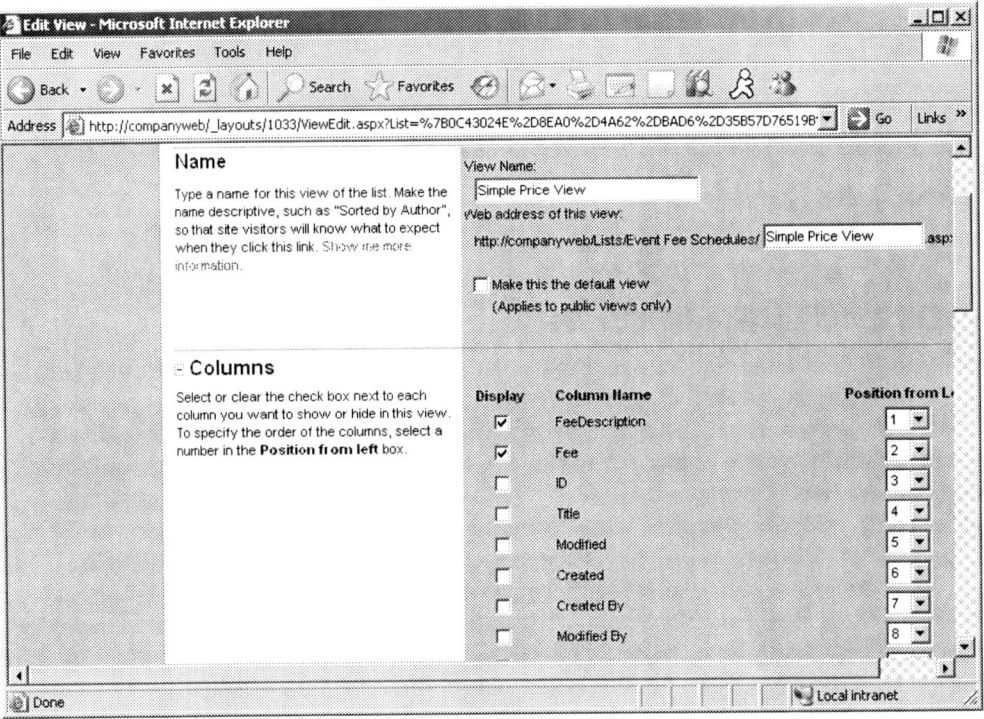

Figure 6-7. *Creating a new view*

9. In the Sort section, you can choose whether to sort by specific columns and the order with which those columns should be sorted. I have no preference for this view, so I have left the default settings intact.

10. The Filter section allows you to actually filter the data in the view that is shown to only that data which meets specific criteria. If you had, for example, a view that only shows items with prices less than $50, you could create a filter here that restricts the view to only items whose Price fields contains a number less than or equal to 50. For my view, I don't really care about filtering, so again I've left the default settings in place.

11. I'm finished creating the view, so I will click OK to publish the view.

When I go back to the original view, on the left pane, I see the Select a View section. The generic All Items view is listed, but the new view I just created shows up there under Simple Price View. Clicking that results in a much simpler view that's easier to refer to at a glance. Mission accomplished. See for yourself in Figure 6-8.

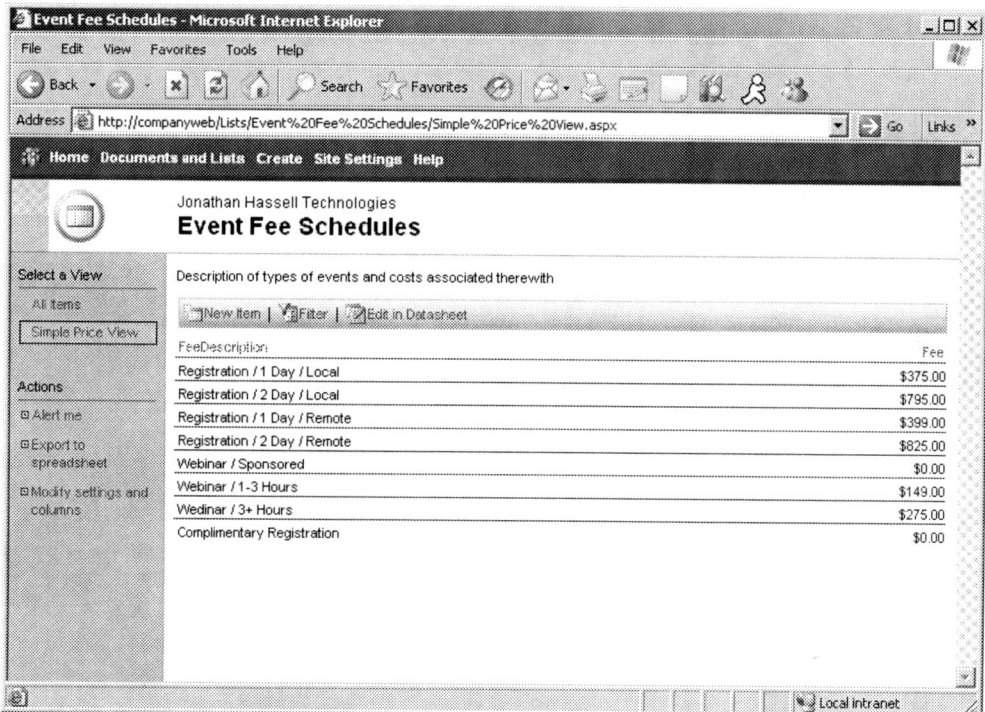

Figure 6-8. *The new view within SharePoint*

Advanced View Creation

There are a few other options I didn't cover in the preceding example that are useful if you have a large list that you're using, or that you're attempting to use to glean statistics about the overall corpus of data contained within your list. To access these advanced features, create a new view as explained previously, but scroll down. Above the OK and Cancel buttons you will see several sections that are collapsed by default. Expand them by clicking the plus sign beside each, and then look at the options offered to you.

- **Group By**: This setting will allow you to group items that have the same value together in the list. For example, if your list has a column indicating a type of item, and you want all the items with a type of Portable to be grouped together on the list, you can select that type here and determine the order in which those items are grouped.

- **Totals**: In this section, you can specify to display totals for each column and choose how those totals will be calculated (either as addition or as a count of the items).

- **Style**: This option lets you pick how the list will be presented. You can choose from a basic table, a box with no labels, a box with labels, a newsletter, a newsletter without border lines, a shaded list, or the default view.

- **Item Limit**: You can use this feature to limit the number of items displayed, an especially useful option if you have a particularly large list. You can choose a hard limit or allow each user to view that particular number of items per screen and present the data in batches of that number.

You can see these advanced switches in Figure 6-9.

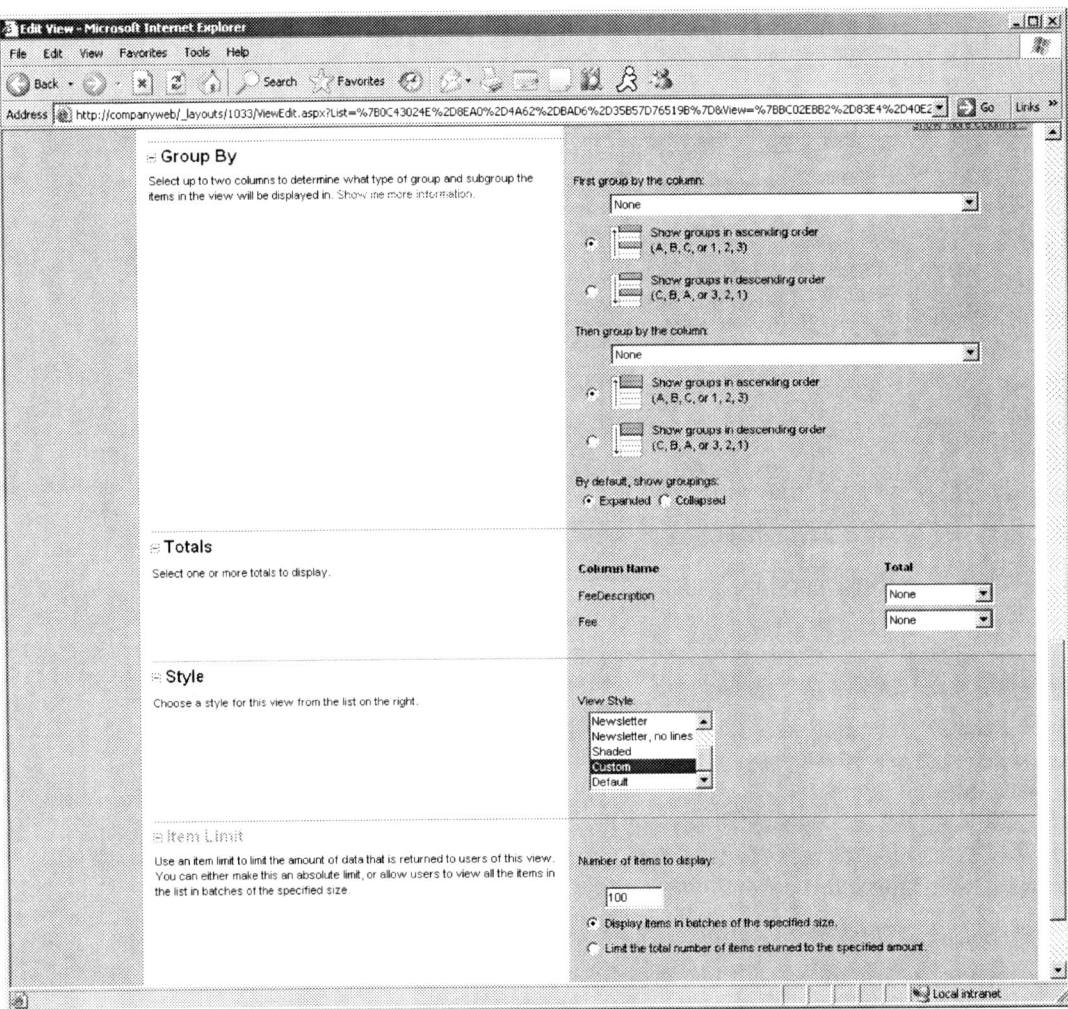

Figure 6-9. *Toggling advanced view options within SharePoint*

Customizing Themes in SharePoint

You may want to customize the colors, fonts, and icons used within your SBS server's Share-Point sites to further reflect the look of your company. Or, if you have several SharePoint sites, color coding them may be a route you'd like to go in order to make it easier for your employees to distinguish the different sites and their purposes.

To customize themes within SharePoint, you use Microsoft Office FrontPage 2003. Front-Page contains a collection of themes that encompass design elements like buttons, hover buttons, bullets, backgrounds, horizontal lines, page banners, and font and formatting options. Again, because of the integration between Office and SharePoint, it's very easy to change themes on SharePoint-based sites with FrontPage.

The process of applying a theme changes all design elements contained within the theme simultaneously—you can't just pick one change and apply it, and then pick another, and so on. It also changes all the elements on all pages of the site, so you don't have to waste your time reformatting each page within the site.

Basic Customization

The easiest way to get started is to start with an existing, preformatted theme bundled with FrontPage. You can then make changes to that existing theme and create your own custom look. To get started:

1. Open your SharePoint site in FrontPage 2003 by selecting Open Site from the File menu.

2. From the Format menu, choose Theme. On the right side of the screen, the Theme task pane appears.

3. Scroll down through the list and select the theme you would like to begin customizing. Click it, and select "Apply as the default theme."

4. Click Yes to confirm you want the changes applied across the site.

5. Now that your selected theme is applied to the site, you can start making changes to the theme. First, click the Create new theme link at the bottom of the Theme task pane.

6. The Customize Theme screen appears. Click the Save As button, and then type a name for the theme you're creating.

7. Click OK to save your custom theme. Now you can get started making real changes.

In this section, I'll focus on changing three elements of the theme: colors, graphics, and text. Let's get started.

Changing Colors

In the Customize Theme dialog box, click the Custom tab. The Custom properties screen appears, which is shown in Figure 6-10.

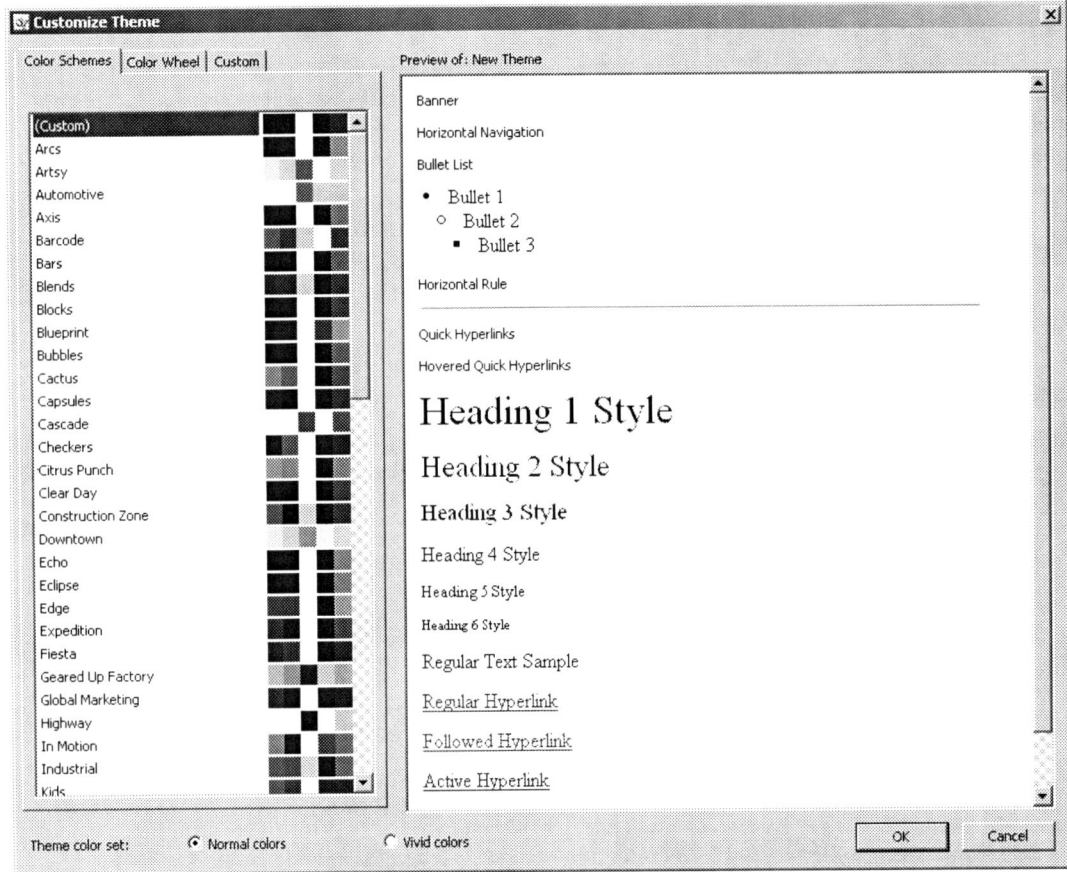

Figure 6-10. *Changing colors on a SharePoint site*

From here, you can change the colors of hyperlinks, horizontal rules, headings, body color, banner text, button text, and background colors. Just select an element, change the color, and then click OK. Lather, rinse, and repeat as needed.

Changing Graphics

With the Customize Theme dialog box, click the Graphics button. The Graphics screen appears, which is shown in Figure 6-11.

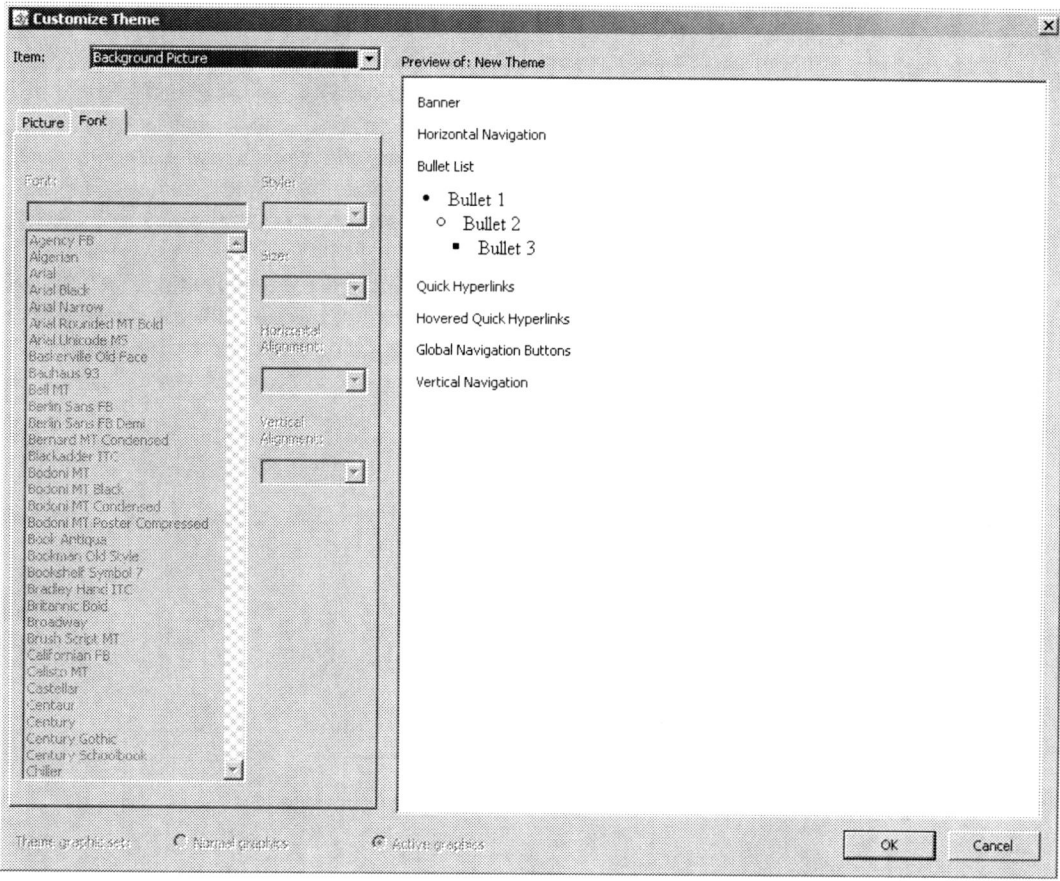

Figure 6-11. *Changing graphics on a SharePoint site*

Again, to change any element here, just click the element you want to change—this could be the picture on the background of the page, a banner image on your pages, or navigation buttons—and specify where the new graphics for your site are stored. Click OK when you have completed your changes.

Changing Text

In the Customize Theme dialog box, click the Text button. The Text screen appears. From here, you can change the font used in body text and headings on your pages. Just click the element to change, select the new font and size, and then click OK.

You might also want to specify multiple fonts for users who might be using systems that don't have many custom fonts installed. To do this, select the preferred font, and then type in a comma, a space, and the alternative, "safe" font in the dialog box. For example, if I want Georgia but would like to default to Arial if Georgia is not available, I would type **Georgia, Arial** in the box. Click OK when you're done.

Advanced Customization: Using Cascading Style Sheets

Don your web designer hats! The themes in FrontPage 2003 use web standards called Cascading Style Sheets, or CSS, to apply font and formatting rules across your entire SBS SharePoint site. FrontPage hides a lot of the complexity behind CSS from you, so in most cases you have no need to worry about it. However, if you want to really dig deep and change just about every element of your SharePoint pages, you'll need to identify what CSS elements define the styles used on the pages and then learn how to change those elements to your own personal specifications.

The central point where you can change the formatting specifications defined by CSS use in FrontPage is the Style dialog box, which is found within the Customize Theme screen with which you're already familiar. From the Customize Theme dialog box, click the Text button, and then on the resulting screen click More Text Styles.

The Style dialog box opens, which is shown in Figure 6-12.

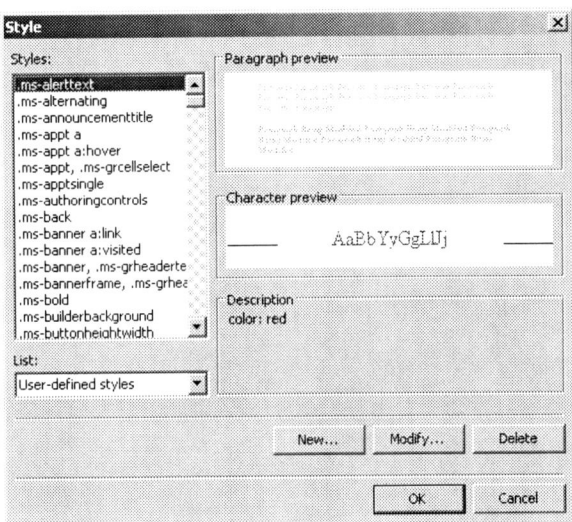

Figure 6-12. *Changing CSS-defined text styles*

You can scroll through the styles to select the element you'd like to change. The formatting that corresponds with them is previewed to the right, so you don't have to keep closing the box, checking the change, and then going back and tweaking the change—a definitely frustrating process! Once you have selected the style you want, click the Modify button, which opens the Modify Style dialog box, as shown in Figure 6-13.

Click the Format button to change the font, paragraph, border, numbering, and position for this style. Once you've made your changes, click OK to back out of all the open dialog boxes, and then click Yes to confirm your change.

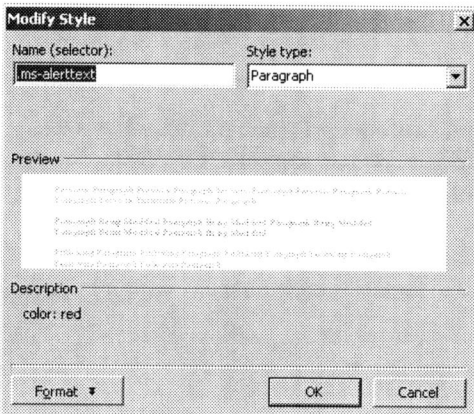

Figure 6-13. *The Modify Style dialog box*

Backup and Restore Options for Windows SharePoint Services

Disaster recovery is always a tenuous topic to cover, and SharePoint-specific backup method-ologies are no exception, mainly because SharePoint itself is such a complex beast, with a lot of moving parts that can break. Because of this, you want a complete backup solution—but it shouldn't be difficult, either. My law of the universe, Hassell's Law, holds that with the increasing difficulty of a task and the increasing importance of a task, the less often that task is actually carried out. Don't agree with me? When do you file your tax return? And when was the last time you made a full backup?

Of course, since SharePoint is a complex beast, there are lots of strategies—and lots of advantages and disadvantages to weigh—in backing up data contained in your site. The three main options are as follows:

- **Use the STSADM.EXE command-line tool to back up individual sites**: You can get a full-fidelity, complete backup or restore of an entire site by using the STSADM.EXE command-line tool with the backup and restore operations. The good news here is that you don't have to have SQL Server 2000. However, you must still be an administrator on the local server computer that is running Windows SharePoint Services in order to per-form this method of backing up and restoring, which might be a bit much for client sites or junior users in your small business. After all, you don't give the keys to your kingdom to just anyone, right?

- **Use the Microsoft SQL Server 2000 tools to back up the databases**: You can use the backup tools included with SQL Server 2000 to get a full-fidelity, complete backup of the databases used by Windows SharePoint Services on your SBS server. When you use this method, you back up and restore the entire configuration database and each con-tent database on your server, and from that point, you can then restore any or all of these databases. The good news is that this is the best way to get a complete backup.

The bad news is twofold: you must be running SQL Server 2000 to be able to use this backup method, and you must be an administrator on the local server computer that is running SQL Server. It also takes a heck of a long time if you have a large database.

- **Use the Microsoft SharePoint Migration Tool (smigrate.exe) to back up individual sites and subsites**: You can back up and restore individual sites or subsites by using the SharePoint Migration Tool. The bad news here is that you may lose some customizations or settings in the process. For example, security settings for the site, such as user membership in site groups, are lost in the restoration. The good news, though, is that you don't need to be an administrator on the local server computer.

Using STSADM.EXE for WSS Backup and Restoration

Site backup and restore is intended to help you reconnect sites that have become corrupted or need to be restored to a previous state. This process is not intended for moving a site to a new server.

When using site backup and restore, keep the following items in mind:

- You can automate this process through the use of the Scheduled Tasks feature within Windows Server 2003, and through a batch file or a script.

- When you are performing a backup or restore, memory usage and CPU performance are affected, so be sure to schedule these procedures for a time when the WSS site usage is the lightest. This will prevent disruption of users.

- If you are trying to restore a site that uses a different language pack than one that is installed on the target computer, you will need to install that language pack on the target computer for the restore to be successful.

The STSADM.EXE utility uses several parameters within the program to perform operations. We're interested in the backup operation, but first, we need to see which sites are available to back up. You'll find the STSADM.EXE program in the C:\Program Files\Common Files\Microsoft Shared\web server extensions\60\BIN directory. Running the following command from the command line will tell us that:

```
stsadm.exe -o enumsites -url <url>
```

In the preceding command, replace <url> with the name of the web server on which your SharePoint sites reside.

Once you know the names of sites, to perform a simple backup of a site, enter a command like the following:

```
stsadm.exe -o backup -url http://server_name/site -filename backup.dat
```

For example, to back up my local WSS site, I would issue the following command:

```
stsadm.exe -o backup -url http://companyweb -filename backup.dat
```

This command will back up the entire contents of the `http://companyweb` URL to a file named BACKUP.DAT, which will be located in whatever directory I'm currently in on the command line. If you'd like to overwrite a backup file with the same name—for instance, if you always name the latest backup current.dat and you run this command each night—then use the following command:

```
stsadm.exe -o backup -url http://companyweb -filename backup.dat -overwrite
```

When you want to restore a site, you have three options: you can restore a site and overwrite the contents of an existing site, you can restore the backed-up site to a new site on the same server, or you can restore the backed-up site to another server that uses a copy of the original server's configuration database. If you overwrite a site, then you completely get rid of whatever was in the site before you began the restore operation. The latter two methods are useful when you're trying to restore data to a corrupted site.

To restore a site from a backup file, either to a new site or a separate server, you would use syntax similar to the following:

```
stsadm.exe -o restore -url http://backup-server/companyweb -filename backup.dat
```

That command would restore my backup.dat file to a separate server, called BACKUP-SERVER, and the WSS site called Companyweb on that server.

Alternatively, if you want to overwrite your site with the backup data, you can use a command similar to the following:

```
stsadm.exe -o restore -url http://companyweb -backup.dat -overwrite
```

Using the SharePoint Migration Tool for Backup

When you use the SharePoint Migration Tool, you must actually perform two separate operations: first, you back up the site to a file, and then you restore the site to the new location. During the backup process, you specify the URL for the web site and the backup file to create. You can also specify the scope of the site migration (whether to migrate just the top-level web site, or whether to migrate the top-level web site and any subsites). During the restore process, you specify the new URL and the backup file to restore from.

If you use the SharePoint Migration Tool to migrate a site based on Windows SharePoint Services to another server running Windows SharePoint Services, security settings, SharePoint Central Administration settings, personalizations, and web part customizations are not migrated.

To back up a site to a file, use a command like the following:

```
Smigrate -w http://companyweb -f backup.dat
```

And to restore a file to a site, use a command like the following:

```
Smigrate -r -w http://companyweb -f backup.dat
```

With this tool, you can choose subsites to back up. For example, if you have a subsite on your SBS server named "partners," you can choose to back up only that subsite—something you cannot do with the STSADM.EXE tool described previously in this chapter. To back up a subsite, issue a command like the following:

```
Smigrate -w http://sbs-server/partners -f partners-backup.dat
```

And to restore it, use a command similar to this:

```
Smigrate -r -w http://sbs-server/partners -f partners-backup.dat
```

Using the SQL Server 2000 Tools for Backup

If you are lucky enough to have purchased the SBS 2003 Premium Edition and have migrated your databases to SQL Server 2000, then using SQL Server's built-in tools is the most complete way to back up your WSS configuration and content. However, it's also the most costly: such an operation is both time- and computing power-intensive, so it's best to use this method sparingly.

The first step of this method is distinguishing which databases you need to back up. The most common choices are outlined here:

- The configuration database is named sts_config.mdf by default. Note that this is only the default name. When you created the configuration database, you had the option to specify a different name.

- The content databases are created with names based on the server name by default. For example, STS_server_name_1.mdf, STS_server_name_12.mdf, and so on. The database names are not sequential. Again, you may have chosen a different naming scheme for the content databases when you created them.

Once you have identified the appropriate database, you can use SQL Server's tools to back up the database.

A practical and effective backup strategy for your Windows SharePoint Services installation is to use both of these tools. At longer intervals, such as monthly, back up your entire set of databases using the Microsoft SQL Server tools. At shorter intervals, such as weekly, run STSADM.EXE to back up just those site collections that have changed. This will facilitate quick recovery of lost items with a minimum of space usage, while the Microsoft SQL Server tools backups are available for large-scale disaster recovery.

Helpful SharePoint Customizations

To this point I've covered a few ways in which you can use SharePoint as a foundation and build upon its functionality to create custom web-based collaboration solutions for your small business. In this section, I'd like to highlight some of the most efficient and productive customizations of Windows SharePoint Services on SBS that have been brought to my attention.

Contact and Service Management

Chad Gross, a small business consultant, has customized the Help Desk feature of his SBS server's internal web site to use as a contact management and service management tool. According to Chad, this homegrown SharePoint customization has actually replaced the venerable Goldmine software in their small business.

Chad has linked custom customer lists and created custom views among other things. Chad says, "We use the Help Desk for scheduling. We added various fields that made sense with the way we work, including fields for technician, customer, service call notes, arrival time, finish time, total time on site, and a billed flag, just to name a few. We then created a new view that shows us the schedule in a calendar view. We also created a few other views to help with our workflow. For example, 'My Active Tasks' shows the user their calls that have not been completed in a list view, which helps us keep up on our paperwork. I open that view, and see immediately which calls I need to complete."

In true team spirit, the Help Desk customizations that Chad has created work around the company to everyone's advantage. Chad again: "Another view we created is 'Ready to Bill.' This is a list view of our calls that are marked Completed but not flagged as Billed. This gives [our billing manager] a one-stop spot for calls that need to be billed. Plus, with all the call details on there, she can copy/paste into the invoice right from SharePoint." Obviously this process saves the billing manager quite a bit of time.

Action Points

Here are the main changes that Chad has implemented to create his contract and service management tool within SharePoint:

- Customize the Help Desk feature (which is unique to SBS) to have a few extra columns. The most useful are technical, total time on site, and a flag whether the customer is billed or not. You can, of course, add others as you see fit.

- Create a couple of extra views: one, as a calendar view of the company's current service call schedule, and another that shows each individual employee's active tasks to help him keep track of them.

- Create workspaces within SharePoint for each customer site to store contract information, templates, past invoices, notes from previous service calls, and other tools.

- Link the Customer field within the Help Desk to the appropriate customer workspace for easy navigation between each part.

- Save the custom Customer Workspace as a template, so you can use it over and over again with each new client you retain.

Figure 6-14 shows a sample of Chad's customized solution for SharePoint.

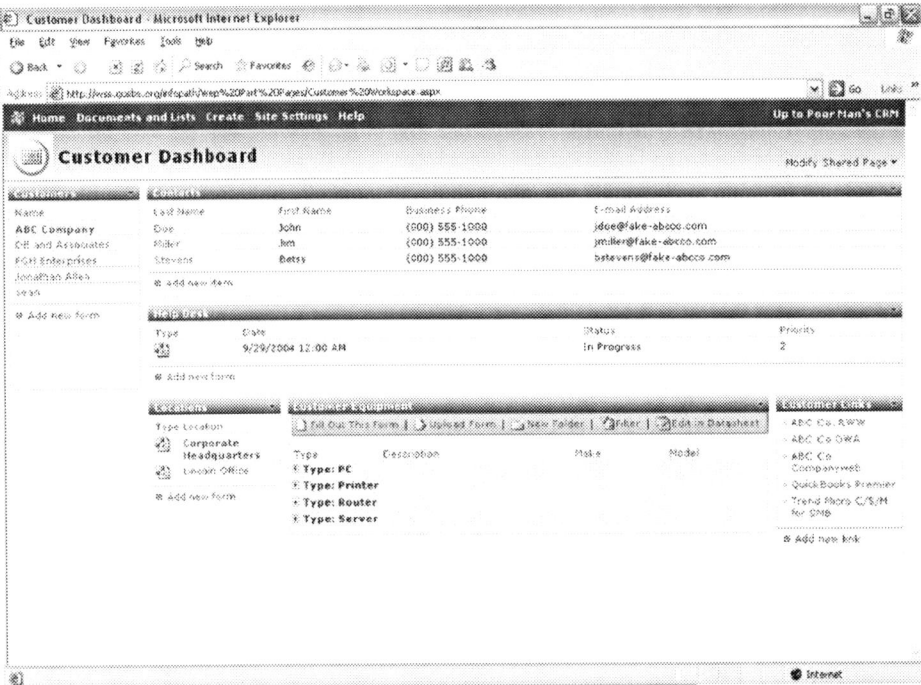

Figure 6-14. *Contract and service management with SharePoint*

Human Resources Management

A big focus in corporate America these days is on human resources management, and virtu-ally every company is examining ways in which it can save money on managing its people and the resources associated with maintaining employees. So what better way to interface with employees, provide them with the tools and forms they need at ready disposal, and take the heat off your HR manager at work than to digitize human resources with SharePoint?

Take a look at the SharePoint-based HR portal shown in Figure 6-15.

You can see the quick launch menu has been modified to provide easy access to benefits information, compensation, matching programs, hiring and acquisitions, and policies and procedures. The Events part in the middle can contain interesting and/or otherwise note-worthy dates, such as insurance open enrollment or 401(k) mass vesting dates. And the announcements part is a great way to provide links and timely information to surfers.

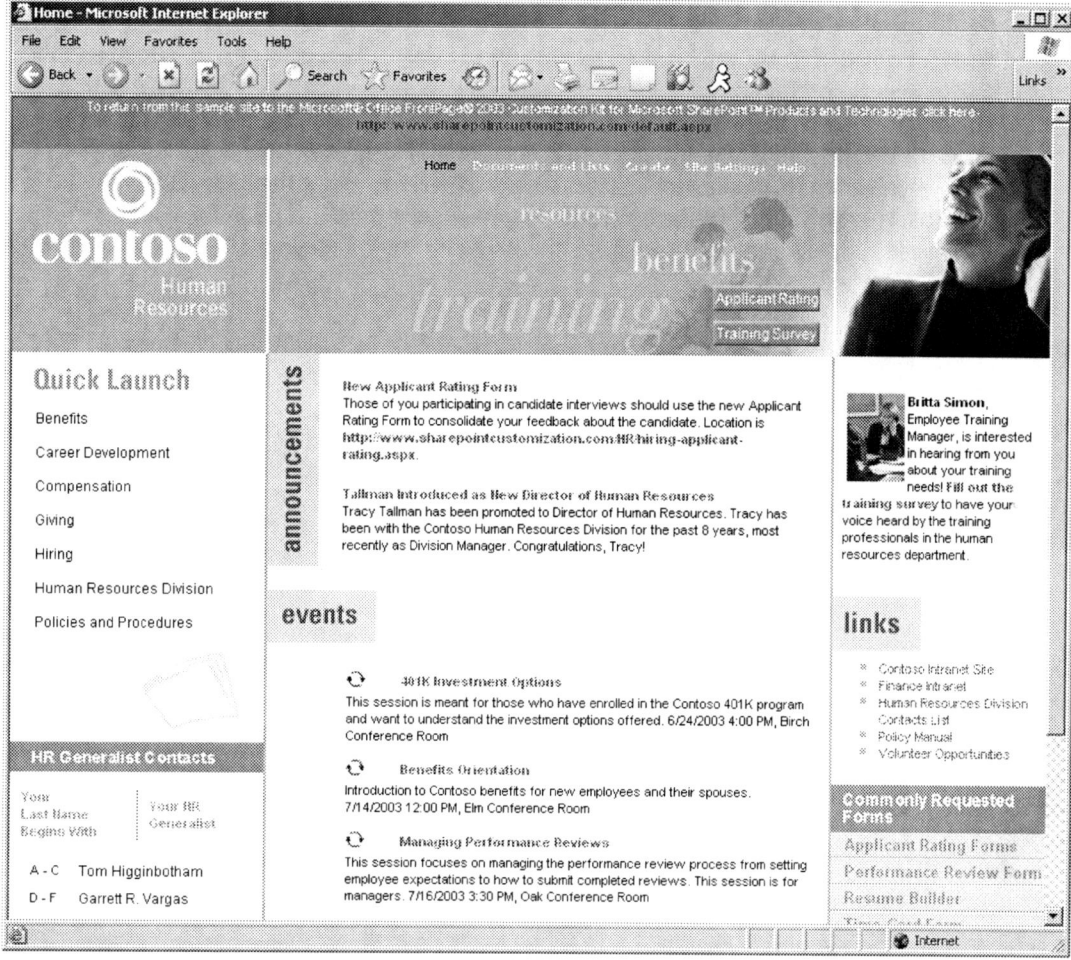

Figure 6-15. *Human resources management with SharePoint*

Action Points

Here are the main items to consider in order to create a custom HR portal within SharePoint:

- Create custom quick launch links to different sections or workspaces for each HR item (benefits, policies, and so on).

- Make a quick contacts part with key names, numbers, and e-mail aliases for your HR team so employees can get in touch if need be.

- Provide a document workspace or library for commonly requested forms, like performance reviews, resume templates, time cards, travel requests, and expense reports.

- Offer a survey section to get feedback on programs from your employees.

Sales and Marketing Portals

"Generate leads!" "Drop your new collateral off by Friday." "We have a big customer meeting in two weeks—are you ready?" Do any of these lines sound familiar? Perhaps you—or your customer—have teams of sales and marketing people who need to get together with each other. Or maybe your teams are separated geographically, and everyone needs a place to come together and drop documents, ideas, calendar events, and other items.

That is exactly the situation for which SharePoint was made—a point for sharing. With a bit of time and skill, you can create a custom sales and marketing portal like that which you see in Figure 6-16.

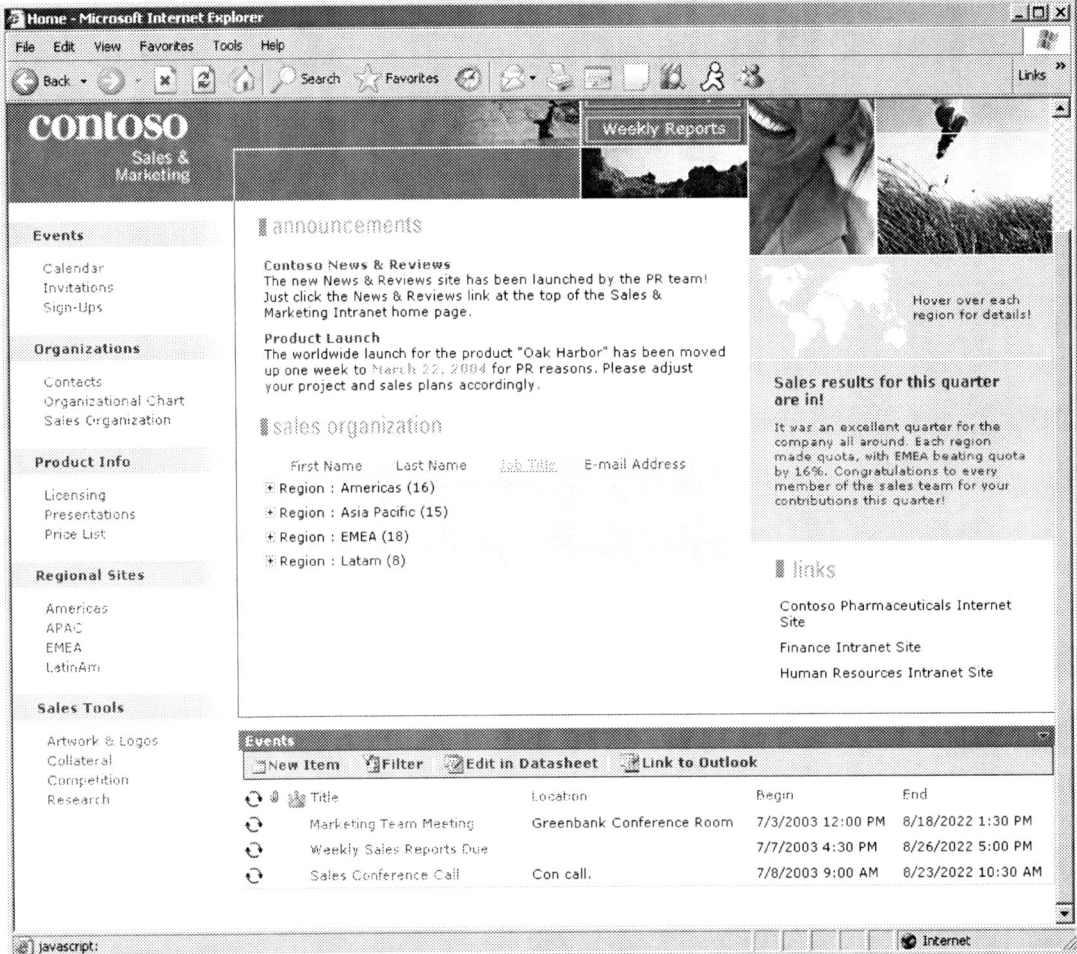

Figure 6-16. *Sales and marketing resources with SharePoint*

The quick launch menu has been customized into categories to show events, organizations, product information, regional sites, and sales tools. The announcements pane lists upcoming press events and product launches, and the sales organization part lists key contacts on the sales and marketing team. The Events pane is a list view of meetings, due dates for important deliverables, and conference calls so everyone can be kept on the same page.

Action Points

Here are the main items to consider in order to create a custom sales and marketing portal within SharePoint:

- Customize the quick launch bar and categorize it into different sections and different types of resources.

- Include a contact list for the front page for critical contacts on the sales and marketing team, including names, phone numbers, and e-mail addresses.

- Make document libraries to store drafts of collateral materials, contact lists for partners and printers, and other sales information.

- Provide a links page to product information on the corporate web site, competitors' web sites, and interested marketing and sales strategy pages.

- Create libraries for presentations, price lists, competitive analyses, weekly sales and marketing reports, news and reviews, etc.

- Finally, include a discussion board for a central place to exchange ideas between team members.

About Windows SharePoint Services Service Pack 1

To deploy or not to deploy? In mid-September, Microsoft released a batch of fixes for rather smallish bugs found in the original release version of Windows SharePoint Services, and true to its common form, Microsoft called the updates a service pack. Here's a list of the bugs the service pack squashes, direct from Microsoft:

- When you type **//localhost** in the Address box of Internet Explorer on your Web server, you receive the following error message: "HTTP 400 - Bad Request Internet Explorer."

- When you try to add a web part to your online Web Part gallery, the web part is not added. This issue may occur if the file name of the web part contains international characters or language-specific characters.

- When you restore your Microsoft SQL database to your Windows SharePoint Services web site, the links that are at the root of your web site are broken.

- When you relink a form in your Windows SharePoint Services web site that contains Rich Text format, all Rich Text formatted text is moved from its original position, and it appears after the text that is in plain text format.

- When you try to sort items in the Threaded view in a discussion board, the oldest item is always listed first.

- When you try to back up your Windows SharePoint Services web site to a network location, you receive a "Write error" error message, and the backup is not completed successfully.

- When you try to create a new Windows SharePoint Services web site on a Microsoft Windows Server 2003–based computer, you receive the following error message: "HTTP Error 403.1 - Forbidden: Execute access is denied. Internet Information Services (IIS)."

- After you install a language-specific Windows SharePoint Services template pack, the language of the pack does not appear in the Select Language list on the Sites and Work-places page.

- When you try to upload a large file to your Windows SharePoint Services web site, you may receive the following error message: "Form Validation Error. Please correct the information you provided by following these steps, then submit the information again. The URL 'Unified Lab Library/docname.doc' is invalid. It may refer to a nonexistent file or folder or refer to a valid file or folder that is not in the current Web."

- When you try to search for events in your Windows SharePoint Services web site, you cannot find past or future events. The search results return only the next event.

- When you install an update to a Windows SharePoint Services server that contains a nonprovisioned web site, the web site is provisioned by the update.

- When you install an update to a Windows SharePoint Services server that has some IIS services stopped, those services may restart automatically after you install the update.

- FrontPage may quit unexpectedly when you try to open a Windows SharePoint Services web page that contains a URL to an image that starts with certain characters and that contains more spaces in the URL than the length of the file name of the image.

- When you publish a disk-based web site in FrontPage that contain pages that have a theme applied and that have a page banner, FrontPage may quit unexpectedly, and you receive an error message.

- When you install an update that contains the Mso.dll file, an incorrect service pack level may appear in the About dialog box of a Microsoft Office program such as Front-Page. This service pack corrects this issue by using the earliest date of the Mso.dll file that is installed on your computer.

- After you install an update to Windows SharePoint Services, some files, such as the Sqmsto.dll and the Sqmstoup.dll files, may have an earlier certificate expiration date than you expect.

- When you locate a home page for a user who was added to Windows SharePoint Services by using a Microsoft Windows group, the UserInfo field for that user appears to be cor-rupted.

- You receive an access violation error message when multiple threads access the same document at the same time in a Windows SharePoint Services web site. This issue may occur if the following functions access the same document at the same time: Put, Get, Copy, Rename, PropFind, Unlock.

- When you locate a Windows SharePoint Services web site by typing **//localhost** in the Address box of Internet Explorer on a Windows Server 2003–based computer, you receive the following error message: "You are not authorized to view this page."

- When you try to paste text in the body of a new announcement in a Windows SharePoint Services web site, text that contains extended characters is not pasted.

- When you type a nonbreaking space in the properties of a file in a Windows SharePoint Services web site and then save the changes to the XML file, the file is corrupted and Microsoft Word, Internet Explorer, or any XML reader cannot read the file.

Not too small of a list, is it? Fortunately, the download of the service pack is easy and the installation is even easier. Point a web browser to the following long URL (make the URL all one line; it's broken here for printing purposes):

```
http://www.microsoft.com/downloads/details.aspx?
FamilyId=875DA47E-89D5-4621-A319-A1F5BFEDF497
```

Once the file has downloaded, double-click it and run through the installation process. As always, make a backup.

Conclusion

There is a lot of room for extending the functionality of SharePoint. In this chapter, I've shown you a lot of techniques, including the following:

- Importing and exporting data to and from Access

- Linking data within an Access database and a SharePoint list

- Customizing views within SharePoint pages

- Three different methods to back up and restore your SharePoint site and its contents

- Customizing SharePoint for contact and service management, human resources management, and sales and marketing portal creation

- Assessing the scope of Windows SharePoint Services Service Pack 1 and downloading and deploying it

We covered a lot of material in this chapter, but all of it is worth your attention. Enhance the marketability and productivity of your firm by personalizing SharePoint within your small business. Good luck, and happy customizing! Please feel free to share your customized SharePoint installs with me—I'm always interested.

CHAPTER 7

■ ■ ■

Exploring SBS Standard Security

In this chapter, I've chosen to highlight several very useful tools for managing and automating Windows security using SBS and its components. I've also included some references to security policy settings that most small businesses will find helpful and necessary.

I have not included an exhaustive reference to every security setting to be found in Windows. There are so many options that would be unique to many different environments that I've found the best procedure is to give a broad overview of security policy management tools, some general settings that can increase security greatly, and then let you explore Windows' security features yourself, or with the firm but gentle guidance of a qualified value-added provider (VAP) representative or consultant.

Let's begin.

Understanding Security Considerations

Most small businesses have several issues to keep in mind when securing their configurations, some of which might be the following:

- There are multiple servers within the organization, and many have distinct roles independent of the others.

- There are older operating systems and applications in use.

- There are legal procedures, protections, and consequences to deal with in some markets and professions.

- There may be a lack of physical security at the site, which makes moot any computer-based security configurations you may plan to make.

- There may be a lack of security expertise within the technical employees at your company. (Of course, this chapter will help.)

- There may be threats, either internal, external, or even accidental, that could damage your systems or harm the valuable data contained therein.

- Lastly, and most commonly, there are likely limited resources—both of the monetary and labor natures—to implement secure solutions.

Of course, not all of these conditions apply to all businesses, but it's very likely that each of these points is an obstacle that most organizations run into. In this chapter, I'll provide cost-effective ways to address some of these obstacles.

Principles of Server Security

Server security operates off the CIA principle. CIA stands for confidentiality, integrity, and availability. *Confidentiality* is the method by which information access is protected and restricted to only those who should have access. *Integrity* is the function that protects that information from being tampered with or otherwise modified without prior authorization. And *availability* refers to ensuring that access to the information is ready and accessible at all times, or at least as much as possible.

Keeping the CIA framework in mind, consider the different approaches one could make to security at the server level. One of the most successful methods at preserving confidentiality, integrity, and availability is the layered approach, which both reduces an attacker's chance of success and increases his risk of detection. In the layered approach, you have seven layers that all have their own methods and mechanisms for protection:

- **Data level**: The data level guards against malicious activity done to the actual data itself. Protection at the data level includes ACLs and encrypting file systems.

- **Application level**: Application-level security protects individual programs from attack. Security at this level can include hardening applications themselves, installing security patches from the vendors for them, and activating antivirus software and performing regular scans.

- **Host level**: Protection at the host level secures the computer and its operating system from attack, which nearly eliminates the attack of the two levels above this one. Protection at this level includes hardening the operating system itself (which is the primary focus of this chapter), managing security patches, authentication, authorization, and accounting, and host intrusion detection systems.

- **Internal network level**: The organization's network is the next level, which protects against intruders entering within the perimeter and sniffing traffic, possibly keys to accessing levels higher than this one. Protection at this level includes segmenting your network into subnets, using IPSec, and installing network intrusion detection systems.

- **Perimeter level**: The perimeter is where the internal network connects to other external networks, including those to other branches of the same corporation and connections to the Internet. Perimeter-level protections might include firewalls and quarantining VPN and dial-up access.

- **Physical security level**: The physical security level involves protecting the real estate that the business is practiced in. Guards, locks, and tracking devices all comprise protection at this level.

- **Policies, procedures, and awareness level**: This level involves educating users about best practices and acceptable and unacceptable methods of dealing with information technology.

Security Policy

The rest of this chapter depends on a fundamental understanding of how to manage security policies and configurations. SBS 2003 comes with two basic tools that will help you create, distribute, and automate security configurations: security templates and the Security Configuration and Analysis tool.

Using Security Policy Templates

Security templates list all possible security attributes and settings for a given system and their associated configurations. By using the Security Templates snap-in, you can easily provision a standard collection of security templates across multiple systems using either remote registry editing or Group Policy.

You can begin using security templates by loading the Security Templates snap-in:

1. Run mmc /s from a command line to load the Microsoft Management Console in author mode. Author mode allows you to construct new consoles from scratch and add snap-ins to them.

2. From the Console menu, select Add/Remove Snap-in. Then select Add. This raises a dialog box entitled Add Standalone Snap-in.

3. From the list, select Security Templates, click Add, and then click Close.

4. Click OK in the next box to confirm the addition of the snap-in.

You now have the Security Templates snap-in added to a console. From this snap-in, you can expand the Security Templates section in the console tree on the left, and then expand the C:\WINNT\security\templates folder to view the predefined security templates.

There are seven configurable areas inside the Security Templates snap-in, which you can display by double-clicking the label in the right-hand pane inside the snap-in after selecting a template from the list in the left pane. The areas are enumerated and described in Table 7-1.

Table 7-1. *Template Policy Areas*

Framework Area	Description
Account Policies	This area applies security configuration to user accounts, including passwords, account lockouts, and Kerberos ticket policies. Password and account lockout policies apply to workstations and servers; Kerberos ticket policies apply only to domain controllers.
Local Policies	This area allows you to set auditing and event logging policies, user rights assignments, and registry keys that directly affect system security. It also controls auditing of events, including application actions and security notifications. Note that settings in this area apply to all Windows 2000 or later systems, and not to only a specific type.
Restricted Groups	This particularly useful area allows you to define policies regarding a user's membership into security groups that allow elevated privileges. It's simple to define a policy where domain users can never be members of the local Administrators group; other policies are equally easy.

Continued

Table 7-1. *Continued*

Framework Area	Description
System Services	This area contains startup options for services and access controls on them.
Registry	In this area, you can configure access permissions on specific keys in the registry. In addition, you can audit access and modification of registry entries.
File System	This area allows you to preconfigure access permissions on selected file system directories.
Event Log	In this area, you can specify how the Application, Security, and System event logs fill and rotate and what their maximum size might be. You can also configure who has access to view the logs.

The compatible security template, COMPATWS.INF, is meant to allow ordinary applications to run on a system without being inhibited by security features. It discerns between ordinary users, who can only run certified Windows applications (those earning the compatibility seal that's usually displayed on the packaging of the software), and power users, who can run uncertified and potentially problematic software. It also allows a certain subset of registry keys, initialization files, and other folders to be modified by otherwise unprivileged users.

The secure security templates—SECUREWS.INF for workstations and ordinary servers and SECUREDC.INF for domain controllers—are designed to provide a middle-of-the-road amount of security. The secure templates offer more stringent password policies, restricted guest access, audit policies that cover most important security events, and increased account lockout policies. However, files, folders, and registry keys and their security settings are not configured with this template, since they are configured securely out of the box. For your environment, you may wish to modify this.

The highly secure template—HISECWS.INF for workstations and ordinary servers—focuses on securing transmissions between workstations and servers running Windows Server 2003. It also removes the Authenticated Users group from the Power Users group on all machines that use this template.

Finally, the default security template, SETUP SECURITY.INF (note the space), restores the default security settings for an initial installation of Windows.

Note Do not apply the domain controller template (SECUREDC.INF) to your SBS server; it is already securely set up and doesn't need any modification on your part. If you apply the template, you may break Group Policy and other server-side business applications!

Creating a Custom Security Template

You may wish to make your own customized policy modifications that go above and beyond those made in the templates shipped with Windows Server 2003. Creating a custom security template affords you an easy way to package, deploy, and apply these modifications with a minimum of administrative headache. Best of all, you can use these templates in conjunction with a utility called the Security Configuration and Analysis tool to assess the overall "hardness," or state of security, of your machines.

To create your own security template:

1. In the Security Templates console, expand Security Templates in the tree pane on the left, and right-click C:\WINDOWS\security\templates (this is the default templates folder in the system).

2. Select New Template from the context menu that appears.

You may now make any policy modifications you wish in any one of the policy areas supported by the tool: account policies, local policies, the event log, restricted groups, system services, the registry, and the file system. Your additions, deletions, and other changes are saved directly into the template as they are made.

To take this one step further, you may decide to build on the basic policy settings provided by the basic and incremental templates shipped with Windows Server 2003. In that case, it's quite simple to open the basic or incremental templates, resave to a different name, and make further modifications to it to create your own custom template. To do so:

1. Select an existing template inside the Security Templates console. In this example, I'll use the SECUREWS.INF file.

2. Right-click the existing template, and click Save As from the context menu, as shown in Figure 7-1.

3. Give the new template a name.

4. Click OK. The new template is created with the settings from the old basic template.

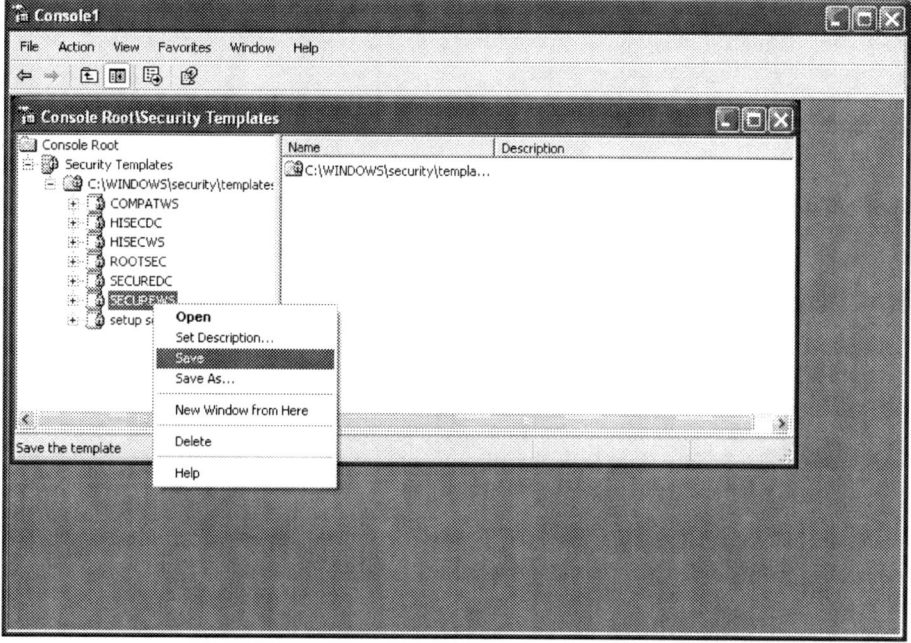

Figure 7-1. *Creating a new security template*

Importing a Template into a Group Policy Object

One of the most common ways to apply a security template to many machines is by importing the template into a Group Policy object. To do so:

1. Select the GPO you want to use inside Group Policy Object Editor.

2. Navigate through Computer Configuration ➤ Windows Settings ➤ Security Settings.

3. Right-click Security Settings and select Import Policy from the context menu.

4. Select the appropriate security template from the list of .INF files, and then click OK.

Security Configuration and Analysis

The Security Configuration and Analysis MMC snap-in lets you compare systems in their current configuration against settings specified within a security template. Using the report generated by that process, you can make wholesale changes to a system's security to bring it up to speed with a template as a whole, or you can modify configurations on an item-by-item basis. This is a great tool for initial rollouts and deployments of systems, since you can have one template that contains your business's entire security policy that can be applied using one simple tool. You can also save the current configuration of systems and export that to a template should a rollback be needed.

To begin using the SCA snap-in, you'll need to add it to a console. To do so:

1. Run mmc /s from a command line to load the Microsoft Management Console in author mode. Author mode allows you to construct new consoles from scratch and add snap-ins to them.

2. From the File menu, select Add/Remove Snap-in. Then select Add. This raises a dialog box entitled Add Standalone Snap-in.

3. From the list, select Security Configuration and Analysis, click Add, and then click Close.

4. Click OK in the next box to confirm the addition of the snap-in.

Creating and Using Template Databases with SCA

SCA uses databases, which have an .SDB extension, to store security templates for faster access and data retrieval. You can either create a new template database, if this is your first time using SCA, or open an existing SDB file by doing the following:

1. Right-click Security Configuration and Analysis in the left pane of your console and select Open Database from the context menu.

2. The Open Database dialog box appears. Type a name or select one from the list to open an existing database, or enter a name for a new database.

3. If you enter a new file name, you will be given the option of importing a base security template. Choose either a predefined template that ships with Windows Server 2003 or one you've modified or customized.

4. Click OK.

Your database is now ready for use.

Once you've created a database with an initial security template inside it, you can import any number of other templates into it as well. Simply right-click Security Configuration and Analysis and from the context menu, choose Import Template. From there, select the .INF file that is the template you want, and click OK. The settings are added to the database; they do not replace or otherwise modify any preexisting settings within the database.

Keep in mind that when you make changes to a security policy from within SCA, those settings are saved to the database and not to a template file that you could import into a GPO or otherwise apply to other systems. You'll need to export any saved settings to another template in order to use it in other systems. To do so, right-click Security Configuration and Analysis, and from the context menu choose Export Template. From there, choose a file name with an .INF extension for the exported template, and click OK.

Scanning System Security

To analyze a system using SCA, right-click Security Configuration and Analysis in the console and select Analyze Computer Now from the context menu. The Perform Analysis dialog box will appear. Select a file name for the results and accompanying log and click OK.

Two reports will be generated: events are written to a log file to correspond with each success and failure of a component analyzed by SCA. Secondly, SCA writes the current state of each component to the configuration trees within SCA, as shown in Figure 7-2.

To view the log file, right-click Security Configuration and Analysis in the left pane, and then select View Log File. Windows will load the log file into the right pane and show generally what portions of the computer's security policy don't match up to a certain baseline as set in the database. For a more exact analysis, you'll need to examine the policy tree itself. To do so, expand Security Configuration and Analysis and select one of the seven security areas to consider. In the previous figure, the password policy tree under Account Policies is shown.

Note, in the right pane, the two columns, Database Setting and Computer Setting. These indicate exactly which configuration options match between the current computer and the settings configured in the SCA database. Settings that agree are preceded by an icon with a small green checkmark. Likewise, settings that disagree are preceded by a small red X mark. Settings that don't appear in the database are not analyzed and thus are not marked.

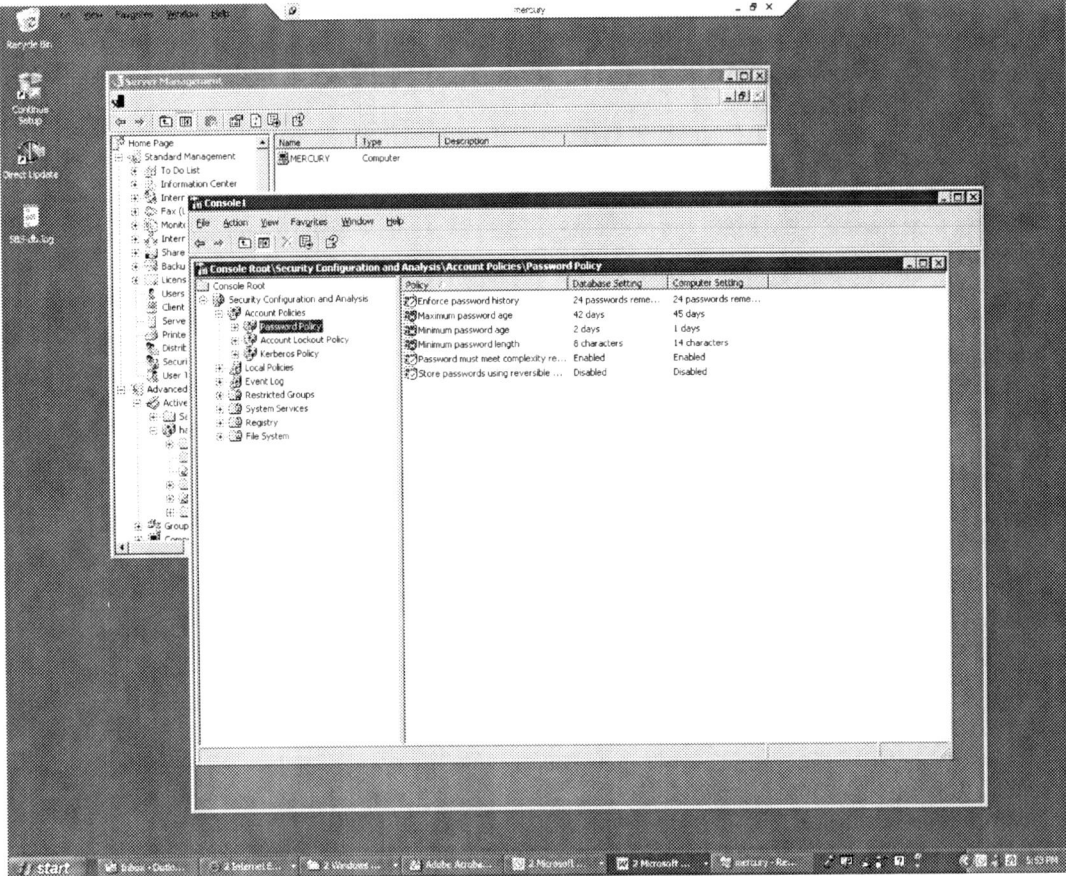

Figure 7-2. *Using SCA to compare system status with a baseline*

Correcting System Security

If you would like to make the changes to a computer's security policy as specified by SCA in a wholesale manner, simply right-click Security Configuration and Analysis and select Configure Computer Now. The changes will be effected on the local computer.

If you'd like to make a change in the database based on an actual configuration object, you can right-click the attribute in question to raise the Analyzed Security Policy Setting dialog box, as shown in Figure 7-3.

Simply adjust the settings in the box and then click OK. The change will be committed to the database, but not to the local computer, and all future computers you examine with that SCA database will be analyzed with that change committed.

Figure 7-3. *Changing a policy setting in the SCA database*

Microsoft Baseline Security Analyzer

The Microsoft Baseline Security Analyzer, or MBSA, is an excellent tool that you can use to assess your network and the effects of your security policy. MBSA works by scanning a machine or range of machines for specific policy problems, security updates that aren't present, Microsoft Office updates that aren't present, and other red flags that may indicate security risks. It then lists all of the problems in a simple-to-read report that makes it easy to simply go down the list and rectify each problem.

The MBSA can scan for problems in the following products:

- Windows NT 4.0

- Windows 2000

- Windows XP

- Windows Server 2003

- Internet Information Services (IIS)

- SQL Server

- Internet Explorer

- Office

The MBSA 1.2 will also scan for absent security hotfixes in the following products:

- Windows NT 4.0

- Windows 2000

- Windows XP

- Windows Server 2003

- IIS

- SQL Server

- Internet Explorer

- Exchange Server

- Windows Media Player

- Microsoft Data Access Components (MDAC)

- MSXML

- Microsoft Virtual Machine

- Commerce Server

- Content Management Server

- BizTalk Server

- Host Integration Server

- Office

The MBSA is essential to ensuring the computers in your organization remain in compliance with any security policy you may have in place. The tool can be downloaded from the Microsoft web site at `http://www.microsoft.com/technet/security/tools/mbsahome.mspx`.

Using the MBSA

Running a scan on a computer or set of computers using the MBSA is simple. In the following example, I'll assume we're only scanning a single computer. First, open the MBSA program. Then follow these instructions:

1. Click Scan a computer to scan a single computer.

2. The Pick a Computer to Scan screen appears, as shown in Figure 7-4.

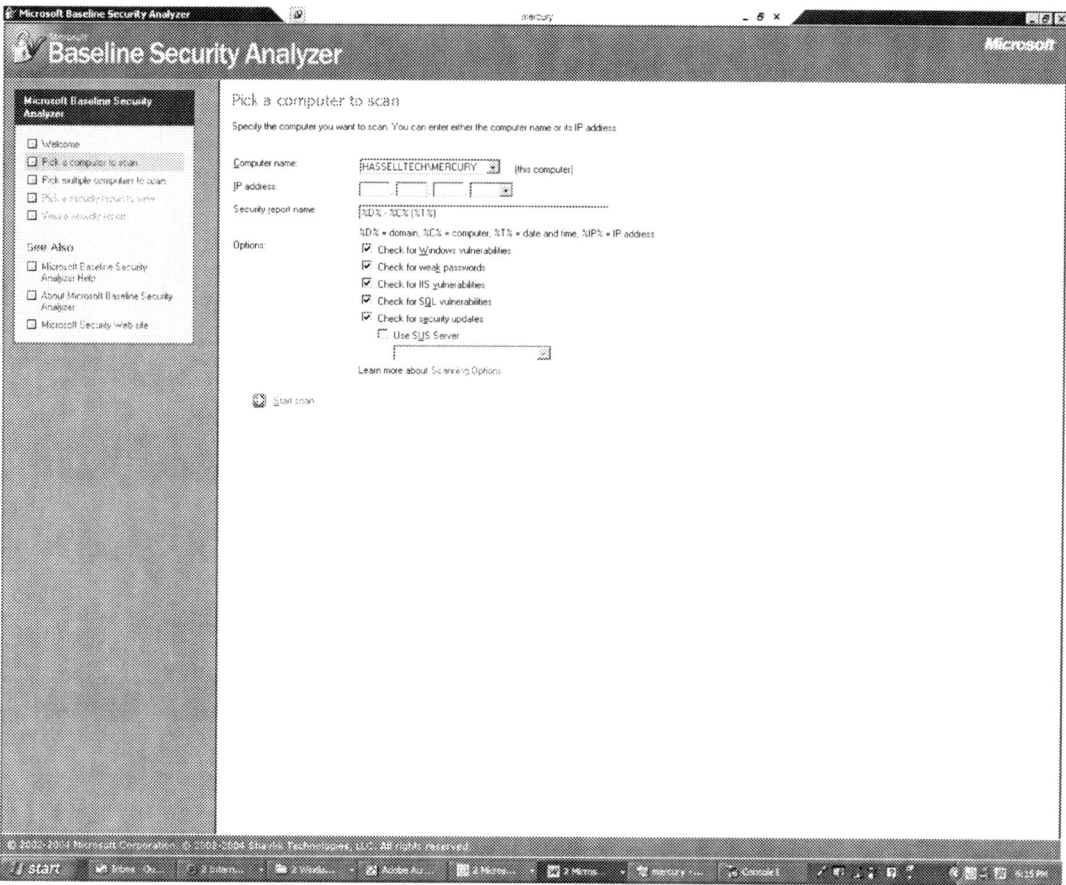

Figure 7-4. *Scanning a computer using MBSA*

3. Ensure the correct computer name is listed in the Computer Name field. You can also specify an IP address. Additionally, enter a name for the resulting report; you can use any of the options listed there—domain, IP address, date and time, and computer name.

4. Select the scope of the scan. You can choose to scan for Windows vulnerabilities, weak passwords, IIS vulnerabilities, SQL vulnerabilities, and security updates. (You can use a Software Update Services server if you wish. SUS is covered later in this chapter.)

5. Click Start Scan to begin the scan.

6. When the scan is complete, you'll see the View Security Report screen. A sample screen is shown in Figure 7-5.

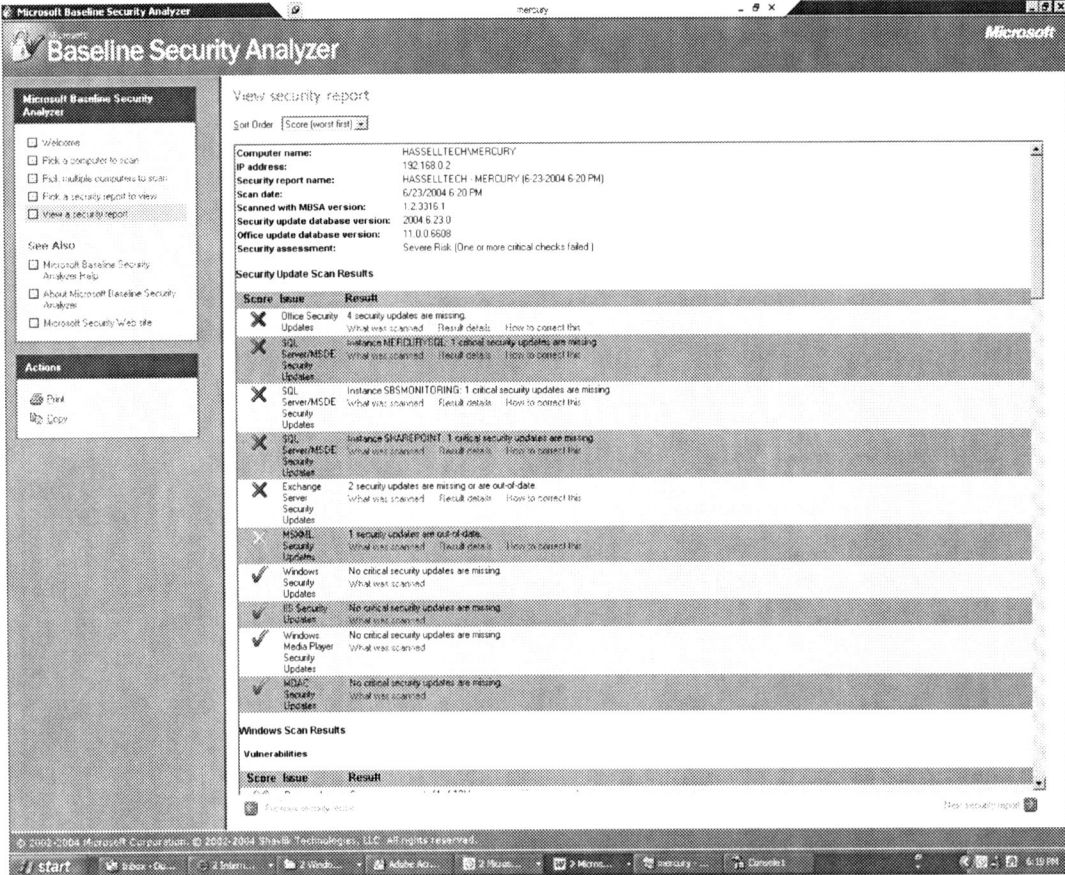

Figure 7-5. *MBSA scan results*

You can see each issue that the scan identified, how serious the issue is, and a link to information on how to correct it.

A suggestion about security strategy: I'd recommend that you use the MBSA before applying your security templates to know what issues to address, and then run it once again after your templates have been applied and tested to identify what may have slipped through the cracks.

Locking Down Windows

Multiuser systems are security holes in and of themselves. The simplest systems—those used by only one person—are the ones most easily secured, since there's much less diversity and variance of usage on the part of one person than there is on the part of many. Unfortunately, most of our IT environments require multiple user accounts, so the following section focuses on some prudent ways to lock down Windows systems, including Windows Server 2003 machines and associated client workstation operating systems.

Password Requirements

Long passwords are more secure, period. As you might suspect, there are more permutations and combinations to try when one is attempting to crack a machine via brute-force, and common English words, on which a dictionary attack can be based, are generally shorter than eight characters. On the same token, aging passwords are insecure. While most users grudgingly change their passwords on a regular basis when encouraged by administrators, some accounts—namely the Administrator and Guest accounts—often have the same password for life, which makes them an easy target for attack.

To counter these threats, consider setting some basic requirements for passwords. To set these restrictions on individual workstations and Windows Server 2003 servers:

1. Open the Microsoft Management Console and navigate to the Local Computer Policy snap-in. This is normally under Start ➤ Programs ➤ Administrative Tools.

2. Navigate down the tree, through Security Settings, to Account Policies.

3. Click Password Policy.

4. Enable the "Passwords must meet complexity requirements" setting.

5. Change the "Minimum password length" to a decent length. I recommend 8 characters.

6. Change the "Maximum password age" setting to a fairly conservative setting. I recommend 90 days.

You can accomplish the same through Group Policy by selecting an appropriate group policy object and loading the Group Policy Object Editor as I've explained in previous chapters. The configuration tree remains the same.

Account Lockout Policies

Three old-fashioned methods to gain unauthorized access to a system are to attempt authentication using

- A known username

- A username not known but derived logically

- A different password for the username on each attempt, repeating as often as possible

Windows can thwart these styles of attack using an account lockout policy, which will disable an account for a specified period of time after a certain number of unsuccessful logon attempts.

To set the account lockout policy:

1. Open the Microsoft Management Console and load the Group Policy Object Editor for an appropriate GPO, or navigate to the Local Computer Policy snap-in.

2. Navigate down the tree, through Security Settings, to Account Policies.

3. Click Account Lockout Policy.

4. Set "Account lockout threshold" to a reasonably small number. I recommend 3 bad login attempts.

5. Set both the "Account lockout duration" and "Reset account lockout after" options to 15 minutes. This setting resists attack while not seriously imposing on users who just suffer from "typo syndrome."

Windows Component Selection and Installation

Security usually takes a minimalist approach: that is to say, when you harden a system, you want as few basic entry points as possible. This effectively shortens the length of the playing field for an intruder: he has fewer processes and fewer software products whose flaws he can exploit, and there's less chance of you, the administrator, configuring something improperly or not at all. Windows Server 2003 makes this a little more difficult, in that at install time, it is not possible to select components that you would like *not* to be installed.

If I might offer a slight editorial aside, this is a serious flaw in Windows and a rather large mistake on Microsoft's part. It would have been bad enough if Microsoft decided that none of its operating systems should ever present the user with component installation options. But this functionality remains available in the Windows 9x line and even in Windows NT! And yet mysteriously, it's not present in Windows 2000 or Windows Server 2003. It's baffling to me why these options were removed at the point of installation. If anyone from Microsoft is reading, please return the power of choice to me, the user!

Local Options

In addition to securing local accounts, the newer Windows platforms give you the ability to lock down certain rights and configurations on the local computer, aside from any domain security policy that might be configured. Several of the options available do little to thwart attacks, so in this section I've covered the six most effective changes you can make to your local security policy.

All of the hardening suggestions in this section can be enabled through the Security Options section of the Local Computer Policy snap-in to the Microsoft Management Console. This snap-in can be found normally under Start ➤ Programs ➤ Administrative Tools. To get to the appropriate section, navigate the snap-in tree through Computer Configuration ➤ Windows Settings ➤ Security Settings ➤ Local Policies. Then click Security Options, and the different configuration switches will appear in the right-hand pane.

The instructions in this section will assume you have already loaded the snap-in and navigated to the appropriate section.

Anonymous Access

Windows allows access by an anonymous user to many shares and files through the use of a null user account; this is a security hazard, of course. You can still enable anonymous access to files and directories by explicitly granting rights to the ANONYMOUS USER account in Windows inside the appropriate access control list (ACL). This setting merely disables it by default, so you know exactly where connections are being made.

To fix this hazard, set Additional Restrictions for Anonymous Connections to "No access without explicit anonymous permissions."

Shutdown Without Logon

Windows 2000 and Windows XP Professional machines come in a default configuration that allows you to shut down the system through the use of the Shutdown button on the logon screen. Windows 2000 and .NET Servers disable this out of the box. Despite the convenience factor that this feature affords, it's best to leave rebooting a machine to an aware user.

Change "Allow system to shut down without having to log on" to Disabled to secure this.

Automatic Logoff

Some users log on to the network and then don't log off for months. This is a prominent security hole, as when that user leaves her desk, she is still authenticated to the network with her credentials. These can be used to do destructive things: file deletion and transfer, planting of a "root kit" or backdoor program, or password changing.

The way to fix this security hole is twofold: first, each valid user needs to have a time where she is not permitted to log on. This can be somewhere in the morning for standard 9 a.m. to 5 p.m. office, perhaps at 3 a.m. to 3:30 a.m. Then, a change to the local security policy needs to be made so that when the user's logon time expires, she is not permitted to log on.

To set up a logon time restriction on a domain controller for an Active Directory–enabled domain:

1. Go to the Active Directory Users and Computers snap-in.

2. Expand the icon for your domain, and click the Users container.

3. Right-click a user, and select Properties.

4. Click the Account tab, and then click the Logon Hours button.

5. Select the appropriate region of time in the calendar block, and click the radio buttons to the right to either permit or deny logons during that time.

6. Click OK, and then OK once more to exit the user property sheet.

▓**Note** This option is only available on Active Directory–enabled machines.

Now, make the change to the computer's local security policy. Inside the Local Computer Policy snap-in, change "Automatically log off users when logon time expires" to Enabled. If you do not have a domain, instead change "Automatically log off users when logon time expires (local)" to Enabled.

Digitally Signing Communication

It's a good idea these days for a computer to authenticate itself to other computers during communication. Otherwise, a technique called "spoofing" could be used, and a cracker's computer could pose as the remote end of a connection and receive potentially sensitive information. Using digital signatures can prevent this. However, these are not pervasive; Windows compensates for this limited use by providing two options in the local policy: require it when possible, or require it, period.

I recommend requiring the signatures when possible on both ends of a connection (the RPC protocol refers to the requesting end as the "client" and the responding end as the "server," no matter the systems' usual roles). Unsigned transmissions should only occur when signatures are not available, supported, or possible.

▓Note Be aware that this setting will probably break communications between Windows Server 2003 machines and older, less secure client operating systems, including Windows 95, Windows 98, and Windows Me.

To require digitally signed communication when possible, change "Digitally sign client communication (when possible)" to Enabled and "Digitally sign server communication (when possible)" to Enabled.

Requiring the Three-Keystroke Salute at Logon

The logon screen is one of the most trusted aspects of a computer to a normal user. He trusts it enough that he gives his password and username, and then the computer trusts him, too, if all of that is correct and verified. A cracker can take advantage of this mutual trust by writing a program that runs as a system service—that is, it doesn't need user privileges—that will mimic the logon box, grab the user's input, and do something with it. "It" could be e-mailing the password to the cracker, saving the credentials to a backdoor program data file, or any number of other nefarious things. However, pressing Ctrl+Alt+Del brings Windows itself to attention, and you get the authentic Windows logon and not a shell of one that a cracker creates. This is an easy step that makes your system much more secure.

To require this keystroke to begin, change "Disable CTRL+ALT+Delete requirement for logon" to Disabled. (Yes, that's right. Microsoft uses some questionable terminology.)

Last Username Display

By default, Windows displays the username of the last successfully authenticated person to use that particular system on the logon screen. This is giving needless information away, although some of your users are probably accustomed to it.

To disable the last username from being displayed, change the "Do not display last user name in logon screen" setting to Enabled.

Password Expiration Prompt

Earlier in this chapter I discussed setting password policies to prevent brute-force attacks. Of course, changing passwords is a problem for some users, who'd rather not be bothered with IS minutia and would like to simply use their computers to be productive. With this policy setting, you can tell the system to automatically remind a user when his password will expire and prompt him to change it. Setting this value to 14 days gives a user ample opportunity to change his password, since that is in excess of most scheduled vacations and business trips.

To enable the password expiration prompt, change the "Prompt user to change password before expiration" setting to 14 days at minimum.

Network Options via Group Policy

Windows Server 2003 and Group Policy allow you to configure security options that reside inside group policy objects that will apply to groups of computers. Centrally managing security settings using the Group Policy Framework defines seven areas in which Group Policy can manage security settings across an Active Directory structure. They are shown in Table 7-2.

Table 7-2. *Group Policy Framework Areas and Descriptions*

Framework Area	Description
Account Area	This framework area applies security configuration to user accounts, including passwords, account lockouts, and Kerberos ticket policies. Password and account lockout policies apply to workstations and servers; Kerberos ticket policies apply only to domain controllers.
Local Policies	This area allows you to set auditing and event logging policies, user rights assignments, and registry keys that directly affect system security. Settings in this area apply to all Windows 2000 or later systems, and not to only a specific type.
Restricted Groups	This particularly useful group allows you to define policies regarding a user's membership into security groups that allow elevated privileges. It's simple to define a policy where domain users can never be members of the local Administrators group; other policies are equally easy.
System Services	Here you can set startup options for services and access controls on them.
Registry	In this area you can configure access permissions on specific keys in the registry.
Public Key Policies	You can establish settings for encrypted recovery agents for the Windows encrypting file system EFS, certificate authorities for a specific Windows domain, trusted certificate authorities, and other public cryptography options.
IPSec Policies on Active Directory	This area allows you to define IPSec configurations for any given unit in your Active Directory.

Viewing the Default Domain Policy

When you install Windows Server 2003, a default domain security policy is created. It's a simple task to use this default policy as a base and add and customize settings based on your individual implementation. Let's take a look at this default policy first, and then work through customizing it.

To view the default domain security policy:

1. Open the Active Directory Users and Computers snap-in.

2. Expand the domain tree corresponding to your domain's name in the left pane.

3. Right-click the domain name and select Properties.

4. Click the Group Policy tab, select Default Domain Policy in the details box, and then click the Edit button. Windows raises the Group Policy window.

5. To view each of the default domain policies, drill down through Computer Configuration ➤ Windows Settings ➤ Security Settings and click Account Policies.

6. Look at the right pane. You see Password Policy, Account Lockout Policy, and Kerberos Policy, and by clicking each you can view or change the default configuration.

Figure 7-6 shows the default domain policy on a standard, out-of-the-box installation of SBS 2003.

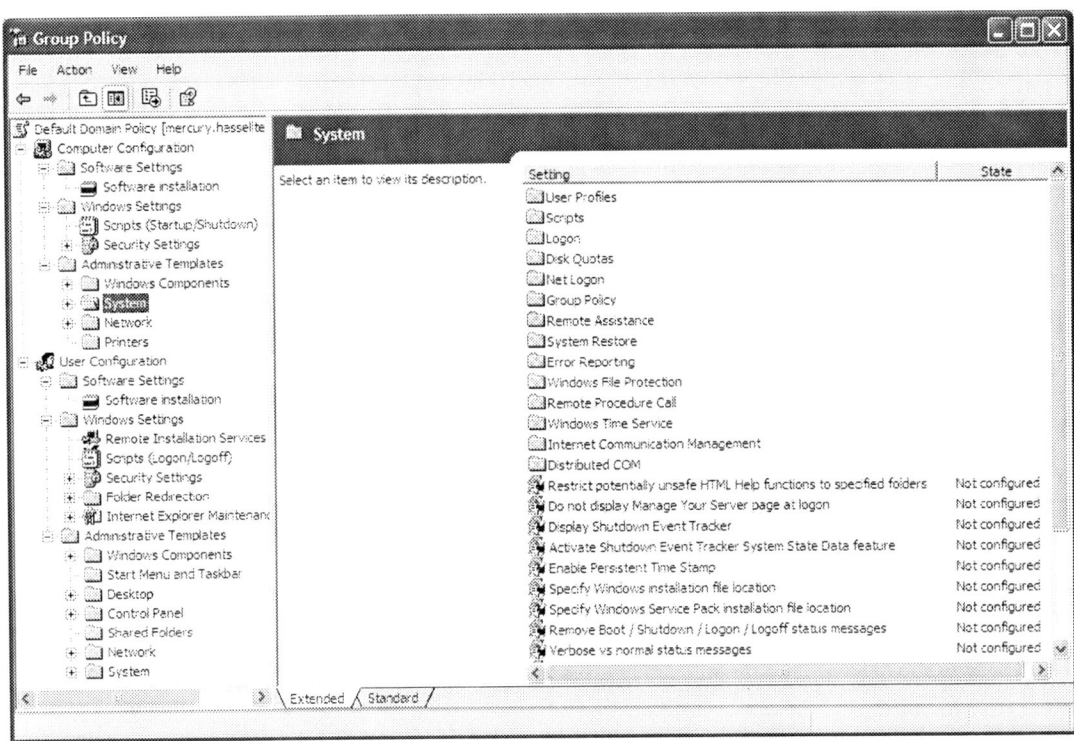

Figure 7-6. *Default domain policy in SBS 2003*

About Software Update Services

Patch management is one of the most difficult but necessary tasks an administrator faces in the wake of viruses and security vulnerabilities that plague our connected world today. However, even though Microsoft operating systems have been the target of many a hacker and virus writer for the past five years or so, there hasn't been a Microsoft-endorsed low-cost method of distributing operation system updates to an installed base of computers—including both clients and servers.

That changed in 2003. As part of its Strategic Technology Protection Program, Microsoft sought to use its popular Windows Update technology—the software that runs the universal update site for all but the oldest versions of Windows. The result of this effort was a new free product called Software Update Services, or SUS. SUS at this point does NOT focus on adding new features to already released software; it only concerns itself with critical updates, allowing administrators to somewhat easily deploy critical updates to servers running Windows 2000 or Windows Server 2003, as well as desktop computers running Windows 2000 Professional or Windows XP Professional. It's designed to work especially in networks with an Active Directory implementation, but it will function without one.

There are two parts to an installation of Software Update Services on your network:

- One server connected to the Internet running the actual server component of Software Update Services. This machine acts as a local version of the public Windows Update site, containing critical updates and service packs for all supported operating systems. This server synchronizes with the public Windows Update site on a schedule that the corporate administrator selects, and then that administrator approves or rejects the availability of certain updates on the SUS server. You can also have multiple SUS servers on an intranet and configure which client machines are directed to specific SUS servers for updates.

- The Automatic Updates feature of Windows 2000 Service Pack 3 and higher or Windows XP Professional at any revision level. Directed by a registry change or by an applied group policy object, the client computers that are running this automatic updates feature are sent to the local network's SUS server on a set schedule to download updates appropriate to their machines. The SUS server will analyze the operating system, service pack level, and currently installed updates and only push those updates that are both needed AND approved by the administrator beforehand.

Using SUS: On the Server Side

There are a few phases to the SUS installation. First, you should download and install the software.

1. Go to the Software Update Services web site at http://www.microsoft.com/sus.

2. Download Sus10sp1.exe to a folder on the server where you want to either install SUS 1.0 SP1 or apply the service pack to an existing installation of SUS 1.0.

3. Double-click the file using the server on which you want to install or upgrade SUS.

4. Click Next on the Welcome screen to continue.

5. Decide whether to accept or reject the license agreement, and click Next.

6. Select the Typical checkbox unless there's a good reason for you to use a custom installation. Click Next.

7. Make a note of the location with which you can direct clients to SUS. Click Install to begin the actual file copy.

8. When the file copy finishes, make a note of the location of the SUS administrative pages. Then click Finish to exit the wizard.

The administrative web site for SUS will open. The default address for these pages is `http://SUSServerName/SUSAdmin`. You can also navigate through Start ➤ Programs ➤ Administrative Tools, and click Microsoft Software Update Services. You'll see something much like that in Figure 7-7.

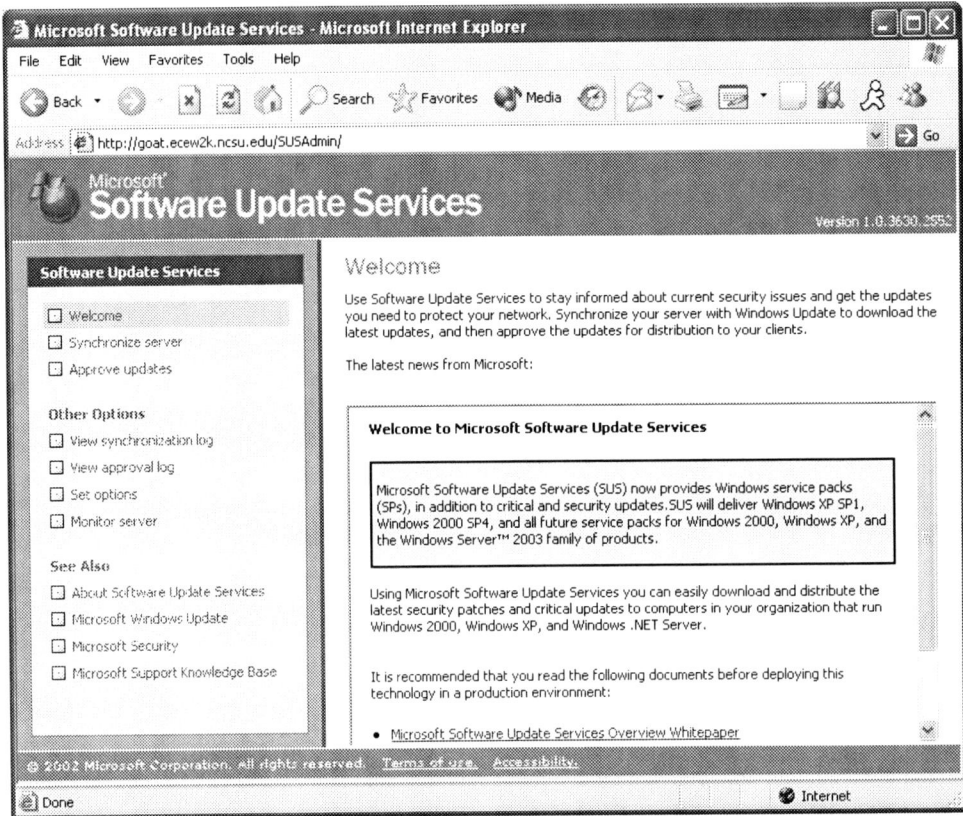

Figure 7-7. *The SUS Administrative Web Site home page*

The first step is to configure the options for your SUS server. In the left pane, click Set Options. The sections on this page are described here:

- **Select a proxy server configuration**: This option is to tell SUS whether to connect to the Windows Update web site using a proxy server or to simply use a direct Internet connection. Fill out this form much like you would inside Internet Explorer itself.

- **Specify the name your clients use to locate this update server**: Here you configure how the server will respond to update requests from client computers on your network. I recommend using the full DNS name here and not just a NetBIOS name for maximum compatibility and performance.

- **Select which server to synchronize content from**: Here you can instruct SUS to download updates to distribute to client computers directly from the public Windows Update site, from another SUS server located somewhere on your network, or from a manually created network share. You can also select whether to use the list of approved updates from other SUS servers, or to use only that server's store in tandem with the local server's list of approved updates.

- **Select how you want to handle new versions of previously applied updates**: If a new version of a patch or other hotfix is issued, you can select here whether to automatically approve the revision for distribution, or to treat it as a new patch that needs to be manually approved by an administrator.

- **Select where you want to store updates**: You can select whether to download the updates from Windows Update in real time or to batch download them and store them on the SUS server. You can also select what localities for which you'd like to store critical updates and security hotfixes (although I've found in my experience that this filter doesn't always work as expected).

Synchronizing and Approving Content

When you start the content synchronization process, the SUS server goes out to either the public Windows Update servers or another local SUS server (as configured in the Set Options section) and downloads the entire library of available critical updates and service packs for each language you have configured. This synchronization usually results in about 150 MB worth of data being transferred for just English updates, or close to 600 MB for updates in every localization.

To synchronize content, surf to the SUS administration web site, and then do the following:

1. In the left-hand navigation pane, click Synchronize server.

2. Click the Synchronize now button in the right pane to begin the transfer.

You can also opt to schedule your synchronizations automatically, so that you don't have to remember to resynchronize every time a new update is released—which is all too often in most of our opinions. On the Synchronize server page, click Synchronization schedule. A dialog box like that in Figure 7-8 will appear.

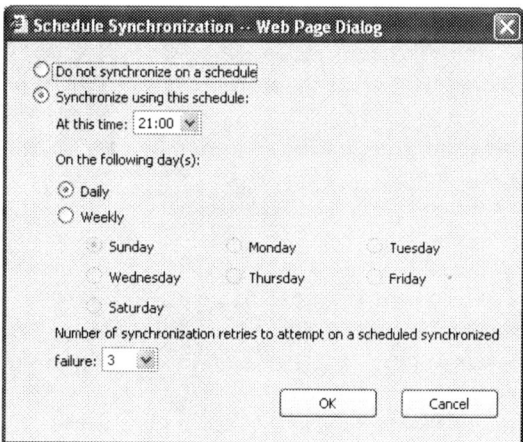

Figure 7-8. *Setting a synchronization schedule for the SUS host machine*

Set your desired options for synchronization and then click OK. Be aware that if the SUS server can't connect to the appropriate upstream update source, it will repeat its attempts four times, spacing out each attempt by half an hour. You can adjust this using the "Number of synchronization retries to attempt on a scheduled synchronization failure" drop-down box on the Schedule Synchronization dialog box.

Now that you have an actual library of updates on or near your SUS host machine, you can approve the updates individually for distribution to client machines within your network. The approval process makes it easy to withhold patches until further testing is done, partly assuaging the general fear that's caused by installing patches that might cause more problems than they fix. To begin the update approval process:

1. In the navigation pane, click Approve updates.

2. In the right-hand pane, select the updates that you would like to approve, and click Approve when you've finished your selection.

SUS will notify you when the approval is complete. In the right-hand pane, where all the updates are shown, each patch's status is shown as one of five possible values. A new update is one that was just recently downloaded and has not been approved yet. An approved update is available for distribution to client machine. An update that is not approved will not be distributed to clients, but the actual patch file remains in the library on the SUS host machine. An updated patch indicates a new version of an earlier patch that currently exists in the library. And finally, a temporarily unavailable patch is one whose dependent files were downloaded incorrectly, could not be found, or are otherwise unable to be located by SUS.

If, for some reason, you would like to clear the list of approved updates, you can clear all check boxes on the list of available updates and then click Approve. This will remove any available updates from the SUS catalog, and your client machines will stop downloading the updates until you approve more fixes. This will not, however, uninstall the patches from the client machines.

The SUS server will record an entry to the synchronization log whenever the server attempts to connect to its upstream provider. This log can be accessed from the SUS administrative web site using any standard web browser; it can also be accessed directly from the SUS host machine in the autoupdate\administration directory of the SUS web site—the file name is history-Sync.xml. The log entry contains the time of the last synch, whether the operation was complete, the date and time of the next scheduled synchronization, the contents of the operation and whether each component was successfully installed, and whether the synchronization was routine or manual.

The SUS server also keeps a log of all approved updates, which can be found in the same place as the synchronization log with the file name history-approve.xml.

Pushing Out the Automated Updates Client

If you are upgrading an installation of SUS 1.0, the Automatic Updates software installed on your client computers will self-update to the latest SUS 1.0 SP1 client software. This will occur after the SUS 1.0 server has been successfully updated to SP1 and synchronized with the latest content available on the Windows Update servers.

You can install the updated Automatic Updates client on your clients by installing the Automatic Updates client using the MSI install package, self-updating from the old Critical

Update Notification (CUN) tool, installing Windows 2000 Service Pack 3 or 4, installing Windows XP Service Pack 1 or 2, or installing Windows Server 2003.

▓**Note** You can download the Automatic Updates client from the Microsoft web site at the SUS web page, located at http://www.microsoft.com/sus. On a standalone machine, the AU client can simply be added by running the WUAU22.MSI file on the machine.

Manually installing a file can quickly become a pain when you have more than just a few machines to handle. Fortunately, with the client installation program being in the form of an MSI, you can easily push the program to clients by using Group Policy. To create a new GPO, assign it to your computers, and then have it installed automatically.

▓**Note** The application will be installed in the context of the local computer, so be sure that authenticated users have rights on the source folders.

Open the Active Directory Users and Computers MMC snap-in, and then follow these instructions:

1. Right-click the domain or organizational unit to which you're interested in deploying the client, and select Properties.

2. Click the Group Policy tab.

3. Click New to create a new group policy object. Type in a name for the GPO.

4. Select the new GPO from the list, and click Edit to open the Group Policy Object Editor.

5. Expand Computer Configuration, and then select Software Settings.

6. Right-click Software Installation in the left pane, select New, and then click Package.

7. Enter the path to the WUAU22.msi. Make sure you use a network path and not a local path to ensure your clients can find the file at boot time. Click Open.

8. Choose Assigned to assign the package to the computers in the domain or organizational unit, and then click OK.

9. Allow time for policies to replicate through the domain. Usually this is accomplished within 15 minutes.

10. Restart the client computers. The client software should be installed before the logon dialog box is displayed.

You can also deploy the client MSI through a logon script by calling MSIEXEC followed by the client software file name as an argument. The software will be installed as requested.

Configuring the Automatic Updates Client

The Automatic Updates client does not have any user interface options for determining the origin of updates to install. You must set this via either a registry change on each of the client computers or through Group Policy, either locally or based through a domain.

Through a domain-based group policy, direct clients to the SUS server using the following procedure:

1. Open the Default Domain Policy GPO in Active Directory Users and Computers and click the Edit button.

2. Expand Computer Configuration ➤ Administrative Templates ➤ Windows Components.

3. Select Windows Update. The right pane will contain four options that pertain to the Automatic Updates client, as depicted in Figure 7-9.

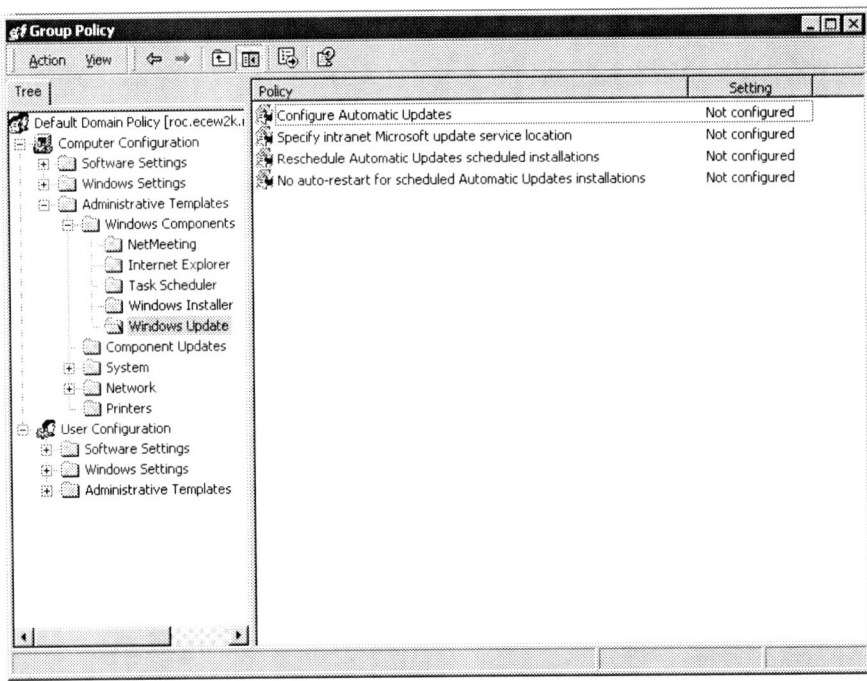

Figure 7-9. *Group Policy options for SUS and AU*

These options are described here in more detail:

- **Configure Automatic Updates**: This option specifies whether this computer will receive security updates and critical bug fixes. The first option has the currently logged on user notified before downloading updates, and notified again before installing the downloaded updates. The second option has updates automatically downloaded, but not installed until a logged on user acknowledges his presence and authorizes the installation. The third option has updates automatically downloaded and installed on a schedule that you can set in the appropriate boxes on the sheet. To use this setting, click Enabled, and then select one of the options.

- **Specify intranet Microsoft update service location**: This option designates an SUS server from which to download updates. To use this setting, you must set two server name values: the server from which the Automatic Updates client detects and downloads updates, and the server to which updated workstations upload statistics. You can set both values to be the same server.

- **Reschedule Automatic Updates scheduled installations**: This option specifies the amount of time to wait after boot before continuing with a scheduled installation that was missed previously, for whatever reason (power outage, system powered off, network connection lost, and so on). If the status is set to Enabled, a missed scheduled installation will occur the specified number of minutes after the computer is next started. If the status is set to Disabled or Not Configured, a missed scheduled installation will simply roll over to the next scheduled installation.

- **No auto-restart for scheduled Automatic Updates installations**: This option designates whether a client computer should automatically reboot or not when an update that is just installed requires a system restart. If the status is set to Enabled, Automatic Updates will not restart a computer automatically during a scheduled installation if a user is logged in to the computer, instead notifying the user to restart the computer to complete the installation. If the status is set to Disabled or Not Configured, Automatic Updates will notify the user that the computer will automatically restart in 5 minutes to complete the installation.

You will want to allow 10 to 15 minutes for the changes to the domain's policy to replicate among all domain controllers.

To adjust the group policy on a machine that is not managed by Active Directory, follow these steps:

1. Click Start, select Run, and type **GPEDIT.msc** to load the Group Policy snap-in.

2. Expand Computer Configuration and Administrative Templates.

3. Click Add/Remove Templates, and then click Add.

4. Enter the name of the Automatic Updates ADM file, which can be found in the INF subdirectory within your Windows root. It can also be found in the INF subdirectory within the SUS server machine's Windows root.

5. Click Open, and then click Close to load the wuau.adm file.

You can now adjust the policy settings as described in the previous subsection.

Finally, to adjust some of these behavior settings through registry changes, use the appropriate key for each setting:

- **To enable or disable Automatic Updates**: Create the value NoAutoUpdate in the `HKEY_LOCAL_MACHINE\SOFTWARE\Policies\Microsoft\Windows\WindowsUpdate\AU` key. The value is a DWORD with possible values zero (enabled) or one (disabled).

- **To configure the update download and notification behavior**: Create the value AUOptions in the `HKEY_LOCAL_MACHINE\SOFTWARE\Policies\Microsoft\Windows\WindowsUpdate\AU` key. The value is a DWORD that includes integers 2 (notify of download and notify before installation), 3 (automatically download but notify before installation), and 4 (automatically download and schedule the installation).

- **To schedule an automated installation**: Create the values ScheduledInstallDay and ScheduledInstallTime in the `HKEY_LOCAL_MACHINE\SOFTWARE\Policies\Microsoft\Windows\WindowsUpdate\AU` key. The value for each is a DWORD. For ScheduledInstall-Day, the range is from 0 to 7, with 0 indicating every day and 1 through 7 indicating the days of the week, Sunday through Saturday, respectively. For ScheduledInstallTime, the range is from 0 to 23, signifying the hour of the day in military time.

- **To specify a particular SUS server to use with the Automatic Updates client**: Create the value UseWUServer in the `HKEY_LOCAL_MACHINE\SOFTWARE\Policies\Microsoft\Windows\WindowsUpdate\AU` key. The value is a DWORD; set it to 1 to enable the custom SUS server name. Then, create the values WUServer and WUStatusServer in the same key, of types Reg_SZ, and specify the name (with the http://) as the value.

- **To specify how long to wait before completing a missed installation**: Create the value RescheduleWaitTime in the `HKEY_LOCAL_MACHINE\SOFTWARE\Policies\Microsoft\Windows\WindowsUpdate\AU` key. The value is a DWORD that ranges from 1 to 60, measured in minutes.

- **To specify whether to restart a scheduled installation with a currently logged in non-administrative user**: Create the NoAutoRebootWithLoggedOnUsers value in the key `HKEY_LOCAL_MACHINE\SOFTWARE\Policies\Microsoft\Windows\WindowsUpdate\AU`. The value is a DWORD that can be 0, which indicates that a reboot will indeed take place, or 1, which indicates the reboot will be postponed while a user is logged on.

Using SUS: On the Client Side

To configure Windows XP to work with SUS, first enable the Automatic Updates feature. In Windows XP:

1. Open Control Panel. Navigate to the System applet and open it.

2. Click the Automatic Updates tab.

In Windows 2000:

1. Open Control Panel.

2. Navigate to the Automatic Updates applet and double-click to open it.

You will see the properties screen for the feature, which is depicted in Figure 7-10.

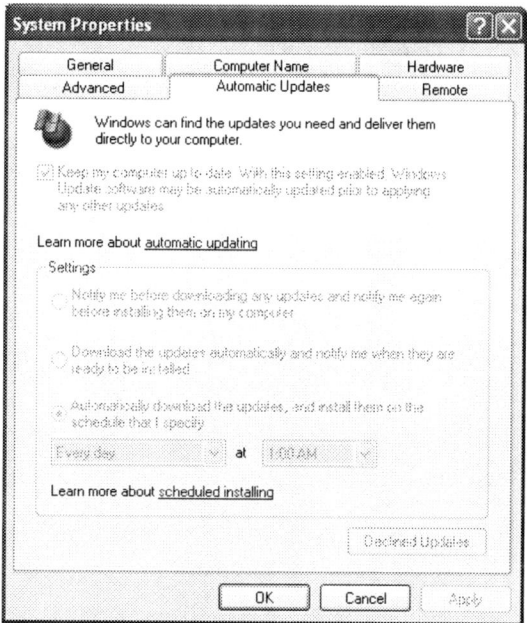

Figure 7-10. *Automatic Updates in Windows XP and Windows 2000*

You, as the administrator, select how updates are downloaded, signaled to the user, and subsequently installed on client machines. The currently logged on user, if that person happens to have administrator credentials, is notified through a small update icon in the system tray as well as an information "bubble" that pops up when the updates' download is complete. In addition, an administrator can determine if updates have been downloaded by looking at the system log. If the current user is not an administrator, Windows will wait until one logs on to offer the notification that updates are available for installation.

Update Download and Installation

The updates are downloaded in the session's background by the BITS, or Background Intelligent Transfer Service, extension to Windows. BITS detects inactivity over a network connection and uses it to download large amounts of data from remote sites. BITS will detect when a user initiates activity over a connection and pause the download process, waiting for the next idle period to resume it.

On the Automatic Updates property sheet, to have the currently logged on user notified before downloading updates, and notified again before installing the downloaded updates, click the first option. Use the second option to have updates automatically downloaded, but to wait until a logged on user acknowledges her presence and authorizes the installation. Finally, click the third option to have updates automatically downloaded and installed on a schedule that you can set in the boxes below.

The update installation process proceeds depending on the preceding selection. When updates have finished downloading, the notification bubble will appear in the system tray area of the machine, and an administrative user can double-click the bubble to raise the Ready to Install dialog box, featured in Figure 7-11.

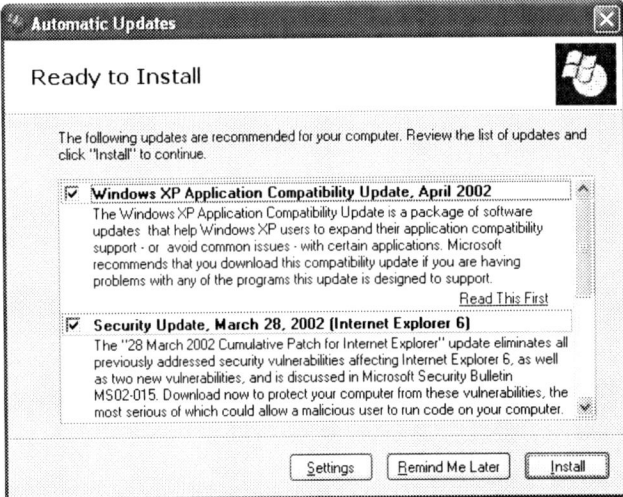

Figure 7-11. *Installation dialog box for Automatic Updates*

You can click the Remind Me Later button to defer the installation of updates for a set period of time, ranging from half an hour to three days from the current time.

If you have configured Automatic Updates to install fixes on a regular schedule, the updates will be downloaded in the background and automatically installed on that schedule. Automatic Updates installs the update and restarts the computer if an update requires that, even if there is no local administrator logged on. If an administrator is logged on, he will have the chance to cancel the process; if a normal user is logged on, he will receive a notification of the impending process and a countdown to its initiation. However, between the set install time and the current time, if updates have finished downloading the notification will appear in the system tray much like described earlier in this section. The user will not have the option to click Remind Me Later, but he can choose to install the updates at that time to have the process over with before the predetermined installation time.

Monitoring the Client-Side System

Software Update Services and the Automatic Updates client provide several event templates that are written to the system event log to describe the current status of the update process, any errors that are encountered, and a brief notation of what updates were successfully installed. You can program an event log monitoring tool to monitor for certain event IDs that are specific to SUS to have a picture of your network's health when it comes to updates. Table 7-3 lists these events and their meanings and context.

Table 7-3. *SUS/AU Client Event Log Messages*

Event ID	Label	Description
16	Unable to connect.	The client can't connect to either the Windows Update site or the SUS server, but will continue trying indefinitely.

Event ID	Label	Description
17	Install ready; no recurring schedule.	Updates have been downloaded and are ready to be installed, but an administrator must log on and manually start the installation process.
18	Install ready; recurring schedule.	Updates have been downloaded and are ready to be installed. The date this install is scheduled to occur is listed within the event description.
19	Install success.	Updates have been successfully installed; these have been listed.
20	Install failure.	Some updates did not install correctly; these have been listed.
21	Restart required; no recurring schedule.	Updates have been installed, but a reboot is required, and until this reboot is complete Windows cannot fetch more updates for installation. Any user can reboot the machine.
22	Restart required; recurring schedule.	Updates have been installed, but a reboot is required and has been scheduled within five minutes.

Common Problems and Workarounds

Using policy settings that control installation of unsigned software can interfere with the ability of the Automatic Updates client to do its job. In particular, if you have the "Warn but allow installation" object set when dealing with code that isn't signed, you will run into problems with some updates. Microsoft occasionally releases unsigned code updates, and since Windows is instructed to prompt for a warning, the procedure stops, waiting for confirmation that it's OK to install the update. Of course, this confirmation can never come since the installation is unattended, so AU simply stops. If you encounter this issue, you need to kill the running update processes using a tool like Sysinternals' Process Explorer. The built-in Windows Task Manager refuses to touch it.

Also, some machines experience an "obsession" over certain patches, which may or may not be caused by SUS but also isn't limited to SUS itself. If a machine tends to require the same patch repeatedly, using both SUS and a manual visit to the Windows Update web site, the best course of action is to clear Internet Explorer's cache: this will typically repair the problem.

If your SUS server doesn't synchronize correctly, make sure the server itself isn't sitting behind a prohibitively tight firewall. To synchronize, SUS only requires communication through port 80, but it also must be able to access the following (nonbrowsable) URLs:

- `http://www.msus.windowsupdate.com`

- `http://download.windowsupdate.com`

- `http://cdm.microsoft.com`

You may also be having a problem, particularly on a low-bandwidth connection, where the currently available service packs are choking your Internet pipe and causing the synchronization process to fail. To turn off the service packs, download the service packs themselves at other times during the day, and then manually copy them to the SUS `content\cabs` folder on the server itself. Finally, rename those files to w2ksp4_en_7f12d2da3d7c5b6a62ec4fde9a4b1e6.exe and XPSP1A_8441053935ADBFC760B966E5E413D3415A753213.exe respectively. You can now continue using SUS without worrying about SUS failing on service pack downloading attempts.

If you are trying to debug client-side SUS problems that may present themselves, you might consider clearing the SUS-related registry keys:

- HKEY_LOCAL_MACHINE\SOFTWARE\Microsoft\Windows\CurrentVersion\WindowsUpdate\ Auto Update\DetectionStartTime

- HKEY_LOCAL_MACHINE\SOFTWARE\Microsoft\Windows\CurrentVersion\WindowsUpdate\ Auto Update\LastWaitTimeout

You can also refresh the Windows Automatic Updates service from the command line by stopping it using net stop wuauserv, following by net start wuauserv. These steps usually solve most client-side SUS problems; to verify things are back to normal, wait 15 to 30 minutes and then inspect the file C:\Windows\Windows Update.log for activity.

Note You have to leave the system alone after you clear the registry keys and restart the AU services, or BITS will never detect a system idle enough to synchronize updates from the SUS server.

If it seems like the Automatic Updates client is simply frozen and lists updates that are available but it never actually downloading them, you can check out the status of any downloads using the Background Intelligent Transfer Service administrative utility, located in the Support directory on an XP CD. Install that, and then after clicking Start Download in the AU client interface when it notifies that updates are ready to install, open a command prompt and type **bitsadmin /list /allusers /verbose**. It may display information on download attempts and why they're failing. It's also prudent to ensure that anonymous access is granted on the IIS root of the SUS server, and that the SUS folder (and in particular, the SUS\Content\Cabs folder) grants Everyone access. BITS attempts to download from that Cabs folder, and issues will result if it can't access it.

Using Auditing and the Event Log

Keeping track of what your system is doing is one of the most important, but tedious, processes of good IT security management. In this section, I'll look at the tools to audit events that happen on your system and the utilities used to view them.

Auditing controls and properties are modified through group policy objects in Windows 2000, XP, and Windows Server 2003. Assuming your computer is participating in an Active Directory domain, you can find the domain auditing policy inside the Default Domain Policy, in the Computer Configuration ➤ Windows Settings ➤ Security Settings ➤ Local Policies ➤ Audit Policies tree. Otherwise, you can view the Local Security Policy through the Administrative Tools applet in Control Panel.

The settings for each group policy object indicate on what type of events and on what type of results a log entry will be written. The options for auditing policies are outlined here:

- Audit account logon events

- Audit account management

- Audit directory service access

- Audit logon events

- Audit object access

- Audit policy change

- Audit privilege use

- Audit process tracking

- Audit system events

You can configure individual objects to be audited by editing the System Access Control List (SACL) for any given object, which is much like assigning permissions, except it is indicating to Windows on what type of access an event log entry should be writing. You can access the SACL for an object by clicking the Advanced button on the Security tab of its properties sheet. On the Auditing tab, you can click Add to include new auditing events for an object, or click View/Edit to modify an existing auditing event. Figure 7-12 shows the SACL for an object.

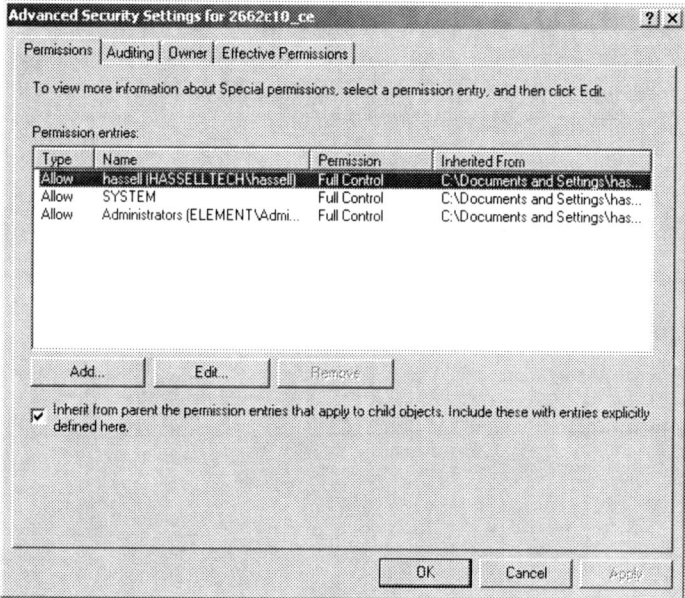

Figure 7-12. *The SACL for an object*

▓**Note** Only NTFS files and folders can be audited. FAT partitions do not contain the necessary permission information to support auditing events.

Recommended Items to Audit

You'll want to take particular note of the following items from your event logs:

- Logon and logoff events, which can indicate repeated logon failures and point to a particular user account that is being used for an attack

- Account management, which indicates users who have tried to use or used their granted user and computer administration power

- Startup and shutdown, which shows both the user who has tried to shut down a system and what services may not have started up properly upon the reboot

- Policy changes, which can indicate users tampering with security settings

- Privilege use, which can show attempts to change permissions to certain objects

Event Logs

Similarly to auditing policies, the policies for configuring the event logs are found inside the Default Domain Policy, in the Computer Configuration ➤ Windows Settings ➤ Security Settings ➤ Local Policies ➤ Event Log tree.

The settings for each of these GPOs indicate the amount of disk space dedicated to storing log events, the permissions granted to view the event logs, how long their contents are retained before rolling over to new logs, and how those event logs are supposed to be retained during that time. The options for event log policies are described here:

- Maximum application log size.

- Maximum security log size.

- Maximum system log size.

- Restrict guest access to application log.

- Restrict guest access to security log.

- Restrict guess access to system log.

- Retain application log.

- Retain security log.

- Retain system log.

- Retention method for application log.

- Retention method for security log.

- Retention method for system log.

- Shut down the computer when the security audit log is full.

The Event Viewer

The Event Viewer allows you to look at events in three event logs. Figure 7-13 shows a typical Event Viewer console.

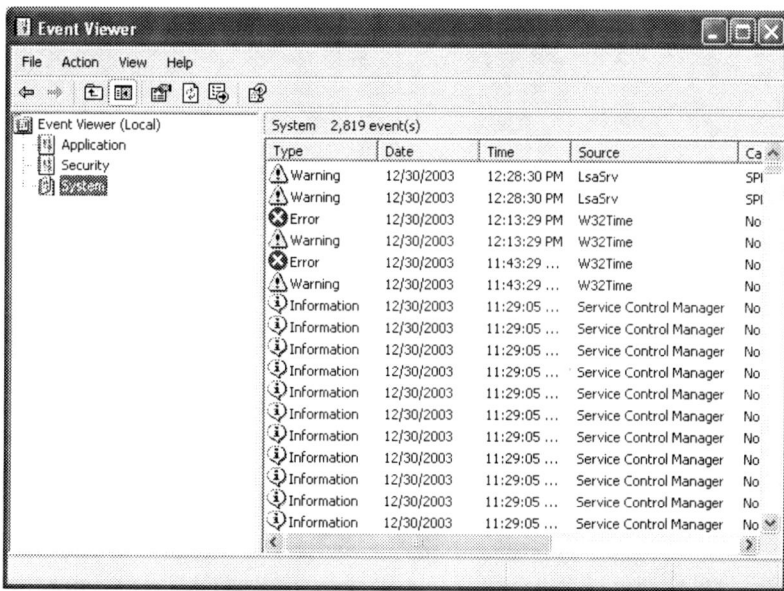

Figure 7-13. *An Event Viewer console*

First, the security log displays successes and failures with regard to privilege use, and classifies them into categories such as object access, account logon, policy change, privilege use, directory service access, and account management. The remaining event logs have three different classes of entries: errors, informational events, and warnings. The application log consists of information reported from programs running on the system. The system log consists of events and exceptions thrown by Windows itself. All users can see the system and application logs, but only members of the administrators group can see the security log.

To clear all events from your Event Viewer console, choose Clear All Events from the Action menu.

Understanding Routing and Remote Access

RRAS, or Routing and Remote Access services, is the component that protects your network from Internet-facing threats in SBS 2003 Standard Edition. In the Internet Connection Wizard that I discussed in Chapter 2, you were asked several questions regarding how you planned to connect your SBS network to the Internet. In this section, we'll delve a bit deeper into how the answers to those questions were translated into settings in the RRAS interface and how you can change some of those settings to better fit your environment.

First, at the server console, open the Server Management Console, and navigate through Advanced Management ➤ Computer Management ➤ Services and Applications. Click the Routing and Remote Access node, and then under IP Routing, select NAT/Basic Firewall. In the right pane, notice that the selection changes to outline the network connections currently installed in your server. Right-click the default LAN connection shown there, and select Properties. The screen in Figure 7-14 appears.

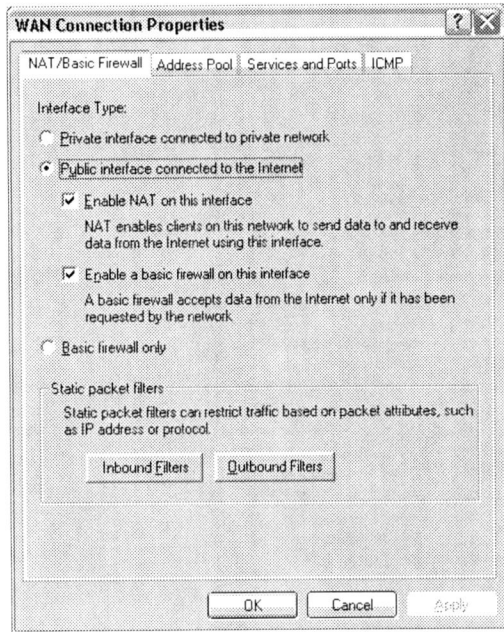

Figure 7-14. *Enabling NAT and a basic firewall*

On the NAT/Basic Firewall tab, you can see that the "Public interface connected to the Internet" option is selected. By default, this enables Network Address Translation, a routing technique that enables you to assign private, nonroutable IP addresses to devices behind a router or firewall and use a single publicly addressable IP address for the entire network. You can also check the "Enable a basic firewall on this interface" option, which simply discards packets from the Internet destined for internal machines unless that data is sent in response to a request that originated from within the network—a "don't speak unless spoken to" sort of policy.

Typically, a firewall works in tandem with a router program to examine each packet of data sent out on a network to determine whether to send that data to its destination. A firewall also includes or complements a proxy server. In addition to aggregating network requests so that all outgoing traffic appears to be coming from one computer instead of from several machines on the internal network, a proxy server also collects and caches all incoming network pages. Administrators often install a firewall on a specially designated computer separate from the rest of the network so that no incoming request can directly access private resources. Let's look at a few of the screening methods firewalls use.

Packet Filtering

The SBS 2003 Standard Edition firewall, using RRAS, uses packet filtering. A dynamic packet filter is a firewall facility that monitors the state of active connections, using this information to determine which network packets to let through the firewall. By recording session information, such as the IP address and port numbers, a dynamic packet filter implements much tighter security than a static packet filter. For example, assume that you want to configure your firewall so that you let all your users access the Internet, but you let in only replies to users' data requests. With a static packet filter, you'd need to permanently let in replies from all external addresses, assuming that users are free to visit any site on the Internet. This kind of filter would let an attacker sneak information past the filter by making the packet look like a reply (by indicating "reply" in the packet header). By tracking and matching requests and replies, a dynamic packet filter can screen for replies that don't match a request. When the system records a request, the dynamic packet filter opens an inbound door just long enough to let in only the expected data. Once the system receives the reply, the filter closes the door, dramatically increasing the firewall's security capabilities.

Stateful Inspection

Stateful inspection is a firewall screening method also used by the RRAS-based firewall in SBS standard edition that doesn't examine the contents of each packet; instead, it compares certain key parts of a packet to a database of trusted information. Stateful inspection monitors information traveling from inside the firewall to the outside, looking for specific defining characteristics, and compares these characteristics with incoming information. If the comparison yields a reasonable match, the firewall lets the information go through; otherwise, it discards it. However, because stateful inspection doesn't examine the entire packet, malformed packets can penetrate this line of defense and cause problems with the servers behind the firewall. A packet's contents can contain information or commands that can cause applications to fail (for example, Active Server Pages—ASP—or Common Gateway Interface—CGI—script on a Web server). In fact, some multimedia applications (for example, Real Audio) require firewall manufacturers to revise their stateful inspection engines. For that reason, large companies and e-commerce and hosting sites use high-end firewalls that are hybrids, offering stateful inspection and proxy applications for specific programs. However, most SOHO applications need only a firewall with simple stateful inspection.

With that out of the way, click over to the Services and Ports tab. On this page, you can enable the different services you'd like to be available and visible to the Internet from your SBS server. Items such as FTP Server, Internet Mail Server (SMTP), Secure Web Server (HTTPS), and others are available on this tab, and are checked based on your answers when you were completing the ICW interview. If you want to add services directly here, simply check the box corresponding to the appropriate service and click OK. The required ports will then open on the firewall, and traffic for that service will be allowed into your network.

■**Note** You'd be better off to rerun the Internet Connection Wizard (ICW) when you decide to run another service, since other SBS components may need to be aware of the configuration change. It's not recommended to make manual changes to the firewall settings without running the ICW first to ensure its changes are made, too.

Using Remote Access Features

The year 2004 was deemed the Year of the Mobile Information Worker. While that sounds like a prestigious title that should be accompanied by a significant raise, a Christmas bonus, and perhaps a company car, it is indeed true that even workers for small businesses are conducting an increasingly large portion of their interactions while away from the office.

SBS 2003 comes complete with several features that allow you to essentially mix and match to re-create your entire office environment from any machine with an Internet connection. In this chapter, I'll look at each of these features in detail, describe how they can help you, and tell you a bit about how they work.

Remote Web Workplace

The Remote Web Workplace (RWW) is the hub of remote user activity. It provides a secure, easy-to-use place to come to access all resources that your users are entitled to use. Figure 8-1 shows the default view of the RWW for a user based on the Power User template.

How Remote Web Workplace Works

In the Remote Web Workplace, your user permissions are examined by the script that controls how the RWW displays. It then gives you only the options to which you will have access. Additionally, if you log in as an administrator, you will have the option to connect directly to the server desktop.

If you want to bypass this automatic detection and have all links displayed for you when you log in, there is a bit of registry editing to do. As always, before making any changes to the registry, back it up first. Then, look at the following location:

```
HKEY_LOCAL_MACHINE\Software\Microsoft\SmallBusinessServer\RemoteUserPortal
```

There are two folders, called AdminLinks and KWLinks, that have associated keys and values. You can adjust the values to display individual links. Set the value to 0 to indicate that you would like the link to display, and set the value to 1 to indicate that you don't want the link displayed.

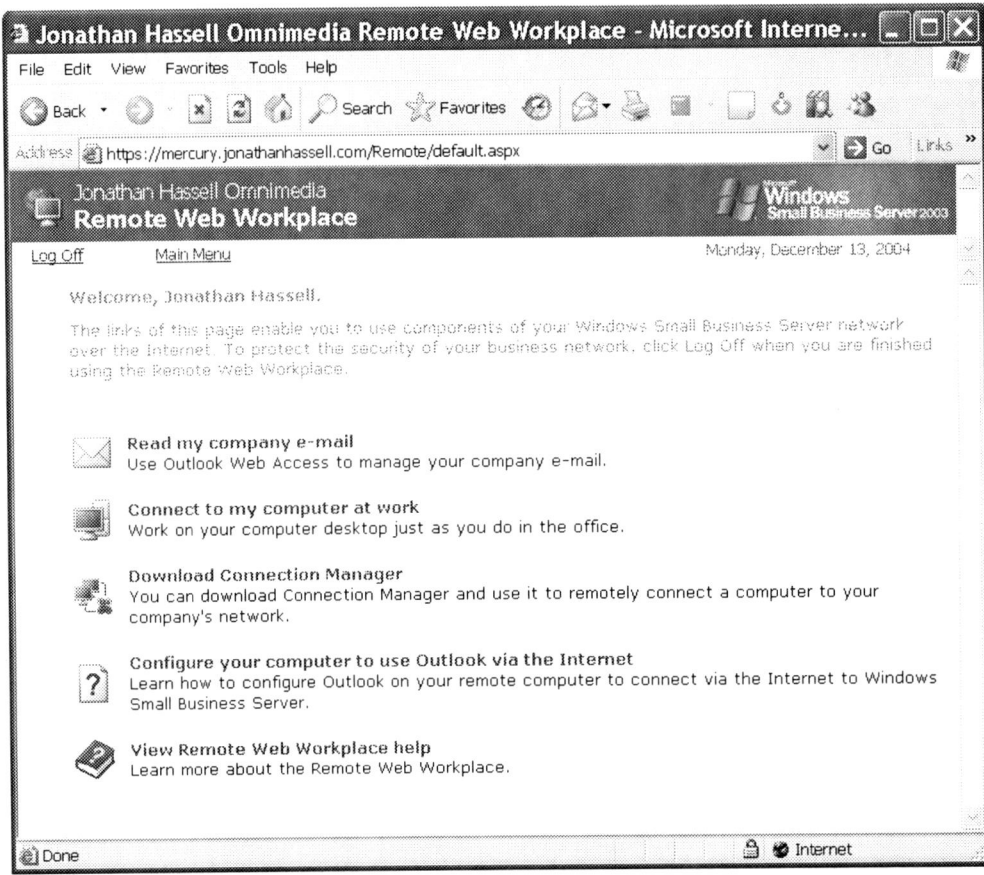

Figure 8-1. *The Remote Web Workplace*

Note Think you can get around licensing requirements by having your users log in to RWW on a daily basis? That won't work. Each user logging into RWW will also be counted against your available CALs, so each remote user is treated like a regular user in the office.

In the remainder of the chapter, I'll take a look at the individual features offered in the RWW. I've tried to structure the chapter so that we build on features in terms of complexity, starting from the simplest remote solutions to the most complex (VPNs, which are actually not part of the RWW). You'll see more of what I mean by this as we go along.

Outlook Web Access

If you're working away from the office and simply need to check your e-mail without frills and accoutrements, then Outlook Web Access will fit the bill for you. Outlook Web Access, or OWA, is a great web-based e-mail client that allows you to access your mailbox using a web browser anywhere, with an interface that is very similar to the Outlook 2003 desktop client that you're used to using.

To access OWA, you can either log on to the RWW and click the Read my company e-mail link or open Internet Explorer and enter your SBS server's full Internet address in the address bar, appending "/exchange" to the end of the address. (With the latter method, you will be prompted to log on to OWA itself, whereas with the former method, RWW passes your credentials on to OWA, eliminating a second logon.) Figure 8-2 shows the OWA interface, and at first glance it might be difficult to tell it apart from the Outlook client.

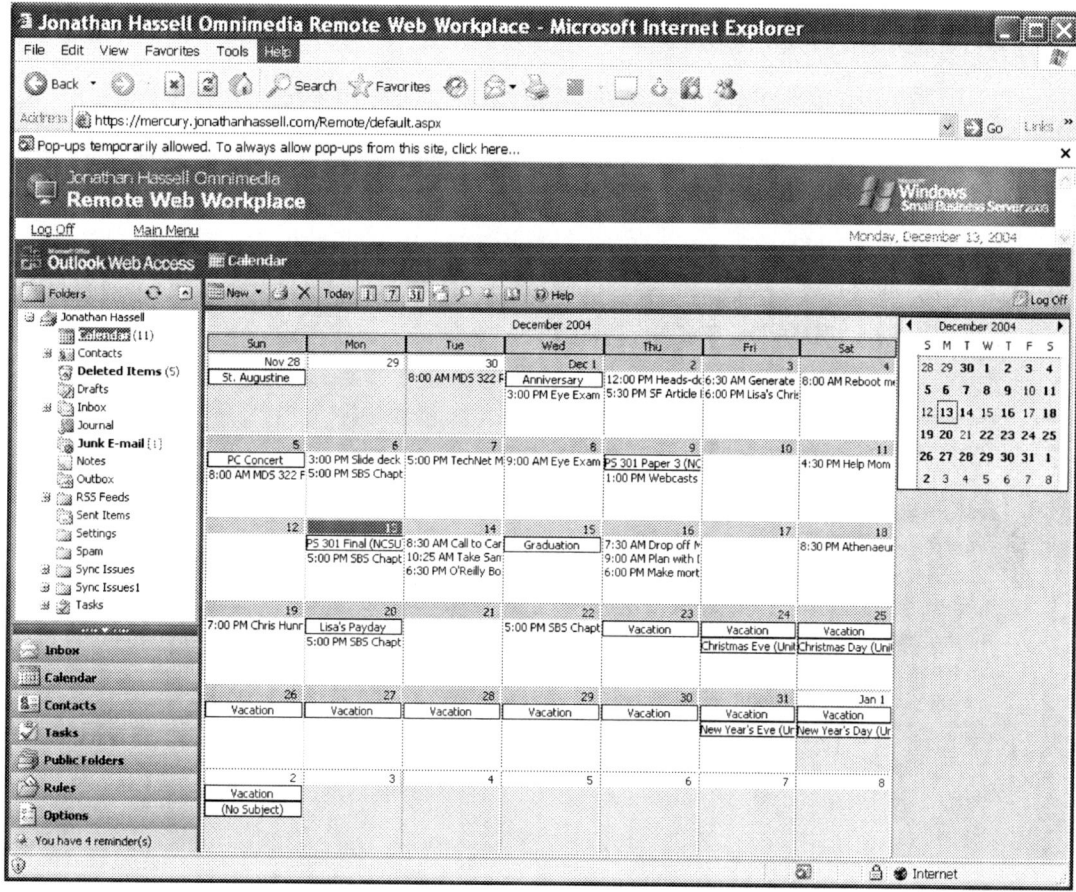

Figure 8-2. *Outlook Web Access*

OWA isn't really a new product, but it has undergone many improvements in its versions. For one, the security surrounding OWA has been improved. In the past, OWA was by default allowed to run over the unencrypted HTTP protocol, but in SBS 2003 you must run OWA with HTTPS, the encrypted form of the protocol, by default. (You can manually change this, however, if you have a good reason.)

Also, in previous versions, the features in OWA were not as plentiful and certainly not as aligned with the full Outlook product as they are in SBS 2003's version. Such nice functionality like the Junk E-mail folder, privacy features that prevent image downloading in HTML-based e-mail, and a better implementation of the rules featureset are now included with OWA. For e-mail users who don't have a lot of special requirements—those factory-floor workers who simply need to keep tabs on messages from management—it is entirely possible to forego installing the full Outlook client for them and to allow them to exclusively use OWA.

However, there are certainly limitations to what OWA can do when compared to the full Outlook client:

- You cannot open multiple mailboxes with OWA. You need to individually log on to each mailbox to access its contents.

- You can't send an e-mail to a contact in a public folder with just a single click. In the full Outlook client, when you view a contact record stored in a public folder, you can click the New Message to Contact button to immediately send a message to that contact. You must manually enter the e-mail address in OWA if you want to send e-mail.

- The search folders feature, covered in Chapter 6 in detail, is not available in OWA.

Premium OWA vs. Basic OWA

There are two specific flavors of OWA: premium and basic. Both of these "modes" of OWA are provided with SBS 2003; it is up to the user each time she connects to decide which to use—the option is under the Client section. You can see this in Figure 8-3.

The basic version of OWA removes some of the more processor- and bandwidth-intensive features to save on download times and link speed, while the premium edition contains all features and is primarily meant for use over a fast connection.

In the premium edition of OWA, you get the ASP-based logon page that allows for your session to be automatically timed out after inactivity, your session to be logged off fully—including the clearing of cached credentials—when you click the Log Off button, the ability to designate whether you are using a public or private computer, the ability to block external content in e-mail, the ability to kill access to potentially nefarious attachments, a junk e-mail filter, and encrypted and signed mail.

In the basic of edition of OWA, you remove from the preceding list the ability to clear your cached credentials upon logoff and the ability to encrypt and digitally sign mail.

Using the Full Outlook Client Remotely

As great as Outlook Web Access is, there are some mobile workers who simply require the rich features of the full Outlook client. Previously, the ability to use Outlook remotely required a VPN connection, which is covered later in this chapter. And while VPNs aren't necessarily a bad thing, they are an additional level of complexity and add another layer of support required for mobile users. And a lot of times, from remote locations, firewalls restrict your ability to initiate an outbound VPN connection. (Some hotels are paranoid, and this can be very frustrating.)

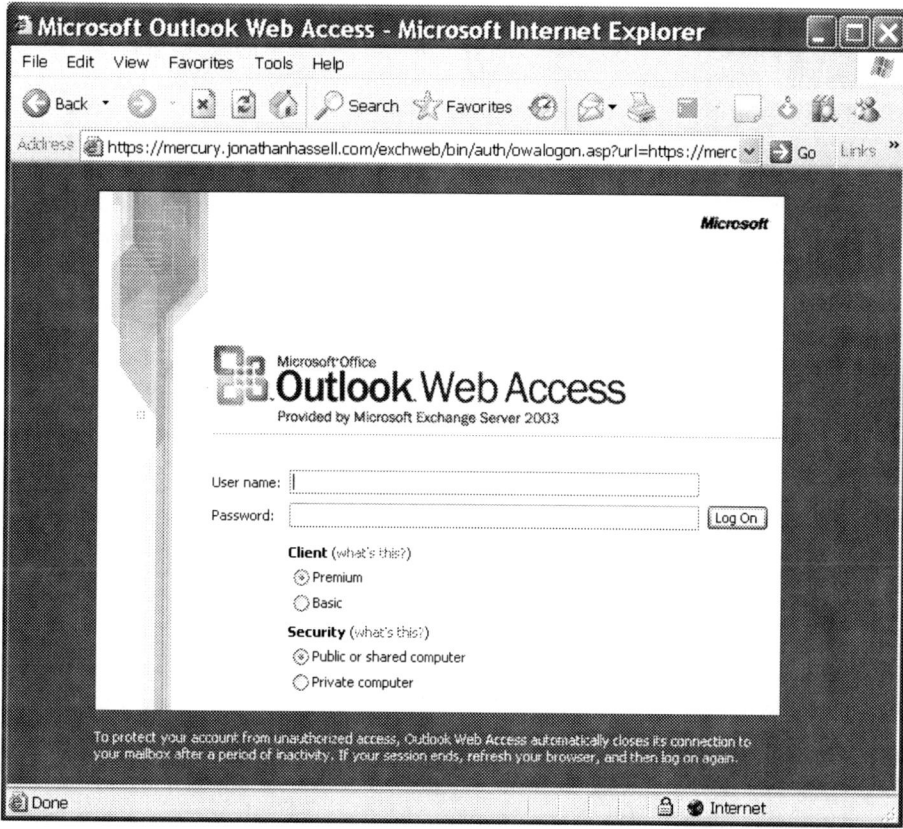

Figure 8-3. *Choosing the OWA mode*

With these issues and problems in mind, Microsoft set out when it designed Exchange 2003 to offer a better way to connect Outlook to the business network when one is away from the office. They came up with RPC over HTTP, which essentially is a technical term that refers to one protocol, which Outlook uses extensively, being wrapped up within HTTP, the standard protocol used over the web. Basically, HTTP acts as a capsule and encases RPC transmissions. The advantages of this are twofold: one, there is no special configuration required on the client end, like a VPN connection profile; two, you can use Outlook from just about anywhere that allows web access. While firewalls range in paranoia, most all of them allow for standard outbound access on port 80.

There are a few initial requirements to set up your clients to use RPC over HTTP capabilities in Outlook. For one, you will need to be running at least Windows XP with Service Pack 1 installed. Your users who might still have Windows 2000 on their laptops can't take advantage of this feature unless they upgrade. If you are not running Service Pack 1 for XP, you'll also need to install the hotfix associated with Microsoft Product Support Services Knowledgebase article Q331320, which you can find—along with more information about what the hotfix does—at http://go.microsoft.com/fwlink/?LinkId=18651. (If you're smart enough and up-to-date enough to be running Windows XP Service Pack 2, you don't need the hotfix, as the necessary changes were included with that.) You also need to be running Outlook 2003—RPC over HTTP is very dependent on the latest version of Outlook, and the necessary parts aren't present in earlier versions.

Once you've found the systems that are up to that baseline, the next step is to install the server's security certificate on each of these systems. This step basically tells each system to trust the server is who it says it is, and to not wonder if the server is actually a rogue machine pretending to be your server with the intent to steal passwords, confidential information, and other sensitive material. To do this, open Internet Explorer and type in the full Internet name of your machine (for example, `https://mercury.jonathanhassell.com/remote`). If you get a security warning, click the View Certificate button, click the Install Certificate button, and then follow the very simple instructions from that point. Now your computer automatically trusts your SBS server, and you won't receive the security warnings anymore.

It's now time to configure Outlook itself to use RPC over HTTP. Follow these steps:

1. On the client computer, make sure Outlook 2003 is closed.

2. Open Control Panel from the Start menu.

3. Double-click the Mail applet. (You may have to switch to Classic view to see the icon.)

4. Click the E-mail accounts button in the Mail Setup window.

5. Click View or change existing e-mail accounts, and then click Next.

6. The E-mail Accounts screen appears. Select Microsoft Exchange Server, and then click the Change button.

7. Make sure your local server name, not the full Internet name, is listed in the Microsoft Exchange Server field. In my case, this would be mercury.hasselltech.local and not mercury.jonathanhassell.com. Then, type your username in the User Name box.

8. Click the More Settings button.

9. Navigate to the Connection tab.

10. Select the Connect to my Exchange mailbox using HTTP box at the bottom of the screen, and then click the Exchange Proxy Settings button.

11. Type your SBS server's full Internet address into the "Use this URL to connect to my proxy server for Exchange" field.

12. Check the Connect using SSL only box.

13. Select "Mutually authenticate the session when connecting with SSL."

14. Type this in the "Principal name for proxy server" field: **msstd:full_Internet_address**. Replace "full_Internet_address" with the full Internet address of your SBS server. Make sure there are no spaces in this field.

15. Select "On slow networks, connect using HTTP first, then connect using TCP/IP."

16. Select Basic authentication under Proxy authentication settings.

17. Click OK twice, and then click Next.

18. Click Finish, and then click Close.

That was a long process, but you've finished configuring Outlook 2003 to use RPC over HTTP to connect to your SBS server. Now, simply open Outlook 2003 and enter your credentials (format the username as SHORTDOMAINNAME\username). You can choose to save the password. You'll then see your mailbox, and from then on, you won't see anything different than if you were directly connected to your SBS network in the office.

Remote Desktop Connection

Allow me to introduce the usefulness of Remote Desktop Connection by relating a true story (and embarrassingly so, at that). I was the on the road on the opposite coast for about a week, and before I had departed I had been working on a fairly complex Excel spreadsheet with lots of formulas and graphs and functions and the like. Sunday came, and I left town.

I arrived at my hotel Sunday night exhausted, but I really wanted to check my e-mail to make sure nothing urgent about my meetings on Monday had been sent to me. I opened my laptop and tried to use Outlook, but something within Outlook had become corrupted and I couldn't open the program to save my life. I tried everything that I knew, every trick I had accumulated over the years, and even burned some incense and had a séance—all to no avail. I wasn't entirely troubled by this, as I knew that I still had access to Outlook Web Access and could check in the morning. (After the séance, I was about to fall asleep in the chair.)

Monday morning rolled around, and I attempted again to retrieve my e-mail. I logged on to Outlook Web Access and successfully checked my e-mail, and then I double-clicked my Excel spreadsheet and was greeted with three different errors—all of which prevented the Excel application from opening. At this point, I was panicking, because the vital data contained in that spreadsheet was the main reason I made this cross-country trip.

What was I to do?

I logged into Remote Web Workplace, and then clicked Connect to my computer at work. I selected my computer from the list of machines on the network at home, and then clicked Connect. Voilà! I had access to my office computer. I logged on, loaded the spreadsheet, and breathed a huge sigh of relief. Since the location where my meeting was being held had wireless access, I was assured that I'd be able to access my Excel spreadsheet through my office computer.

In this case, RWW and the Remote Desktop Connection feature saved my bacon. While the feature is useful in emergency situations when you're in a bind from afar, it's also very convenient if you work from home a lot, or even if you work out of your office but in another room in the building a lot. Your office computer is with you at all times, provided you have some sort of Internet access.

There are a couple of interesting interactions, though, between normal office computer use and other use over Remote Desktop Connection. For one, when a remote user connects to the office desktop and successfully authenticates, if there is currently a user logged on OTHER than the user attempting to connect to the computer, that user logged on to the office computer who is at the office will simply be logged off with no warning whatsoever. (That can be disconcerting.) If the user attempting to connect remotely to the computer is the same user as the one logged on to the machine at the office, that user's remote session will be the same as the actual desktop session (this is technically known as the console session). Finally, whenever a remote user is logged in to a machine, the office computer is locked for use at the office— this is to prevent nasty things from happening if a remote user and a local user both move the mouse at the same time. Who might win? In this case, the local user would never have a chance to log on, much less win the conflict.

It's very easy to use this technology. To do so:

1. Log on to Remote Web Workplace.

2. Click the "Connect to my computer at work" link.

3. The screen you see in Figure 8-4 appears. Select the name of your office computer, and click Next. Your office desktop is now available.

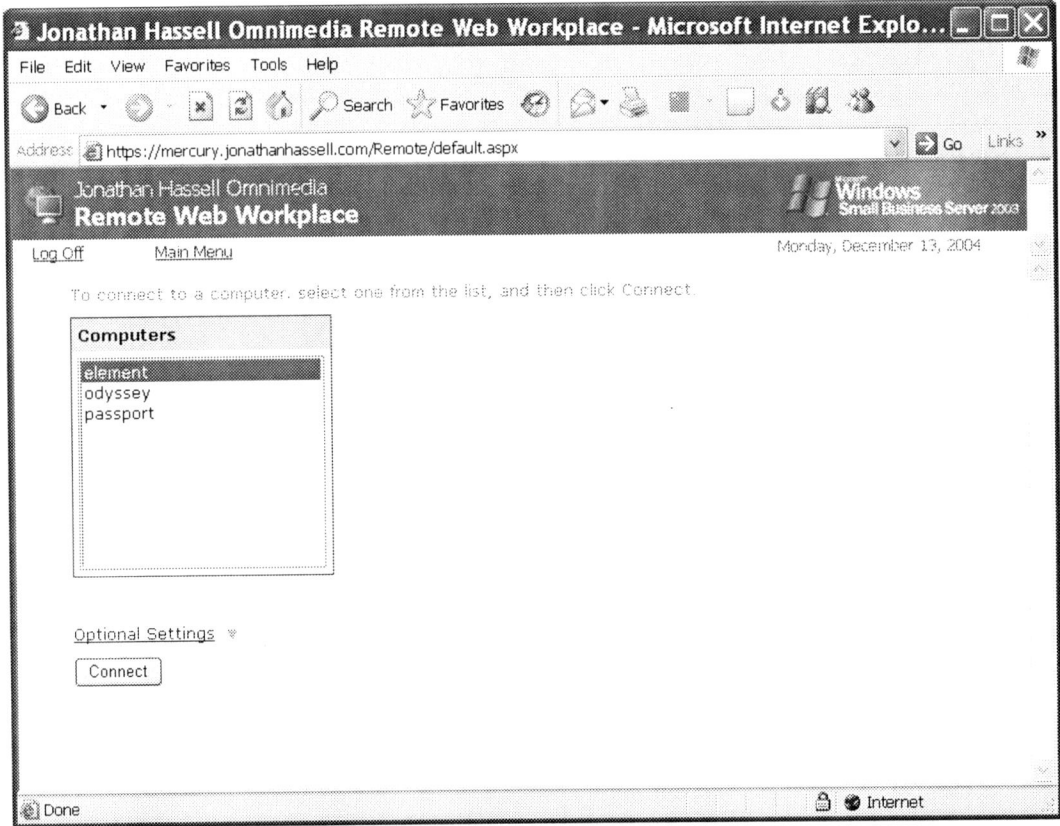

Figure 8-4. *Connecting to an office desktop*

If you click the Optional Settings link, you will see five options. We describe each of them here:

- **Log on to the selected computer as <USERNAME>, where <USERNAME> is the name you used to log on to the RWW**: Select this option if you want to use the same credentials to access your office computer—the username field on your office desktop will be prepopulated when you connect.

- **Enable files or folders to be transferred between the remote computer and this computer**: This feature allows you to access your local computer's drives within the session to your office PC. This is useful if you have files in both locations and need an easy way to transfer them.

- **Enable documents on the remote computer to be printed on a local printer**: Another great tool that lets you print items that reside inside your session to your office computer on the printer that is currently beside you, not at the office.

- **Hear sounds from the remote computer on this computer**: This simply redirects audio from the remote computer to your local machine. If you're working over a fairly slow connection, I would avoid this: the quality isn't all that high and the sound will come out jumbled and slow.

- **Select a screen size for this connection**: This allows you to set the resolution for the session. I recommend 1024×768 for most connections, as this will typically either be full screen or one step below full screen for you.

As you can see, there are several options to customize the session.

▓**Note** The RWW will terminate your remote desktop connection after 20 minutes of inactivity for security reasons. However, the RWW will display a message alerting you that you have one minute remaining in your session, so you can create some activity in time to reset the counter and avoid disconnection.

If you simply close the connection to your office computer, the applications that you were running in that session will stay running. Later, if you go back to RWW and reconnect to your office computer, you will be returned to your session with all the same applications open and your data intact. This is great if you have to run off to a quick phone call, or you want to come back after dinner to continue working on something.

To completely disconnect your session and close the connection (which returns your office computer to a logon prompt), within your remote session select the Disconnect option from the Start menu.

A Little More In-Depth About RDP

The Remote Desktop Protocol, or RDP, is the protocol that drives Windows Terminal Services. RDP is based on and is an extension of the T.120 protocol family standards. It is a multichannel-capable protocol that allows for separate virtual channels for carrying device communication and presentation data from the server, as well as encrypted client mouse and keyboard data. RDP provides a very extensible base from which to build many more capabilities, supporting up to 64,000 separate channels for data transmission as well as provisions for multipoint transmission. The new Terminal Services client software (Remote Desktop Connection, or RDC, which is used in SBS 2003) uses RDP 5.2, and many of the local resources are available within the remote session; the client drives, smart cards, audio card, serial ports, printers (including network), and the clipboard. Additionally, the color depth can be selected from 256 colors (8-bit) to True Color (24-bit), and resolution can be set from 640×480 up to 1600×1200.

RDP basically takes instructions from a terminal server host machine on screen images and draws them onto a client's screen, refreshing that image about 20 times every second if there's activity on the client side. (To save bandwidth, if there is no activity detected on the client side, it cuts the refresh rate in half.) It then notes any keyboard and mouse activity (among other things) and relays those signals to the terminal server host machine for its processing. This two-way exchange of information is wrapped into what's called a session, which consists of the programs running on the host machine and the information being sent over RDP between the terminal server and the client machine.

Using Virtual Private Networks

If all of the features I've discussed earlier in this chapter are just not sufficient for you, and you have to have full access to your office network (read: access that would seem exactly like you were connected to the building network) even though you're working from a remote location, then virtual private networks are your answer. Virtual private networks, or VPNs, are tunnels that are created between a client and a server so that private data can be transmitted through a link carried on a public network. In essence, you're taking advantage of the public Internet to establish a virtual circuit back to your office network.

VPNs are certainly useful, but they come with a slew of requirements and as such are harder to administer and manage than some of the other solutions presented in this chapter. In SBS 2003, VPNs take advantage of the Routing and Remote Access Service (RRAS) that is bundled with Windows Server 2003. RRAS is a complex beast, but fortunately during the initial configuration of your server, the wizards took care of most of the configuration.

■**Note** Firewall alert: you'll need to open port 1723 to allow VPN packets to pass into your network from the outside. If you don't, your remote clients will be locked out and won't get access.

If you want to deploy a VPN solution to your mobile workers, you need to install a connection profile on the machines that will be going outside your building. This connection profile contains all of the necessary settings to create the VPN connection (the tunnel) between the client at a remote site and your SBS server. This is one of the great features of SBS: you don't have to create this connection profile yourself and find out the settings via trial and error; it's already created and you just have to push it out to clients. You can do that pushing in three ways:

1. During the Add Users and Computers Wizard process, you can specify on the Mobile Client and Offline Use screen (see the latter portion of Chapter 3 for a detailed procedure on this) to install the Connection Manager profile on a machine. Doing so results in a shortcut placed on the desktop of that machine that starts the VPN connection.

2. You can create a Connection Manager diskette in the Server Management Console. Under Standard Management, click the Manage Client Computers node, and then click the Create Remote Connection Disk link on that page. Once the diskette has been created, you'll need to take it to each machine and run the program on the diskette on each of the computers that need it.

3. You can download the Connection Manager software from the Remote Web Workplace, which is the simplest way to deploy the software to existing computers, assuming they have Internet access and permission to view the RWW.

With that in mind, let's look at using the Remote Web Workplace to download the Connection Manager profile.

1. Connect to your server's Remote Web Workplace, and log in. Make sure that you uncheck the box for "I'm using a public or shared computer." (If you don't, RWW won't allow you to download the software, since there's no reason for a VPN connection profile to reside on a public machine—it's a security risk.)

2. On the main menu screen, click the link entitled Download Connection Manager. You'll receive a message strongly encouraging you to make sure all users on your SBS network have strong passwords. Click OK to acknowledge the message, and then click Run to execute the program.

3. Acknowledge any security warnings that may present themselves by clicking the Run button.

4. The Connect to Small Business Server message box will appear. Click OK to confirm that you want to install the software.

5. After a few seconds, you'll see the shortcut appear on the desktop. This is a sign the profile is installed. Unfortunately, you won't receive any feedback from the program— it doesn't tell you when it's done.

The profile is now installed. Let's use it to VPN to the network.

1. Double-click the Connect to Small Business Server shortcut on the desktop.

2. You'll see the SBS logo and a box asking for your credentials, as shown in Figure 8-5. Enter your username and password. You can choose to save your password and also to connect automatically in the future when you double-click the shortcut.

3. Click Connect.

You'll see the wizard establish a connection, verify your password, and then register the current machine on the network. After that, the connection is established, and you can see the connection icon in the system tray in the lower-right corner of your screen. The lights on the icon come on and off when data is sent or received over the VPN connection. To disconnect, simply right-click the icon and click Disconnect.

Figure 8-5. *Connecting via VPN to your SBS network*

Conclusion

In this chapter, we've looked at quite a few of the remote access features that SBS offers. Using Outlook Web Access, you can check your e-mail using only a web browser. We also looked at using the full Outlook client remotely, connecting to your office desktop system and working with it from a distance, and using VPNs to connect yourself to your business network like you were sitting in a room in the building.

In short, there is a great deal of focus in SBS 2003 placed on allowing a user to use his normal, day-to-day tools from anywhere, at any time.

CHAPTER 9

∎ ∎ ∎

The Shared Fax Service

BEGINNER SBS ADMINISTRATOR ▪ **ADVANCED SBS ADMINISTRATOR** ▪ **EXPERIENCED CONSULTANT**

Faxing used to be the *de facto* method to exchange messages, and documents between sites and—sometimes—departments within a single larger corporate campus. Nowadays, e-mail has risen to manage our instant message communication needs, but faxing remains an important way to quickly send completed documents for viewing and signing to sites far and away.

Faxing in SBS is much improved over previous versions, where it seemed to take the role of the red-headed stepchild, languishing behind the other core components of the product in polish and stability. However, in SBS 2003, the Shared Fax Service (SFS) is a robust addition to the family and handles its business with aplomb.

In this chapter, I'll take you through the steps to set up the Shared Fax Service, customize it for your needs, and send and receive faxes. I'll also point out how to manage the service for administrative purposes.

SBS Faxing Fundamentals

By using the Fax Service in SBS, you avail yourself of many benefits, including the following:

- Sending outbound marketing flyers, announcements, form letters, and other commonly requested items electronically

- Sending faxes using address data stored within Microsoft Outlook

- Automatic archiving of sent and received faxes, which can be useful for legal reasons

- Automatic routing of received faxes to a file share, to an e-mail recipient, or to a document library within Windows SharePoint Services

- Redirection of faxes to third parties, again entirely electronically, which results in no additional loss of image quality

- Automatic printing of received faxes on a regular printer, thereby saving the expense of special cartridges and paper for a traditional fax machine

- The ability to act on received faxes even when you're not in the office, since you can view faxes over e-mail or within SharePoint

Faxing in SBS is at the courtesy of several basic components, which are outlined next. Each of these core pieces serves either the engine that makes faxing work or the administrator and user in interfacing with the Fax Service.

- **Shared Fax Service**: The Shared Fax Service is the engine that drives faxing in SBS. Much like other services to which you have been introduced, such as the Exchange Information Store service and the Routing and Remote Access Service, the Shared Fax Service resides entirely in the background, and you use other tools to manage it.

- **Shared Fax Service Manager**: The SFS Manager gives you the tools and utilities to configure, customize, and tweak the behavior of the SFS. You can manage the fax modem itself, fax jobs that need to be sent or are being currently sent, cover pages that your employees can use with their outgoing faxes, and the printers on which incoming faxes will be distributed.

- **Fax Console**: The Fax Console is oriented toward users themselves and less toward administrators. Users can see the current activity for the Fax Service, including incoming and outgoing faxes, and archived faxes (sort of like the Sent Items folder in Microsoft Outlook).

- **The fax modem itself**: This is, of course, an integral piece of the SBS faxing puzzle. Essentially, the fax modem requires no configuration—you can simply attach it to the SBS server, and once Windows Server 2003 recognizes the hardware, SBS takes over and automatically adds the modem to the outgoing fax modem pool, meaning that it can be used immediately. Another bonus is that you don't have to have the fax modem connected to the server in order to configure the Fax Service. This is useful for consultants, in that they can set up the Fax Service for a new client even before the client really wants to invest in a fax modem. Then, when one is purchased, the consultant can simply guide the installation of the hardware, and the SFS itself is ready for use without a site visit being necessary.

- **Fax printer**: This is a shared object that clients will print to from their workstations, much like the shared printer object that appears in the Print dialog boxes from standard Windows applications. When a user is ready to fax a document, she can simply use the print functionality from within the program, select the fax printer, and click OK. Windows will automatically prompt for the destination fax number, cover sheet, and so on. It's a seamless integration of faxing capabilities into existing business programs.

We'll step through each of these components in the rest of the chapter. First, though, we need to actually set up the service for use.

Configuring the Fax Service

As part of the To Do list in SBS 2003, Microsoft includes the Fax Configuration Wizard, which helps you through the process of initializing the SFS for use. Let's go through this wizard now:

1. From the To Do list in the Server Management Console, click Configure Fax.

2. The Fax Configuration Wizard appears. Click Next on the introductory screen.

3. The Provide Company Information screen appears, as shown in Figure 9-1. Enter your company's name, phone number, fax number, and mailing address on this screen. This information will be used to populate the library of cover pages available for your users. Click Next when you're done.

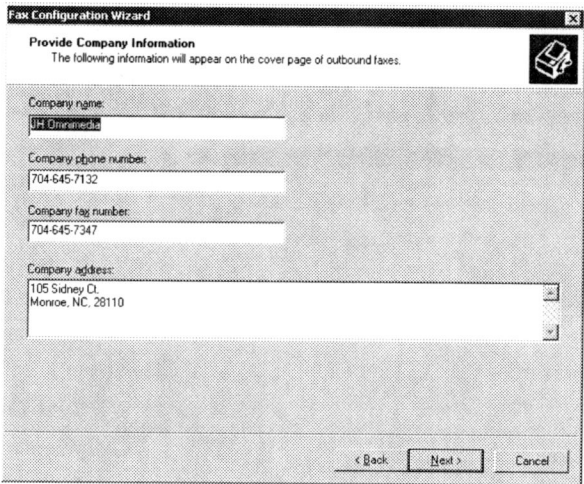

Figure 9-1. *The Provide Company Information screen*

4. The Outbound Fax Device screen appears, as shown in Figure 9-2. The wizard shows the modems that are currently detected by Windows Server 2003. If you have more than one modem, then all will be listed, and outgoing faxes will use the modems in the order they are listed. You can use the up and down arrow buttons on the side of the list to rearrange the order of the modems. Of course, you'll need to specify at least one modem in order for faxing to work. Click Next to continue.

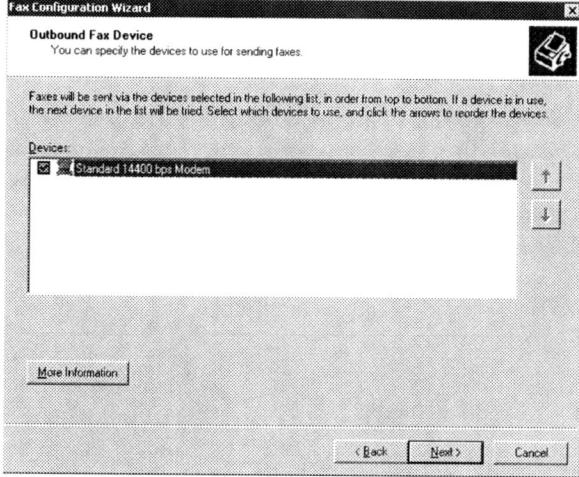

Figure 9-2. *The Outbound Fax Device screen*

5. The Inbound Fax Device screen appears, as shown in Figure 9-3. Like the previous screen, choose the modem to use for inbound faxing. If you have more than one, again you can rearrange the order using the arrow buttons. Click Next to continue.

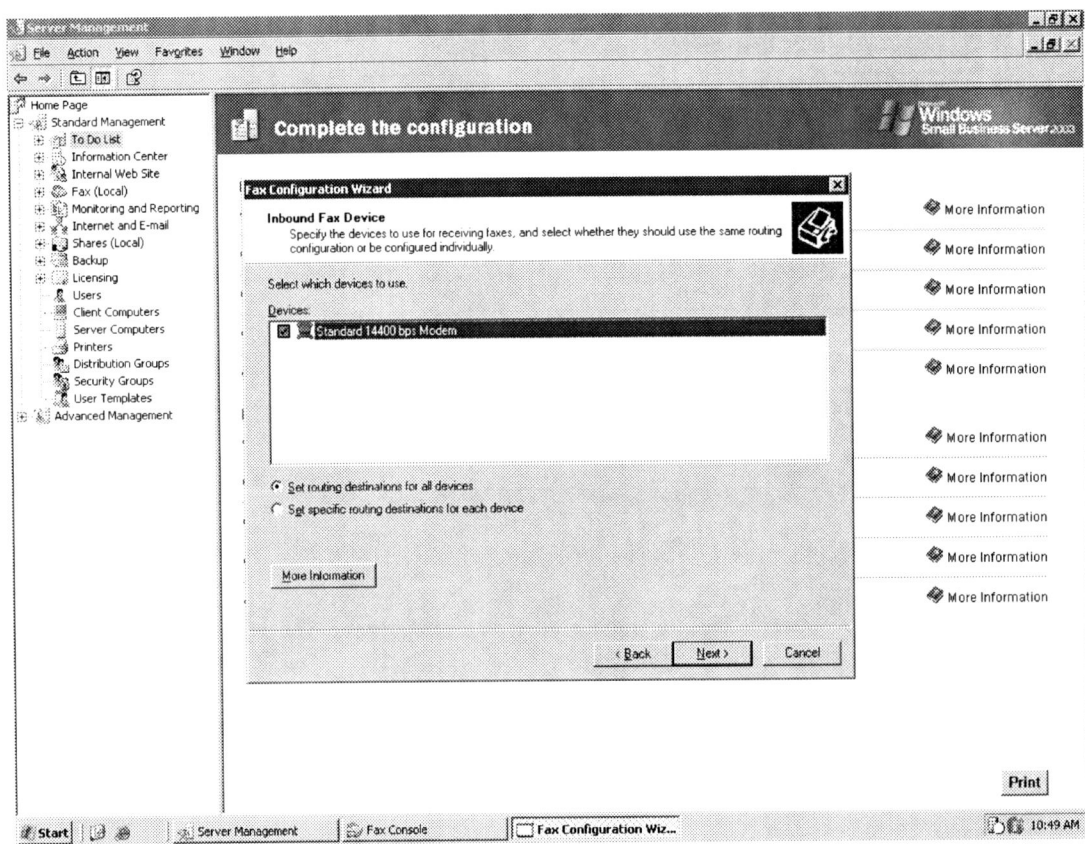

Figure 9-3. *The Inbound Fax Device screen*

6. The Inbound Fax Routing screen appears, as shown in Figure 9-4. Here, you can choose where incoming faxes will be stored. Choose from routing through e-mail, storing them in a folder on the SBS server itself, storing them in a SharePoint document library (there is one created by default, called Incoming Faxes), or printing them immediately on a printer connected to the SBS server. Check the boxes you would like, and then click Next.

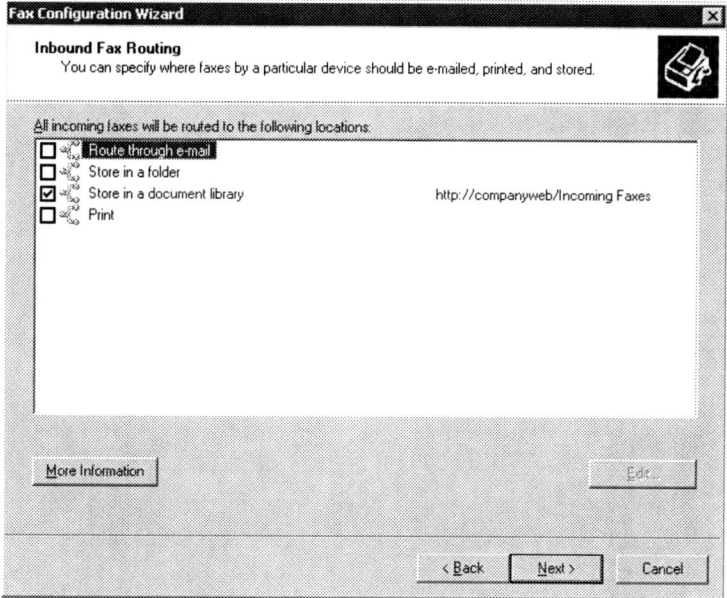

Figure 9-4. *The Inbound Fax Routing screen*

7. The final screen of the wizard appears. Confirm all of the settings you've chosen, and click the Finish button when you're ready to proceed.

Your Fax Service is now set up.

Customizing the Service

While the Fax Configuration Wizard provides a simple interface to get the service up and running quickly, you'll probably want to further fine-tune the behavior of faxing on SBS. The Fax (Local) Console properties is the best way to continue the customization process, as it provides an interface to every setting available from the SFS.

To get to this console:

1. Open the Server Management Console.

2. Under Standard Management, right-click Fax (Local), and select Properties from the pop-up context menu.

Each of the tabs available on this property sheet is covered in the following sections.

General

The General tab is shown in Figure 9-5.

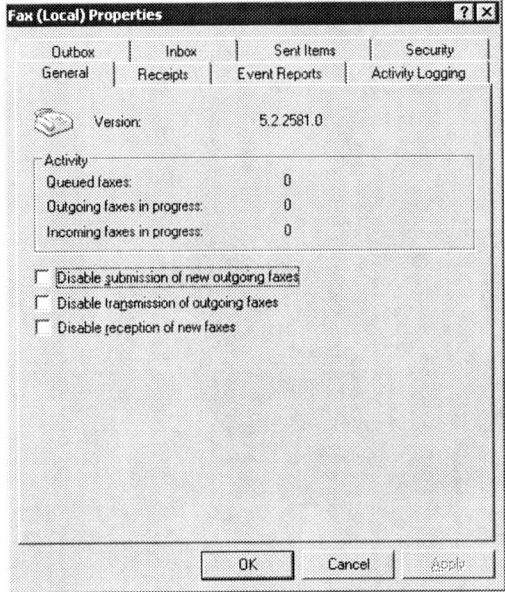

Figure 9-5. *The General tab*

The General tab shows the current status and version of the Fax Service and controls, on a very broad level, the inbound and outbound activity of the service. Take a look at the three check boxes shown in Figure 9-5. From here, you can completely turn off your users' ability to even submit faxes to be sent, or you can disable the actual fax transmission from taking place. You can ignore incoming fax attempts as well. These check boxes are great tools when you need to temporarily ignore fax requests, but you don't want to trigger the Fax Service core engine itself to stop and restart.

Receipts

The Receipts tab is shown in Figure 9-6.

On the Receipts tab, you can select whether users can choose how to be notified when their faxes are successfully transmitted with the first check box, "Enable message boxes as receipts." Under the SMTP E-mail section, you can also select whether to send a simple delivery confirmation e-mail message to a user, what the From address of that e-mail should be, and the outgoing mail server for that message. In most cases, you can use localhost for the outgoing mail server and 25 for the port number.

Note that if you have run the Fax Configuration Wizard, as described earlier in this chapter, the information on this tab is filled in for you based on your responses during that wizard.

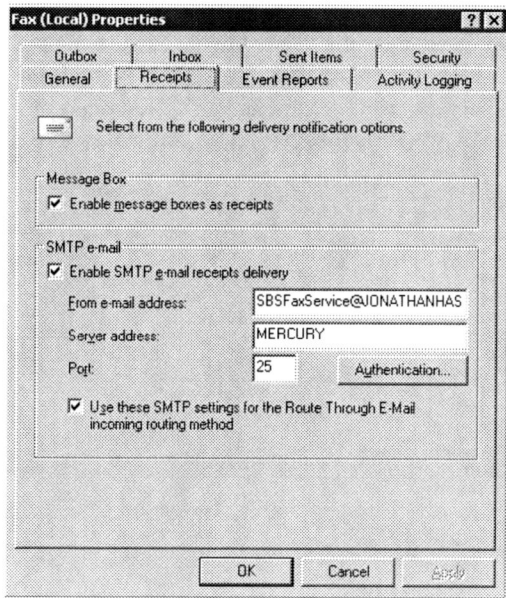

Figure 9-6. *The Receipts tab*

Event Reports

The Event Reports tab is shown in Figure 9-7.

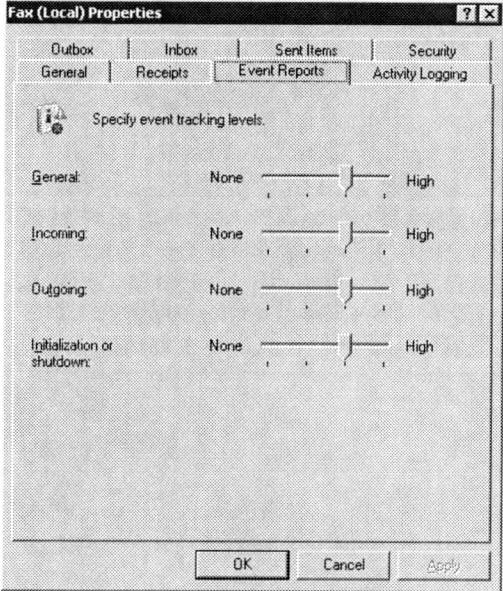

Figure 9-7. *The Event Reports tab*

The Event Reports tab allows you to set the level of logging for the Fax Service that will be put into the Event Log. This logging doesn't generate much traffic (and thus much disk space) at all, so I recommend—for your own peace of mind—that you set each of the four options to at least one notch below High, if not High itself. This can be to your benefit, particularly in sticky legal situations, as you'll now have a record of every fax-based event or error that takes place on your SBS server.

Activity Logging

The Activity Logging tab is shown in Figure 9-8.

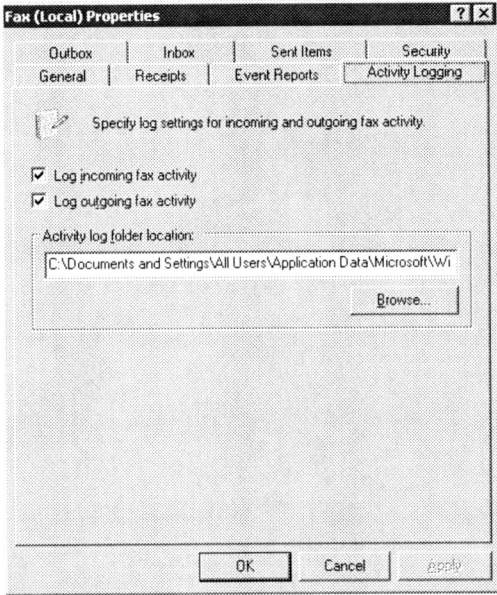

Figure 9-8. *The Activity Logging tab*

The Activity Logging tab allows you to specify whether the Fax Service should write a note to a log file each time a fax is sent or received. This is a bit different than the Event Reports tab, as issues logged in the latter context are written to the system event log. Issues that are logged in the Activity Logging context are simply written to a text file, which can be useful for billing or other analysis. Check the boxes to log incoming and outgoing fax activity, and then choose the location you want these log files to be stored.

Outbox

The Outbox tab is shown in Figure 9-9.

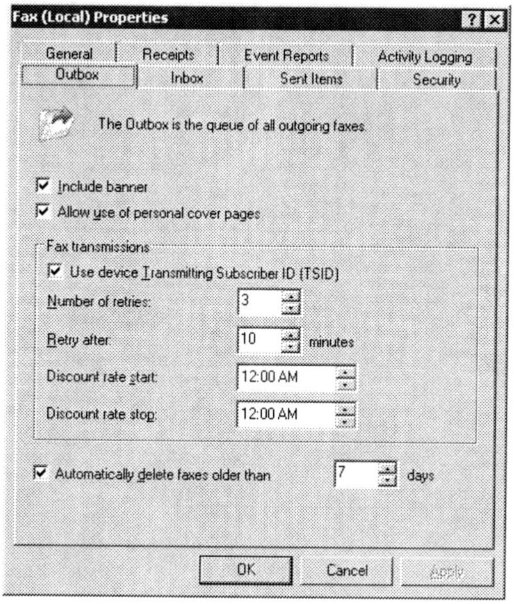

Figure 9-9. *The Outbox tab*

On the Outbox tab, you can configure whether personal cover pages from your users will be allowed, whether failed outbound faxes should be retried and how many times, the period of time to wait between retries, and when your office's cheapest long-distance rates begin and end. The last option on the tab, "Automatically delete faxes older than x days," will delete any fax in the outbound queue that has failed for seven straight days by default. You can change the number of days using the up-and-down scroll box beside the option.

Inbox

The Inbox tab is shown in Figure 9-10.

On the Inbox tab, you can select whether to send a copy of all incoming faxes to a specific directory on your SBS server. You can also tell the Fax Service to send a warning event to the Event Log when the high and low quotas are met, and whether to automatically delete faxes in this folder that are 90 days or older.

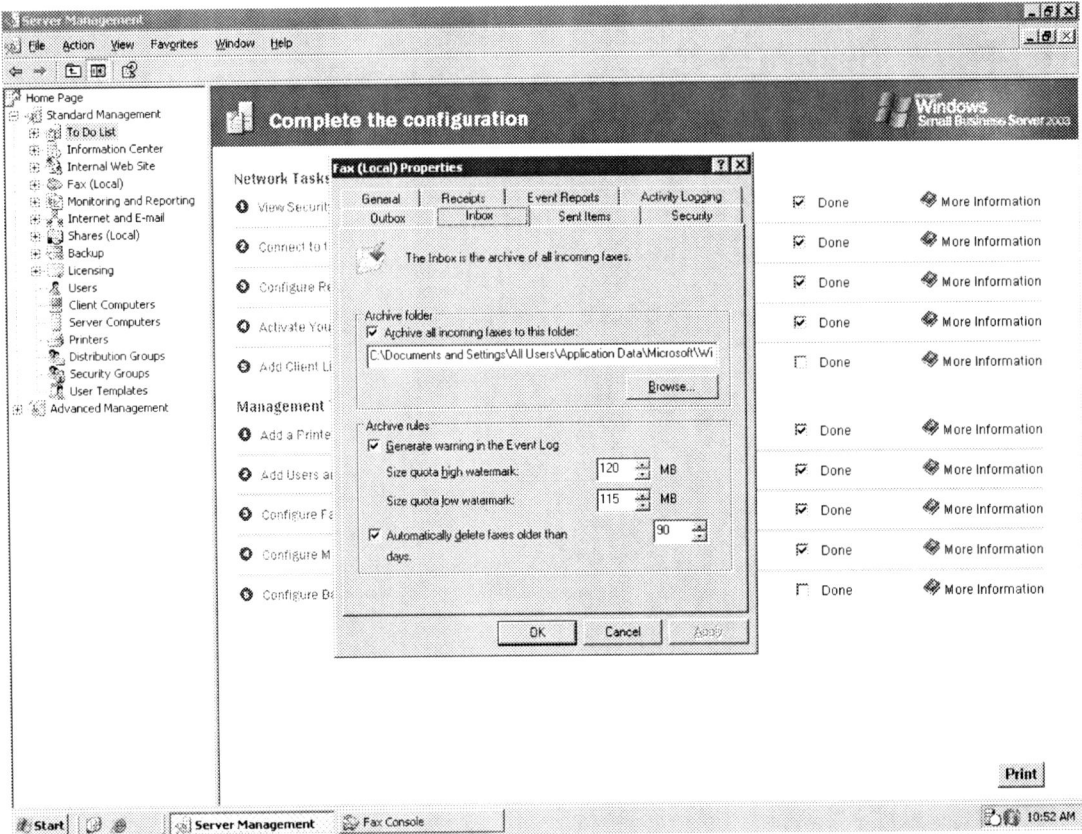

Figure 9-10. *The Inbox tab*

Be sure to watch these values closely over time as you begin use of the service. If these quotas are reached, the Fax Service will shut down, and that can certainly cause you some grief from users and customers.

Sent Items

The Sent Items tab is shown in Figure 9-11.

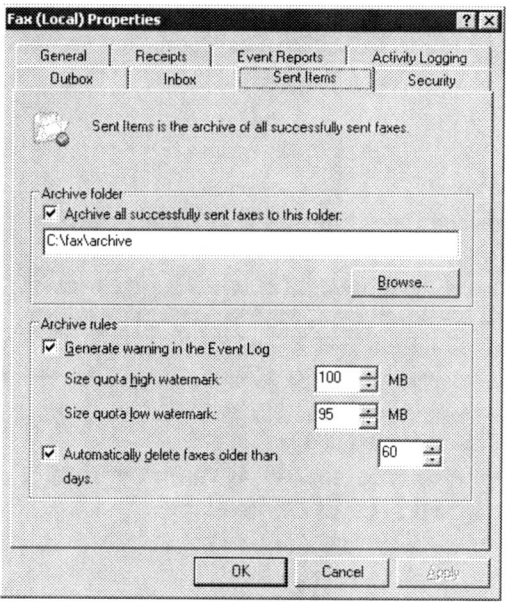

Figure 9-11. *The Sent Items tab*

The same settings from the Inbox tab apply here to the Sent Items tab.

Security

The Security tab is shown in Figure 9-12.

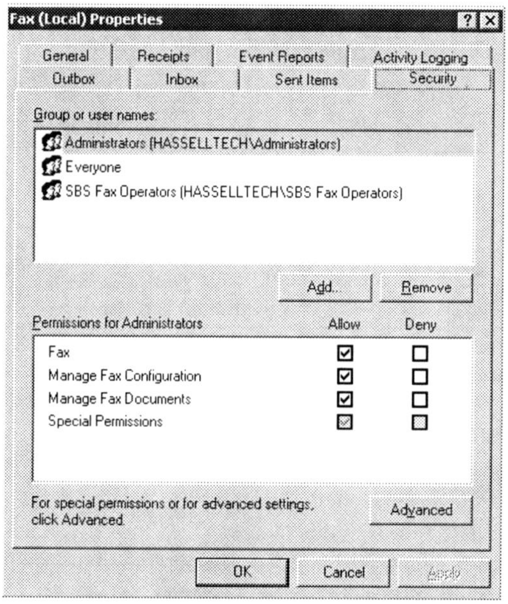

Figure 9-12. *The Security tab*

On the Security tab, you can grant or deny permission for specific users or groups on your SBS machine to send and receive faxes. We'll step through this tab in detail in the next section, where we grant users permission to view received faxes.

Receiving a Fax

Now that the Fax Service is set up, let's look at what happens when an inbound fax transmission is received.

When someone sends you a fax, you receive it either at the printer, in a file system–based share, within a SharePoint document library, or in your e-mail inbox via Microsoft Exchange. If you use any but the latter method of viewing received faxes, you'll receive an inordinate number of support calls, because in Microsoft's recent emphasis on security, by default ordinary users cannot view received faxes. That may seem strange, and I agree. (If anyone from Microsoft is reading this, let's fine-tune that setting in the next release.)

Fortunately, it's a quick change to some security settings to rectify this inconvenience. To grant permission for ordinary users to view received faxes, follow these steps:

1. Open the Server Management Console.

2. Under Standard Management, right-click Fax (Local), and select Properties from the pop-up context menu.

3. Navigate to the Security tab.

4. In the Name field, choose Everyone.

5. Click the Advanced button.

6. The Advanced Security Settings for Fax dialog box appears. Select Everyone in the box, and then click Edit.

7. Under the Permissions section, select View incoming messages archive. Click the check box under the Allow column.

8. Click OK to close out.

Viewing a Received Fax

The most common method to review a received fax is simply to open the attachment to the e-mail message that's sent by the SFS when the fax is received. Faxes attached to e-mails are transmitted in TIF format, which is a popular graphics interchange format. From inside the Microsoft Document Imaging Tool (which is the default fax viewing application on user workstations), you can print or save the file.

If you have chosen to redirect faxes to a network share, the faxes again will be placed in the designated folder as TIF files. Users can browse to that network share, open the TIF file, and perform all of the same functions they would through e-mail. The same applies for documents routed to a document library within Windows SharePoint Services.

One thing to note: if you receive an abnormally shaped fax and have directed incoming faxes to a printer, the fax will be reshaped to fit the default page size of the printer you have selected. So if you receive a legal-sized fax, and you're printing to a laser printer that defaults to letter-sized paper in the tray, the fax will be reduced to fit on the letter page.

Sending a Fax

Receiving a fax is the simplest event that can happen in faxing—there's not a lot of user interaction required. Sending a fax is a bit more time intensive, though it's equally as simple.

There are a couple of different ways to send a fax: from the Fax Console itself, and from within an application. I'll cover both of these methods in the next two sections.

From the Fax Console

As you've learned, the Fax Console is the central place where inbound and outbound faxing can be managed. Let's look at transmitting an outbound fax. To do so:

1. Open the Fax Console. You can do this on the server from the Start menu—select Server Management, then Standard Management, and under the Fax (Local) node, click the Manage Fax Jobs link.

2. From the File menu, select Send a Fax.

3. The Send Fax Wizard appears. Click Next to move on from the introductory screen.

4. The Recipient Information screen appears, as shown in Figure 9-13. You can enter the name of the person to whom you're sending the fax, his current fax number, and the dialing rules that you may need to use in order to, for example, get an outside line. If you have multiple numbers, you can add numbers using the Add button and continue including fax contacts until you have built a complete list. You can also use the Edit button to correct a typo in a name you've already entered. Click Next to continue.

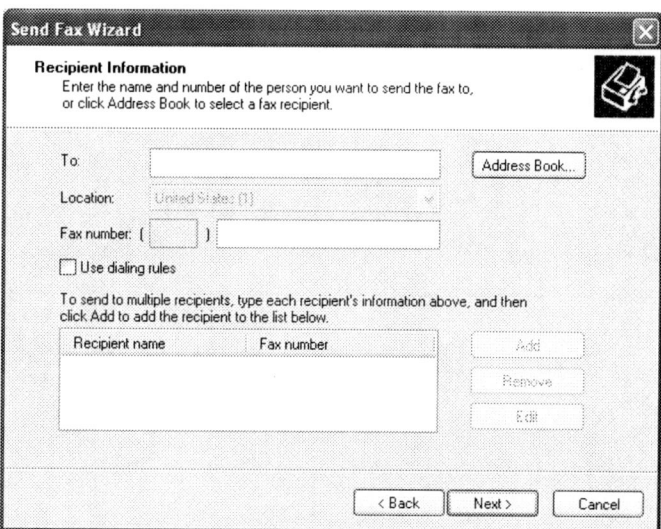

Figure 9-13. *The Recipient Information screen*

5. You'll next see the Preparing the Cover Page screen, as seen in Figure 9-14. Select the cover page template from the drop-down list box—by default, you can choose from Confidential, FYI, Generic, and Urgent—and then enter a subject line and, if you desire, a short note to the recipient about the contents of the fax. Click Next to continue.

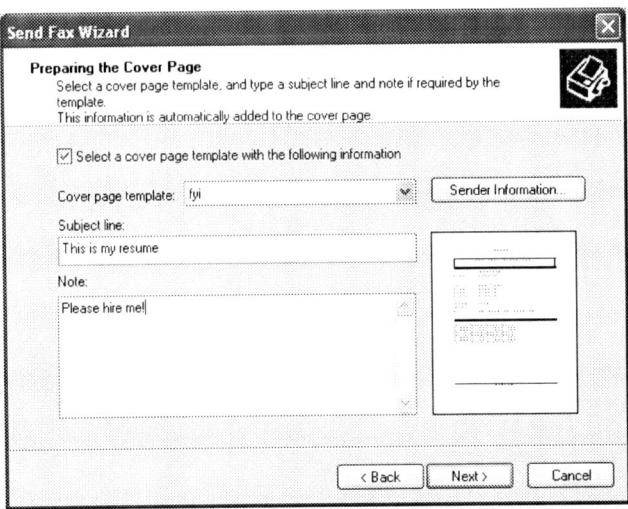

Figure 9-14. *The Preparing the Cover Page screen*

6. The Schedule screen appears, as shown in Figure 9-15. Specify when you would like to send this fax—now, after hours for cheaper long distance, or a certain time within the next day. You can also specify the priority of the fax, which will come into play if there is more than one fax ready to be sent at the same time. (Of course, the fax with the highest priority will be sent first.) Click Next to continue.

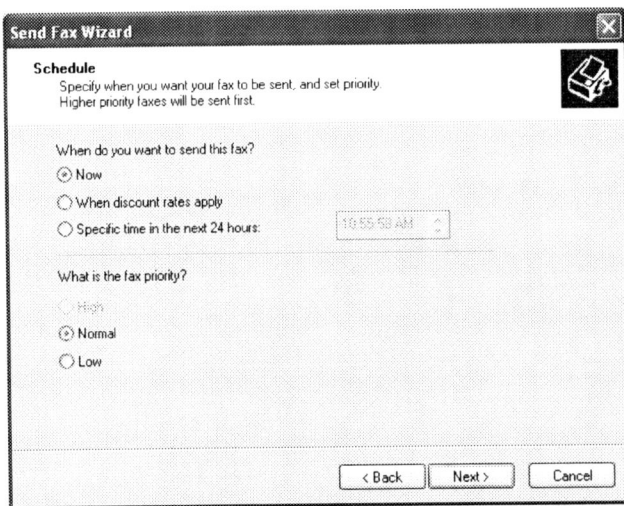

Figure 9-15. *The Schedule screen*

7. The Delivery Notification screen appears, as shown in Figure 9-16. You can tell SBS to send you a pop-up message or an e-mail when the fax is either successfully transmitted or failed. You can also choose to attach a copy of the fax with the e-mail for your own records. Click Next to continue.

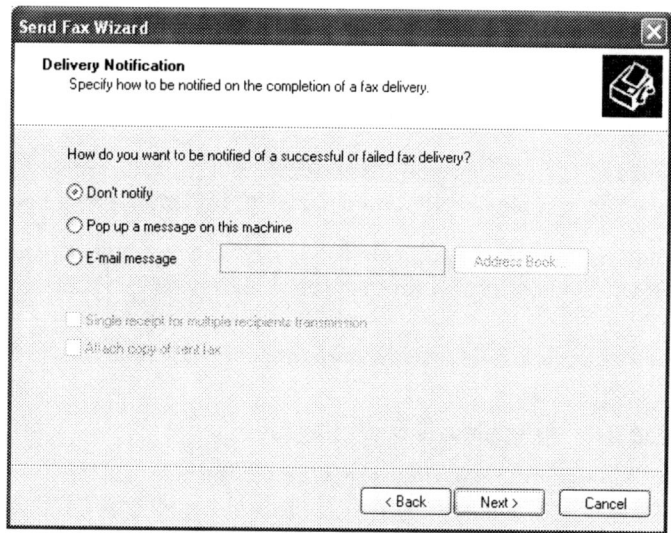

Figure 9-16. *The Delivery Notification screen*

8. The Completing the Send Fax Wizard appears. Confirm all of your settings, preview the fax if you wish using the Preview Fax button, and then click Finish.

Your fax has now been transmitted or is scheduled to transmit at the time you specified.

From Within a Business Application

Most users prepare documents to be faxed from within a business application, and they don't want to spend the time saving the document, launching the Fax Console, stepping through the wizard there, selecting the file, and so on. For these users, SBS provides a seamless way to integrate faxing into existing business applications, like Word, Excel, PowerPoint, ACT!, and so on.

Essentially, all that is required is to set up the Shared Fax Service printer object on your users' workstations. This process is covered in Chapter 3. The SFS masquerades as a printer object to your users, so that they can simply choose to "print" their document to the fax machine. When they do this, Windows will launch the Send a Fax wizard, which you saw in the previous section.

To print from within a Windows application:

1. From the File menu, select Print.

2. Choose the Fax object in the printer selection window, and then click OK.

3. The Send Fax Wizard appears. Click Next to move on from the introductory screen.

4. The Recipient Information screen appears. You can enter the name of the person to whom you're sending the fax, her current fax number, and the dialing rules that you may need to use in order to, for example, get an outside line. Click Next to continue.

5. You'll next see the Preparing the Cover Page screen. Select the cover page template from the drop-down list box, and then enter a subject line and a short note to the recipient. Click Next to continue.

6. The Schedule screen appears. Specify when you would like to send this fax and the priority of the fax. Click Next to continue.

7. The Delivery Notification screen appears. Choose how you want to be notified, if at all, when the fax is either successfully transmitted or failed. Click Next to continue.

8. The Completing the Send Fax Wizard appears. Confirm all of your settings, preview the fax if you wish using the Preview Fax button, and then click Finish.

Your fax has now been transmitted or is scheduled to transmit at the time you specified.

Entering and Personalizing User Metadata and Cover Pages

You'll note that in the previous walkthroughs, there was a lot of information that will likely be the same every time a fax is sent. You can use the Fax Console to enter information to be used over and over—this is known as *metadata*—so that when you go to send a fax, you can cut the time required to step through the wizard and actually send the fax more quickly.

To personalize your outbound faxes:

1. From the client, launch the Fax Console from Start ➤ All Programs ➤ Accessories ➤ Communications ➤ Fax in Windows XP or Start ➤ Programs ➤ Microsoft Shared Fax Client in Windows 2000.

2. From the Tools menu, select Sender Information.

3. The Sender Information dialog box will appear. Fill in all of the pertinent information here, and then click OK.

You will probably also want to create custom cover pages for your outbound faxes. While the ones Microsoft includes with the SFS are useful, you probably want a more professional image, including your company logo, specific contact information, e-mail addresses, and so on.

It's quite easy to personalize cover pages. To do so:

1. From the client, launch the Fax Console from Start ➤ All Programs ➤ Accessories ➤ Communications ➤ Fax in Windows XP or Start ➤ Programs ➤ Microsoft Shared Fax Client in Windows 2000.

2. From the Tools menu, select Personal Cover Pages.

3. The Personal Cover Pages dialog box will appear. From the New menu, select Fax Cover Page Editor.

4. From there, design a custom cover page. Save the cover page when you're done.

5. The new page will be listed in the Personal Cover Pages dialog box you saw in step 3.

Conclusion

As I mentioned at the start of the chapter, the SFS has undergone a major revision and is no longer glued on to the SBS release like an afterthought. It is a worthy member of the SBS feature family, and it's certainly a useful addition to your existing business network.

In this chapter, you've seen the benefits of using the SBS Shared Fax Service as opposed to traditional faxing solutions. I've showed you how you can integrate sending and receiving faxes into both your existing computer investments and your day-to-day workflow style. We've also walked through setting up the SFS, personalizing it, and sending and receiving faxes through it.

■■■

CHAPTER 10

Monitoring SBS Server Health and Performance

In this chapter, I'll examine the monitoring service, the types of reports it creates, how you can configure it to meet your needs, and how you can preserve your custom configuration in case disaster strikes (or in case you need to use it again on other SBS machines).

Let's begin.

Setting Up Monitoring

It's easy to use monitoring in SBS 2003. Microsoft has made it simple to have effective performance monitoring using out-of-the-box defaults that send you performance reports every morning and usage reports every two weeks. However, this performance monitoring isn't turned on and enabled after you first install the product. To use monitoring, you need to enable it. To do so:

1. From the Start menu, open the Server Management Console.

2. In the left pane, expand Standard Management, and then select Monitoring and Reporting.

3. In the right pane, click the Set Up Monitoring Reports and Alerts link.

4. The wizard welcome screen appears. Click Next to continue.

5. The Reporting Options screen appears, as shown in Figure 10-1. Here, you can specify the default options for receiving information on this SBS server's health. You can choose to receive a daily performance report via e-mail, to view the current usage report within the Server Management Console, or to receive a usage report via e-mail as well. Check all the boxes, and then click Next.

6. The E-mail Options screen appears. Enter the e-mail address to which you'd like the performance and usage reports sent. Click Next.

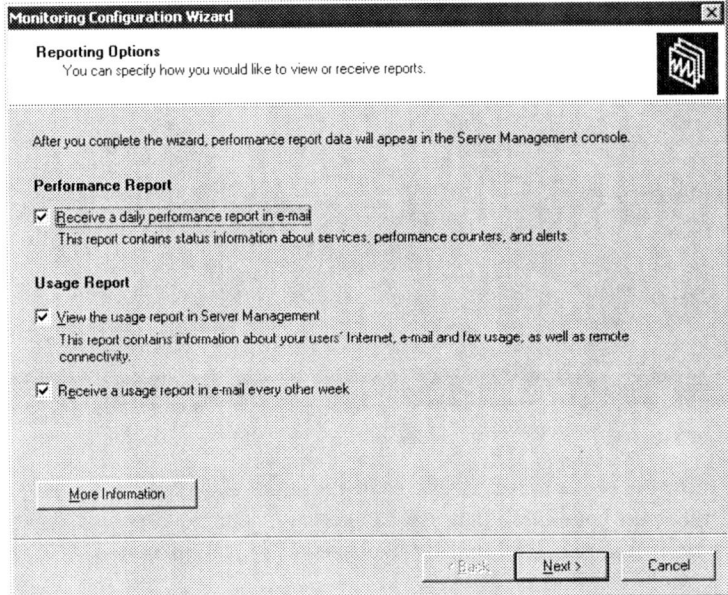

Figure 10-1. *The Reporting Options screen*

7. The Business Owner Usage Report screen appears, as shown in Figure 10-2. Select from the list on the left those users who are authorized to receive and use the information in the usage report, and then move them to the right using the Add button between the two lists. When you're finished adding the appropriate users, click Next.

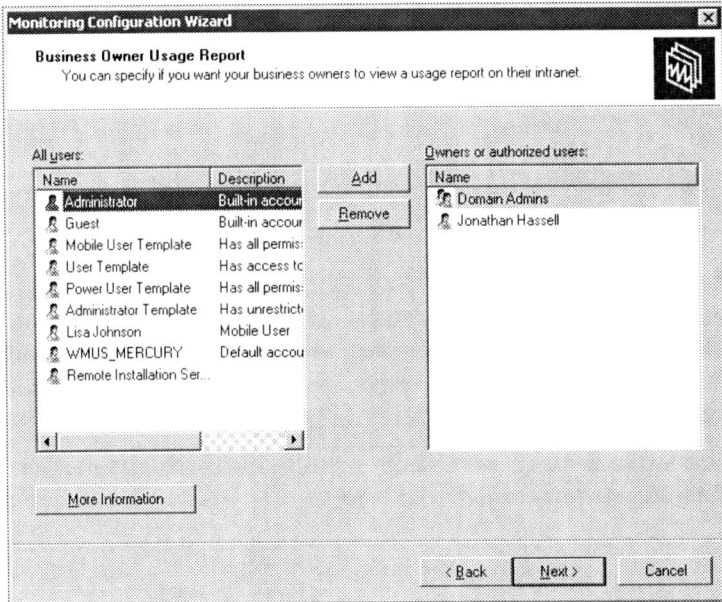

Figure 10-2. *The Business Owner Usage Report screen*

8. The Alerts page appears. You can tell the server to send you an e-mail alert whenever a certain performance parameter drops below an acceptable level. For instance, if available disk space drops below 1 GB, or a process is taking up 100% of the free CPU time for an extended period of time, the server can e-mail you and let you know of this. Check the box to enable this feature, and then enter an e-mail address to which these alerts will be sent. Click Next to continue.

9. Click Finish on the concluding screen of the wizard. The server will adjust the monitoring configuration and show you the progress on screen.

A sample Server Performance Report is shown in Figure 10-3. You'll receive this daily in your e-mail inbox.

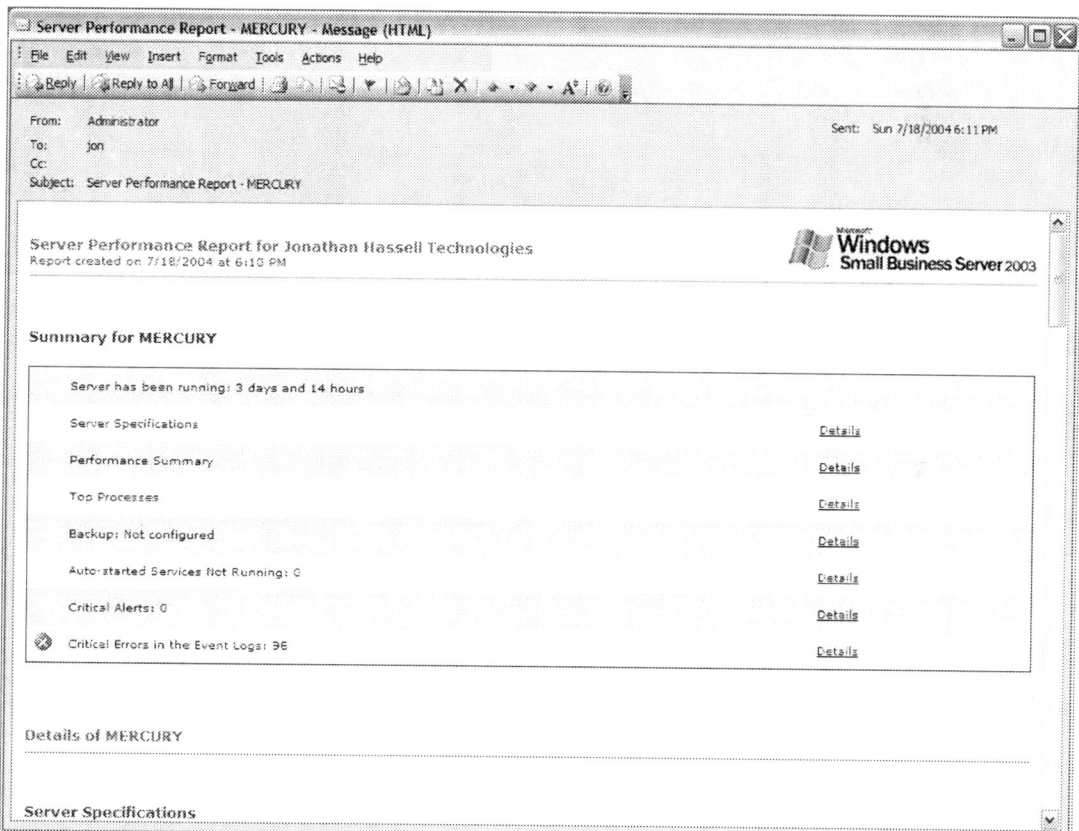

Figure 10-3. *A sample Server Performance Report*

And secondly, the extended Server Usage Report looks a lot like what appears in Figure 10-4, which you receive by default every two weeks (or 14 calendar days).

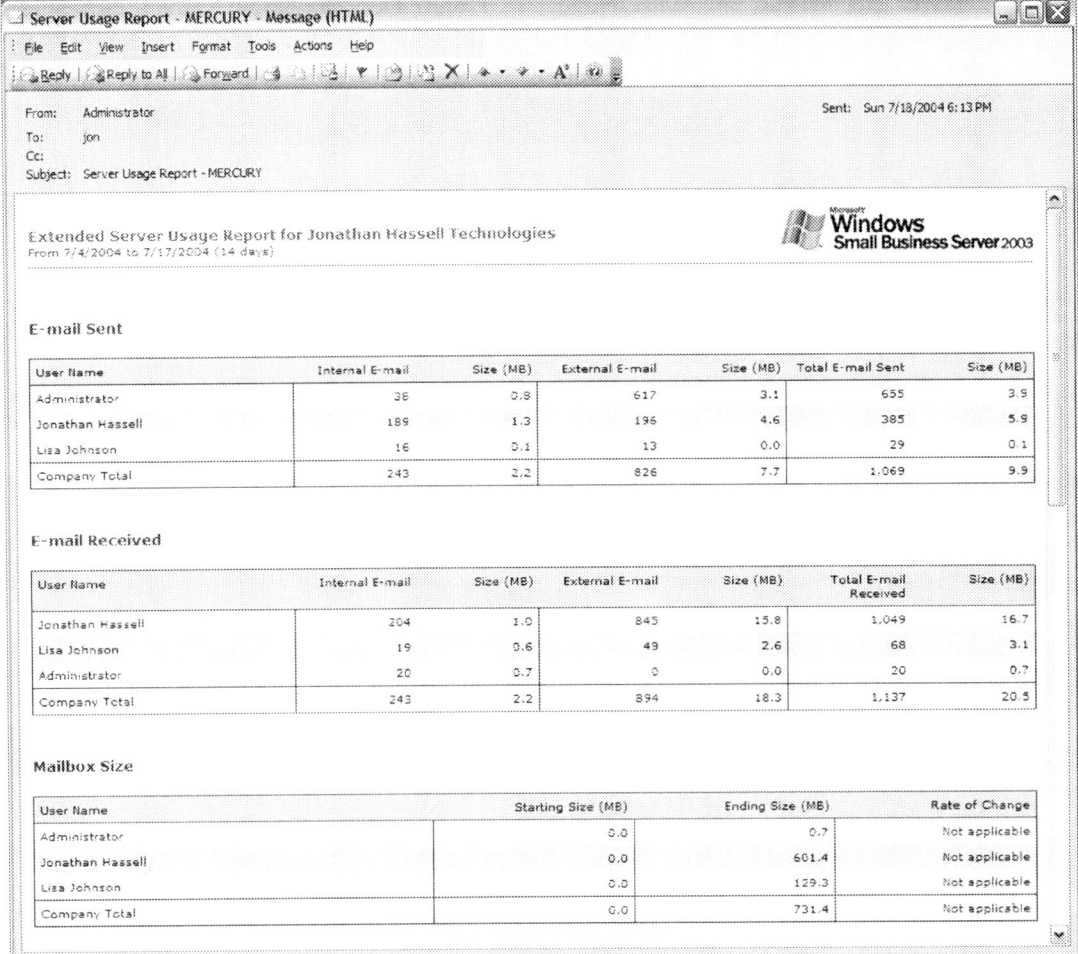

Figure 10-4. *A sample Server Usage Report*

Alternatively, if you prefer, you can view the status reports and the usage report directly from the Server Management Console. Simply click the Monitoring and Reporting node in the left pane, and you will be presented with either the extended usage report or the performance report. To switch views to the opposite report, click the View X Report link in the right pane.

You can also create a different report view, which you may want to do to isolate some statistics from a certain time frame. If this is the case, click the Create New Report button in the top-right portion of the right pane (just below the SBS logo). The Create Your Server Usage Report form will appear, and here you can specify whether to look at a basic view of server usage or the default extended view (which adds information on remote connections and fax activity) and specific dates from which the desired report can be generated. When you've entered the relevant data, click the Create Report button and wait while the report is dynamically built.

Expanding the Scope of the Monitoring Service

In addition to the basic status reports that are sent out via e-mail, you can choose to have certain files attached to those messages as well—useful information such as log files from particular services or third-party applications. This can be especially helpful if you have an agreement with a customer to process their web server logs and produce a statistical analysis of their traffic: you can have the logs automatically sent directly to you without any effort on either the customer's or your part.

To do so:

1. Open the Server Management Console.

2. Select the Monitoring and Reporting node from the left pane.

3. Click the Change Server Status Report Settings link in the right pane.

4. The Server Status Reports screen appears. Select the Performance option to indicate you want to attach files to the Server Performance Report and not the Server Usage Report, and then click the Edit button.

5. Navigate to the Content tab.

6. Next, choose the files you'd like to include. By default, you can attach the application event log, any relevant IIS logs, backup logs, the security event log, or the system event log. If you would like another file, click the Add button at the bottom of the screen and select the appropriate file in its location on the disk. You can use wildcard characters to filter the files to include as well.

7. Click OK to conclude your changes.

The new files will now be attached to the Server Performance Report. If you'd like to attach certain files to the Server Usage Report, simply select the opposite option in step 4.

Adjusting the Schedule for Outgoing Reports

You may decide that, after running through the initial wizard, the SBS default settings for sending out performance and usage reports don't suit you. In this case, it's easy to change the time and frequency that these reports are transmitted. In this example, I'll talk about the Server Performance Report, but you can modify the procedure for the Server Usage Report very easily, as noted later.

Before you change the schedule, though, think about what the default settings do for you. For one, most backup programs are scheduled to run in the real middle of the night—most commonly between 1:30 a.m. and 4:30 a.m., to handle both time zone differences and workers still at their desks late at night. Since most Windows-based backup programs report errors in the event logs that are scanned by the monitoring service, any problems with the backup would be included in a 6 a.m. status report, but not necessarily one generated earlier in the day. In the same vein, problems can creep up overnight that might not necessarily have manifested themselves earlier in the wee morning hours. A 6 a.m. status report is a reliable "green light" message from the server, meaning that it's a reasonably confident guess that everything is all right with your machine and that it's ready for the rush of the workday to set in.

Nevertheless, if you have your own reasons to change the schedule for reports to be sent, you can do it this way:

1. Open the Server Management Console.

2. Select the Monitoring and Reporting node from the left pane.

3. Click the Change Server Status Report Settings link in the right pane.

4. The Server Status Reports screen appears. Select the Performance option to indicate you want to attach files to the Server Performance Report and not the Server Usage Report, and then click the Edit button.

5. Navigate to the Schedule tab.

6. The current configuration is spelled out at the top of the screen. You can adjust the frequency the report is sent using the Schedule Task drop-down box, the time at which the report generation is started with the Start Time list, and the days between reports with the Schedule Task Daily box. Adjust the settings as needed.

7. Click OK to finish your adjustments.

The new schedule will go into effect immediately.

Analyzing the Server Performance Report

Now comes the more tricky part: determining what all the information in the Server Performance Report actually means about the health of your server. Let's take a look at each of the sections and discuss the potential implications the data has on future actions you might need to take.

Understanding the Performance Summary

The Performance Summary section offers five useful metrics to determine whether your server is adequately equipped to handle the load experienced within the past 24 hours (or since the last report was sent, if you've altered the default schedule settings). It also lists the five processes that are using the most memory, as shown in Figure 10-5.

Note the four or five statistics at the top, depending on how many disk drives you have installed in your server: memory in use, which shows how much memory most processes are taking up; the amount of free disk space on each of your volumes; how often the disk is busy reading or writing data (which can indicate problems with swapping); and the amount of CPU time being used on average since the last report was sent. The next section, the top five processes by memory usage, shows which processes are currently occupying most of the system RAM. This can indicate programs with memory leak, particularly if over the course of several days you see the same program occupying excessive amounts of memory. Be careful, though, in assessing this—some programs are meant to occupy large amounts of memory and then gradually expand as the server uptime increases. One example is the STORE.EXE process, which is the Exchange Server 2003 Information Store that handles the contents of all of your users' mailboxes.

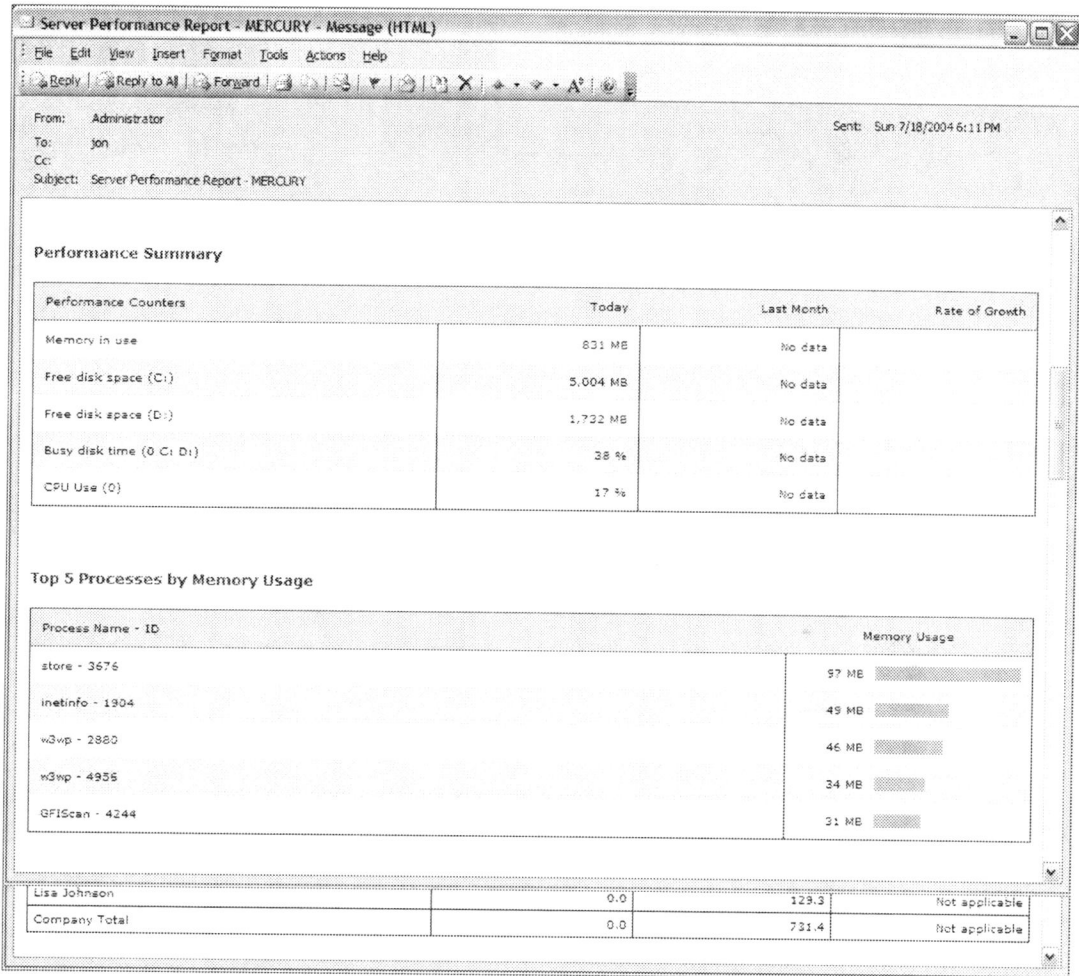

Figure 10-5. *Examining a performance summary*

Moving down the report, we see the sections depicted in Figure 10-6.

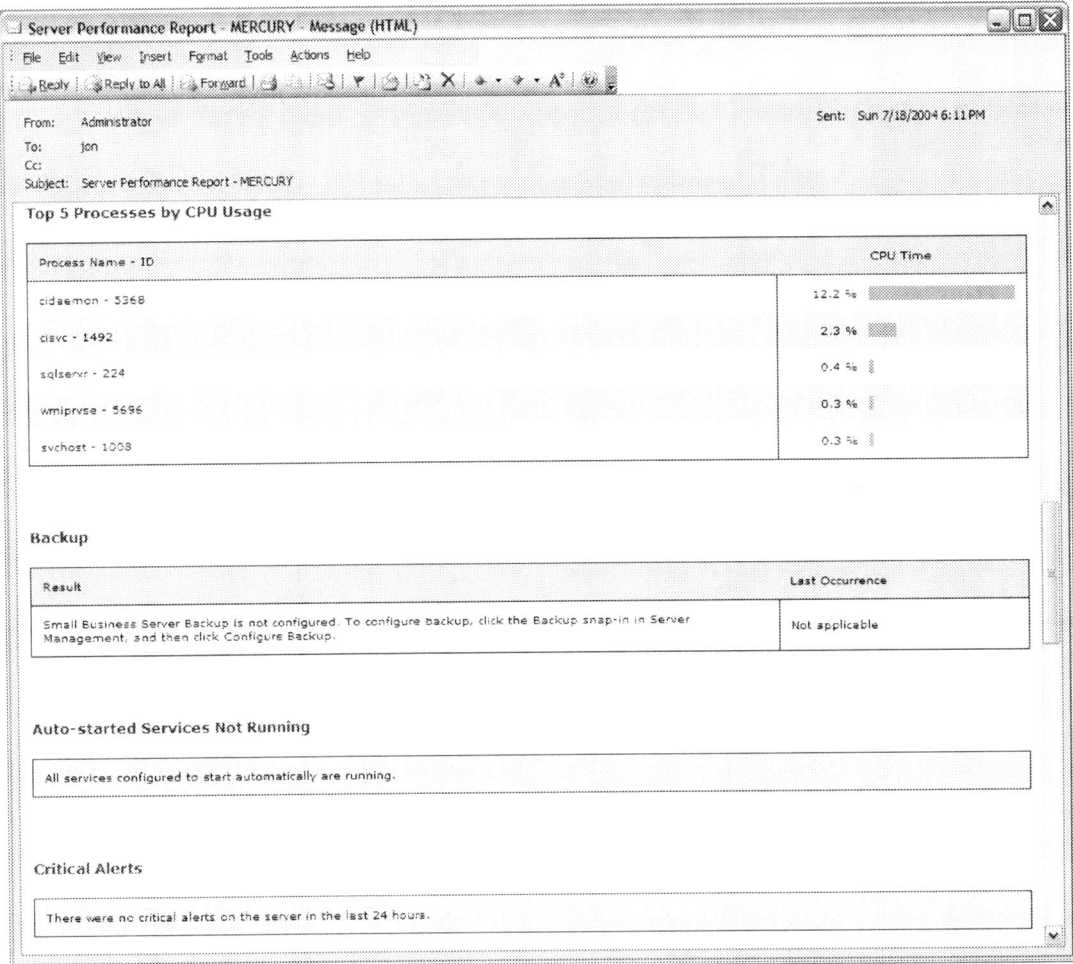

Figure 10-6. *Looking at processes, backups, services, and alerts*

Let's take a look at each of these elements:

- **Top 5 Processes by CPU Usage**: This will show you which programs are making the server do the most work. Disk- and search-intensive programs, like the Indexing Service or a database like SQL Server, will automatically rise to the top of lists like these. In the preceding example, you see the former (cidaemon) used around a tenth of the available CPU time, and the latter (sqlservr) used less than one percent. Clearly none of these is problematic. However, if you start to see programs commonly using more than 60 percent of available time, you might consider either adding a faster processor, adding a second processor, or buying a new server to handle your growing load.

- **Backup**: This shows the result of the most recent backup. In the example report shown previously, this has not been configured, but you can also configure the monitoring service to include the status reports directly from the backup program itself along with these performance reports; you learned how to do that in the previous section.

- **Auto-started Services Not Running**: This shows services that are supposed to start automatically upon a reboot that didn't start. You won't see this populated unless the server has restarted for some reason.

- **Critical Alerts**: This will show any sort of urgent notification, like low disk space or a completely occupied (that is, at 100 percent) CPU, that occurred since the last report was sent.

Examining Error Log Activity

Finally, we get to the juicy stuff: specific errors found in the various event logs. This is shown in Figure 10-7.

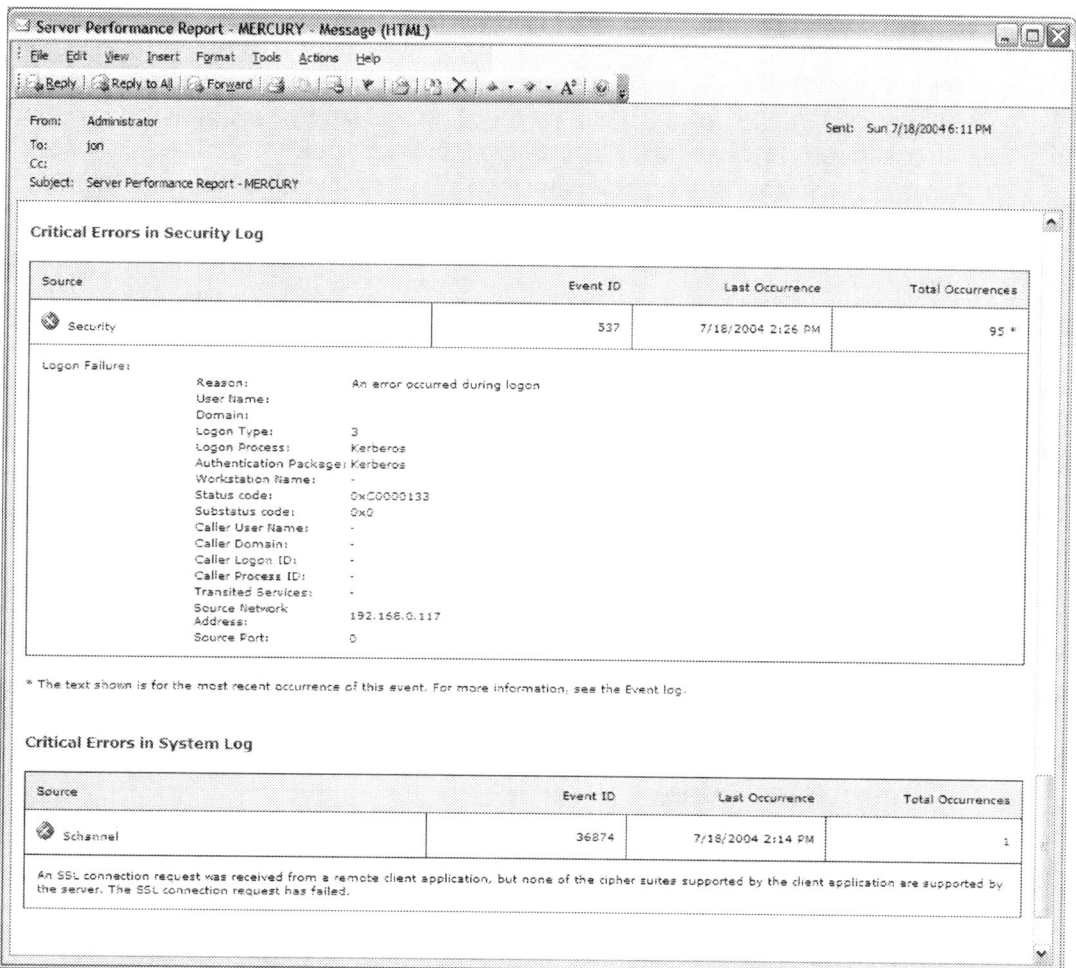

Figure 10-7. *Looking for errors in logs*

VAR CORNER: BUILDING BUSINESS WITH THE SERVER PERFORMANCE REPORT

The Server Performance Report inherently creates a wonderful opportunity for improving relations with your customers. The SPR allows you to proactively manage your customers' machines, with their individual statuses sent directly to your e-mail account each morning. This way, you can head off potential problems, in some cases before the owners and workers of the business come into work.

But there's another angle to this as well—it can be reassuring to a small business owner to receive a simple e-mail each morning from the consultant, commenting that all is well with the technology that runs the business. This simple, 10-second e-mail can improve your bottom line, since your customer will sense that you're always one step ahead, looking for problems before they arise.

Use the Server Performance Report to your advantage, and increase customer satisfaction at the same time.

This section is highly useful for troubleshooting. NT administrators for years have grumbled about managing the deluge of information available within the event logs, filtering it to find problems they need to address, and figuring out an efficient way to streamline that process. This is such a problem that even third-party software developers have created products to assist with this. SBS includes a basic form of this automated event log management within the Server Performance Report itself.

When errors crop up in any event log, they will be included here. The ID number of the error is also reported, as well as the additional information included within the specific event in the log. You can take the ID number and enter it into the form at http://www.eventid.net to find out more about the problem and look at other administrators' experiences in resolving the error.

The monitoring service combs the application, directory services, DNS server, File Replication Service, security, and system logs and reports any errors found therein.

Analyzing the Server Usage Report

The Server Usage Report is a very useful tool that shows what users are doing what activities at what times, and it also shows how often they're doing those activities. A basic usage report includes information on e-mail sent, e-mail received, mailbox size, Outlook Web Access activity by user, Outlook Web Access usage per single hour, and other useful metrics.

A Word on Baselining

Baselining is, in short, taking an initial measure of system usage and activity for later use in comparisons. Creating a baseline is an effective way to document changes that occur to the usage pattern and frequency of certain resources in your infrastructure. To measure these changes, further data collection takes place at measured, regular intervals in the future, and the rate of change is measured from the initial baseline measurement to the new, current measurement.

Baselining is easy with SBS 2003 and the Server Usage Report. As soon as you configure monitoring on the server, the first report that SBS generates is treated as the baseline. From that point on, future usage reports analyze the rate of change of several different statistics from this baseline. This data is great to show to a customer or your boss and outlines exactly what is happening with users and your server. You can say, "Look how disk usage has grown over the last six months," or "We definitely need a couple more modems, since remote connection activity has increased over the past few months."

Determining Available Statistics

Let's look in detail at what metrics are available to be reported on the Server Usage Report:

- **Web activity by computer**: This measures both the average number of hours per day and the total daily hours a client computer was connected to the Internet during the two-week period.

- **Web traffic by hour**: This metric shows both the average number of connections per day and the total number of connections made by all client computers, per hour, during the report's time frame.

- **E-mail sent**: This measures the total number and size of e-mail messages that each user sent outbound to the Internet and to recipients internal to your organization.

- **E-mail received**: This is the count and a report of the size of e-mail received by your users, both from inside your network and from the Internet.

- **Mailbox size**: This measures the size of the user's mailbox both at the beginning and the end of the report dates and then shows a percentage rate of change for the time period.

- **Outlook Web Access activity by user**: This reports the average and the total number of visits each user made to the OWA site.

- **Outlook Web Access usage by hour**: This reports both the average and the total number of visits made to an OWA site per hour.

- **Remote connection activity by user**: This shows the total and average number of times each user made a connection to the internal network from outside the network per day. It also shows the average length of those connections.

- **Remote connection activity by hour**: This shows the average and, again, the total number of remote connections that your users made to the network per hour during the two-week period.

- **Faxes sent**: This measures the total and average number of outbound faxes transmitted to a specific fax number, and the average length and size of all faxes sent to that number during the two-week period. All numbers are listed.

- **Faxes received**: This measures the total and average number of inbound faxes transmitted from a specific fax number, and the average length and size of all faxes sent from that number during the two-week period. All numbers are listed.

- **Faxes sent by user**: This statistic shows the average and total number of faxes sent by each user, per day, during the report's time frame.

- **Fax traffic by hour**: Finally, this statistic shows the average and total number of faxes per day sent by all users, broken down by hour, during the two-week reporting period.

A sample of the Outlook Web Access usage by hour report is shown in Figure 10-8.

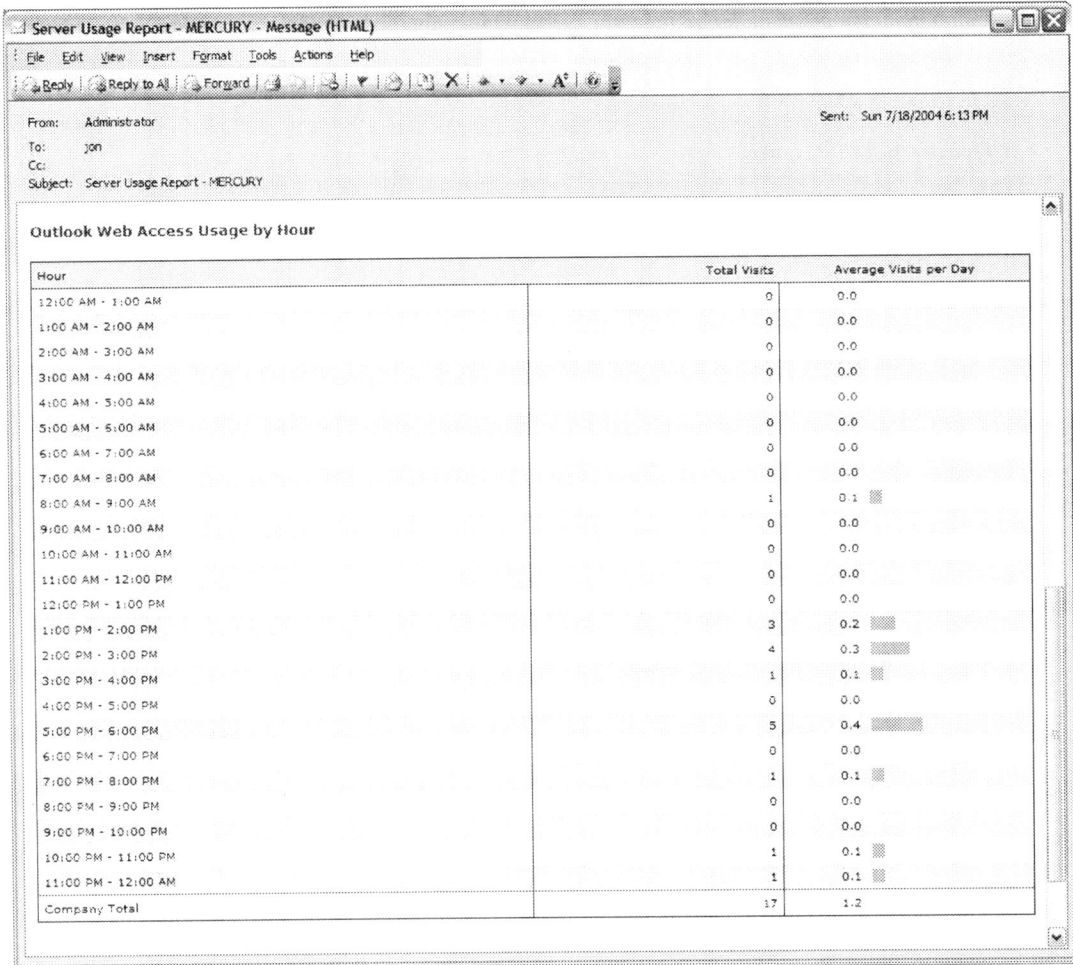

Figure 10-8. *Looking at OWA average access per hour*

Configuring Health Monitor Alerts

There is a special component of SBS, called the Health Monitor, that controls the alert notifications that you receive if something critical goes sour on your server—disk space, free memory available, or processor time being monopolized, for example. You can customize these alerts, adjust their thresholds, or even create your own alerts via the Health Monitor tool.

To access the Health Monitor alerts, go to the Server Management Console, and then view the performance report within the console. Then, click the Change Alert Notifications link in the right pane, and the Alert Notifications screen will appear, as shown in Figure 10-9.

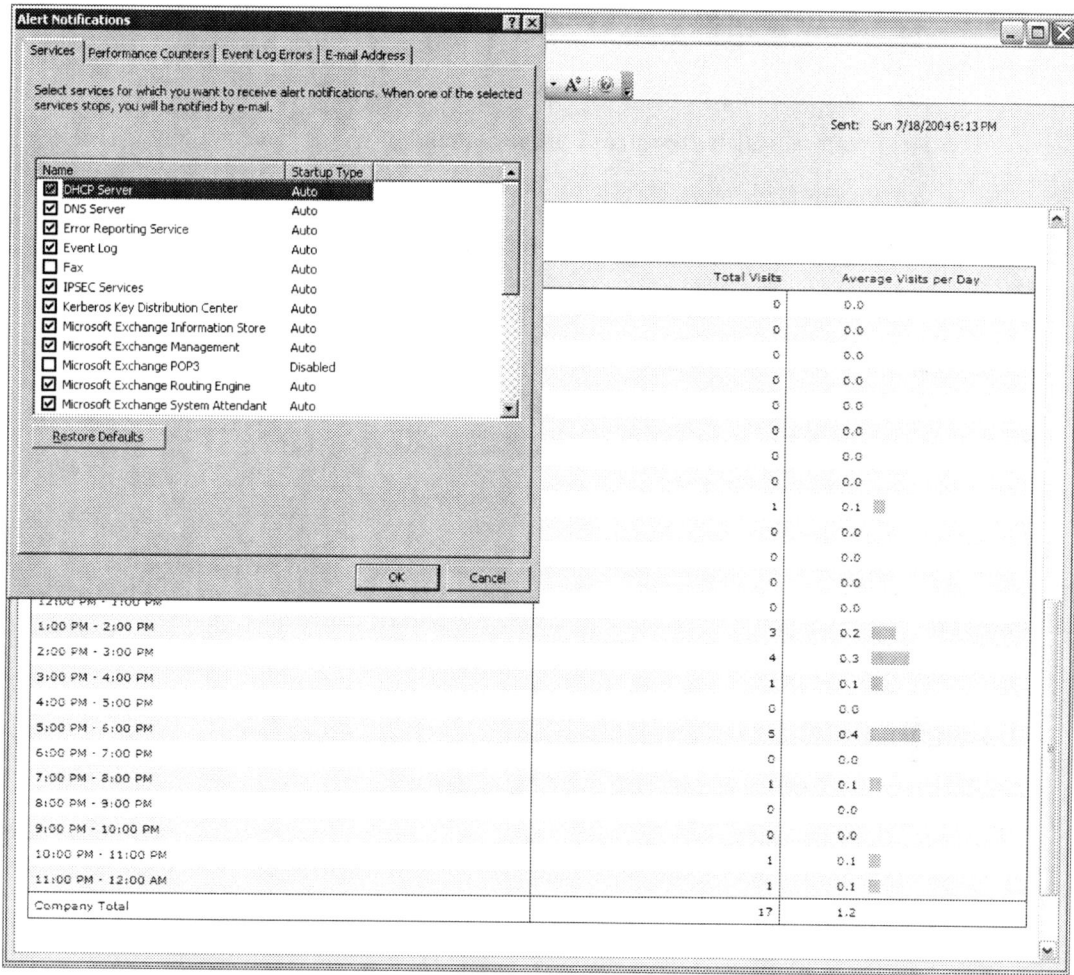

Figure 10-9. *The Alert Notifications UI*

Alerts can be based on service information, thresholds derived from certain performance counters, or errors contained in event logs. There are tabs on the screen corresponding to each of these types of data. On the Services tab, a list of services is presented with check boxes. You can check any service you'd like, and then when that service stops—for whatever reason—you'll receive an e-mail notification to that effect.

On the Performance Counters tab, you can select specific metrics for which you'd like to receive an e-mail alert. In other words, once the value for a particular attribute exceeds a specified amount, the machine will e-mail you a message detailing that. You can choose any one of the following performance counters:

- Allocated memory exceeding a certain amount

- Disk activity less than a certain amount

- IIS memory in use exceeding a certain value

- Disk space less than a certain amount

- Local security authority memory in use exceeding a certain value

- Free memory available less than a certain amount

- Printing errors recorded in the event log

- Processor activity exceeding a given percentage

- Failures for faxes being sent

- Failures for inbound faxes

- Outbound SMTP queue (mail sending) exceeding a certain number of messages

- Exchange Information Store using too much memory

- System up time less than a certain number of seconds

And, on the Event Log Errors tab, you can specify if you'd like to receive e-mail when someone's account becomes locked out (event code 539) or when a backup failed (code 5634). Finally, on the E-mail Addresses tab, you can specify the addresses to which alerts are sent.

Replicating Health Monitoring Settings

If you are a value-added provider or consultant, and you've just created a perfect configuration for your performance monitoring tools and would like to preserve your fine creation for later use—well, up until SBS 2003, this was very difficult to do. There wasn't an automated tool to use. But SBS 2003 includes migration utilities that allow you to export various settings from a production server to a file, which you can then later reimport onto a separate server and establish an identical configuration. As you can imagine, not only is this perfect for consultants, who set up multiple servers a year and probably have an ideal array of settings in mind for their clients, but it's also great for the IT person at the small business as well: now he has a foolproof backup method so if, for some reason, disaster struck his company and he had to build SBS 2003 onto another machine, he could reimport his settings and be back where he was before the problem occurred.

To back up your performance monitoring settings and current configuration, perform the following steps:

1. Open the Server Management Console.

2. Under the Advanced Management section in the left pane, click Migrate Small Business Server Settings.

3. Then, in the right pane, click Export Health Monitor Configuration. The Export Health Monitor Configuration Wizard appears. Click Next to continue off the introductory screen.

4. The Export Location screen appears. Enter the path to the file where you want the settings to be stored. You can use the Browse button to navigate the file systems on your server hard drives. When you've entered an appropriate path, click Next.

5. On the final screen, double-check the file name you've entered, and then click Finish to actually export the settings.

The wizard will export the settings, and then tell you about its progress. When the check mark appears next to the task, click the Close button. The exporting process has completed.

The Indexing Service

Windows Server 2003 includes an index service that catalogs files stored on network drives, corporate intranets, and Internet sites and provides a web-based query form for easy search and retrieval of those cataloged resources.

Part of the power behind the Indexing Service is its ability to catalog documents without needing them reformatted to a special, proprietary format. The service understands most Microsoft Office file formats, including the common Word and Excel documents, and those types of files indexed by the service are available immediately and without any sort of special processing required. This makes the service very useful even beyond its basic premise of indexing plain web sites.

The Indexing Service works by identifying unique words within a document and establishing their location in that document, and then reporting that information back to a central database—the "index," as it were. You, as the administrator, can specify certain documents to either be indexed or be excluded from indexing, and you can also include the properties of a document—consisting typically of title, author, date of creation, date of last edit, and similar bits of information—in the catalog to expand the criteria on which your users can search.

How the Indexing Service Works

The Indexing Service makes use of filters to extract information from documents. The CiDaemon process, created by the parent Indexing Service, runs in the background on the machine where the Indexing Service resides, filtering documents for later indexing by filters. Filters are pieces of DLLs that actually extract information from a document—be it words within a document or the properties of a document—from specific types of files, like Word documents or HTML pages. The service comes with a standard set of filters that can index text; HTML; Microsoft Office documents created in versions 95, 97, 2000, XP, and 2003; and Internet Mail and News clippings and posts. Filters are extensible and can be created by third-party vendors for their specific data types.

After using filters to extract data, the service compares the filtered data against an exception list, which mainly contains a list of commonly used prepositions, pronouns, articles, and other nonessential words. The exception list is called NOISE.XXX, where the XXX represents the language of the document being indexed. When the filtered data has had words that matched entries on the exception list removed, the remaining data is moved to word lists, which are small, temporary, and nonpersistent stores of index information that only serve as holding bins. About once a day, a shadow merge takes place to aggregate the information within shadow indexes and remove data from the "holding bin," to both free up memory taken up by nonpersistent word lists and to make data that is filtered persistent by saving it on a disk. Shadow indexes are created when word lists and other shadow indexes are combined into a single index.

At a separate time, the Indexing Service initiates master merges, which take place when individual shadow indexes are aggregated and infused into a current master index to create a single master index. The master index is a permanent index of a larger collection of documents. In a truer sense, the master index is the only index, containing pointers to resources within the corpus, much like the index of this book points you to certain words and phrases at specific points within the body. Picture a set of indexes, each for a certain chapter of this book. One could take these individual indexes (the "shadow indexes") and combine them into a master index, which would then be placed at the back of this book—this is the process of master merging. These indexes are stored in the catalog, a specific folder that contains all indexes, either temporary word lists or more permanent shadow and master indexes.

Other terms you may run across while administering the Indexing Service:

- The **corpus** is an entire collection on HTML pages and other indexed documents that comprise the base of the indexed material.

- A **query** is simply a certain request to the Indexing Service to retrieve files or data that match certain criteria.

- **Saved indexes** are just highly compressed indexes that are stored on disk media and not simply placed in memory; thus, saved indexes persist after reboots. Saved indexes come in two flavors—shadow indexes and master indexes.

- A **scan** takes place when the Indexing Service wishes to determine what files in a particular location have changed or otherwise been modified.

- The **scope** of an index is simply the range of documents and files to be searched when satisfying a query.

- A **virtual root** is an alias to a certain directory on a disk. The Indexing Service can index any location defined as a virtual root.

Performance Considerations

Obviously, the single largest requirement of any indexing service is its disk space—the service will need room to store its indexing files. Microsoft recommends that you allocate about 35 percent of the size of your corpus for the indexing service—I would allocate about 45 percent, simply to provide your service with room to grow. As more electronic information hits your disks, you'll want to have ample space to index that data optimally. Master merges typically require large amounts of disk space on a temporary basis, as much as 50 percent of the corpus size.

Perhaps the greatest demand on your machine's CPU from the Indexing Service comes from master merges, which are very intensive and require large amounts of CPU time. Because of this, master merges are scheduled automatically by the Indexing Service for midnight local time. However, if there is a better time when your machine's CPU load is low, you can change the time at which master merges will start by doing some Registry editing. The MasterMerge-Time value, located in `HKEY_LOCAL_MACHINE\System\CurrentControlSet\Control\ContentIndex`, allows you to specify the number of minutes after midnight local time that the master merge should commence. For this value, you can enter any number between 0 and 1439 (24 hours).

Common Administrative Tasks

In this section, I'll go through some common administrative tasks you will encounter with the Indexing Service. To use most of these, you'll find it easier to create a custom view within Microsoft Management Console to access the Indexing Service controls, since there isn't a clean default view of these options built into SBS 2003. To do so:

1. From the Start menu, select the Run option.

2. Type **mmc** in the Run box and press Enter.

3. The Microsoft Management Console starts with an empty console, as shown in Figure 11-1.

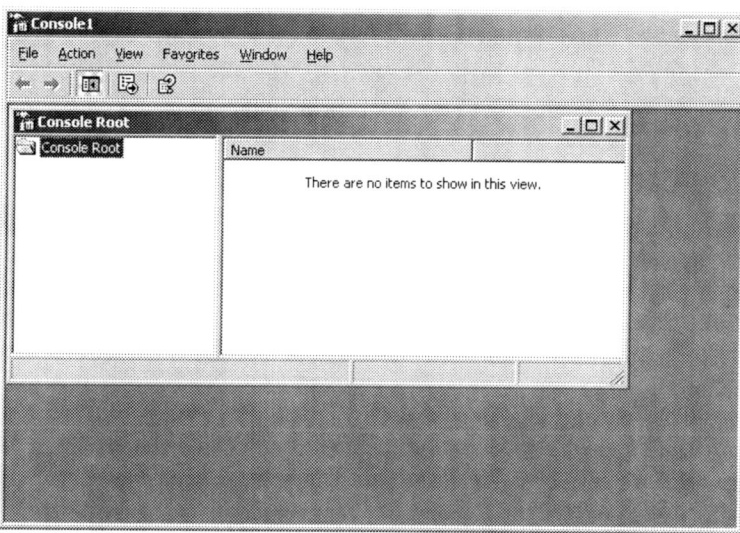

Figure 11-1. *Adding a node to a blank MMC window*

4. From the File menu, choose Add/Remove Snap-in, and then click Add.

5. The Add Standalone Snap-in box appears. Select Indexing Service and click Add, as shown in Figure 11-2.

6. Select Local Computer when prompted, unless you're installing this set of tools to administer the Indexing Service on a remote machine; in that case, enter the name of the remote computer.

7. Click Close, and then click OK, and you'll be returned to the console with the Indexing Service node now added to the left pane.

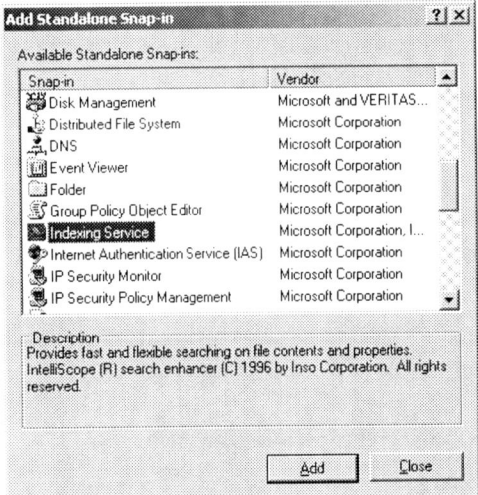

Figure 11-2. *Adding the Indexing Service to an MMC window*

You're now ready to manage the service, as described in this section.

Administering Catalogs

As you read previously in this chapter, a catalog is a specific folder that contains all indexes, either temporary word lists or more permanent shadow and master indexes. When you first add the Indexing Service to a computer, the service creates a default index, named System, that includes all directories on all local drives attached to the system, and another default index, named Web, for any IIS-based web sites that might be running on that particular machine.

For security reasons, I recommend deleting both of these default catalogs. They are too encompassing, particular for web servers. It's best to create your own catalogs that index only certain data on your disk and not every file it can find. However, you may have a completely sanitized system and find that the defaults work well for you—if this is the case, then by all means go for it. But for most people, I would recommend deleting the default catalogs and enabling more specific, focused, and restrictive catalogs.

Creating a Catalog

To create a custom catalog, use the custom MMC that you created with the Indexing Service snap-in and highlight the Indexing Service node in the left pane. Then, select the Action menu, and choose Catalog from the New menu. The Add Catalog screen displays, as shown in Figure 11-3.

Enter a name for the new catalog in the Name box and then enter the path to the folder that will house the contents of the catalog in the Location box. You can use the Browse button to graphically navigate your directory structure. Click OK when you've entered this information. Keep in mind that if you're managing the service on a remote computer, that remote computer must have the default administrative shares (that is, C$, D$, and the others, as discussed in Chapter 4) intact; otherwise, the operation will fail.

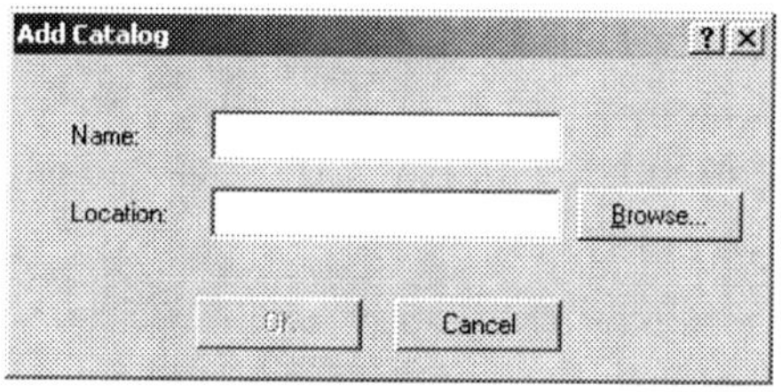

Figure 11-3. *Creating a custom catalog*

░**Note** Avoid putting the catalog in the directory that you're cataloging. For example, if you're trying to catalog D:\DOCS\SBSBOOK, do not put the catalog you create for that directory in D:\DOCS\SBSBOOK. You'll create a near-perpetual loop, since the catalog is always changing, and the service will attempt to index the changing catalog and recatalog the catalog, and so on.

Also, avoid putting a catalog in the WWWROOT directory where IIS webs live. It's fine to catalog the web sites; just don't put the catalog itself there.

Before the new catalog will become active, you must restart the Indexing Service. To quickly restart the service, right-click the Indexing Service node within the console window and select Stop. Once the service has stopped, right-click in the same place again and choose Start.

Catalog Configuration

After catalogs are added, they need to be configured to act as you want. Within the Indexing Service console, right-click the catalog to be configured and select Properties. The screen shown in Figure 11-4 appears.

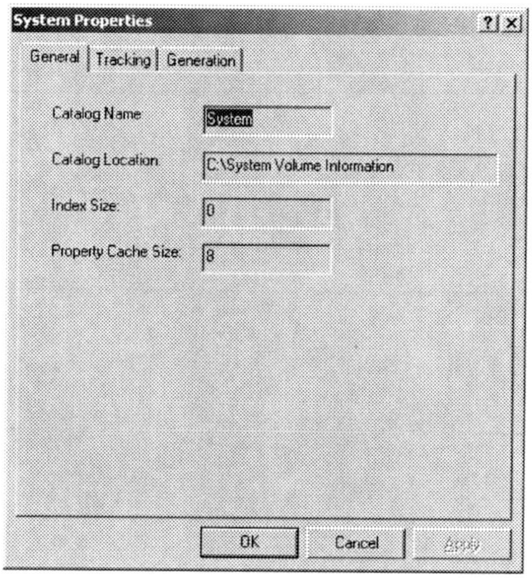

Figure 11-4. *Adjusting the properties of an individual catalog*

A discussion of the features available on each tab follows:

- **General**: On the General tab is information about the catalog that cannot be modified, including the name and location of the catalog, the number of documents in its corpus, and the size of the property cache.

- **Tracking**: On the Tracking tab, you can elect to automatically add and remove aliases for shared network drives and specify whether to inherit the setting for that option from the overall Indexing Service configuration. Simply put, this means that if the service indexes data on a mapped drive, it will remember both the mapped drive and the full UNC path to the data. If you wish to turn it off, you'll need to disable the inheritance feature with the second check box and then disable the automatic alias function by unchecking the first box. If you have IIS installed on the machine that is running the Indexing Service, you can select which web site to index from the drop-down list labeled WWW Server, and you can do the same for any news (NNTP) server running on the machine as well. If IIS is not installed on the machine, the option is grayed out and unavailable.

- **Generation**: On this tab, you can elect to index files that have extensions that aren't covered by the filters currently installed within the service. You can also specify whether the Indexing Service should generate abstracts for files returned from a query and present them on the results page. These two options are by default inherited from the overall Indexing Service configuration; to turn them off, deselect the "Inherit above settings from Service" check box and then adjust the settings individually. You can also adjust the size of abstracts returned to the results page; since the bigger the abstract, the more time needed for a query to be returned, it's best to leave this at the default 320 characters unless you have a specific business need to change it.

Figure 11-5 shows the Tracking tab.

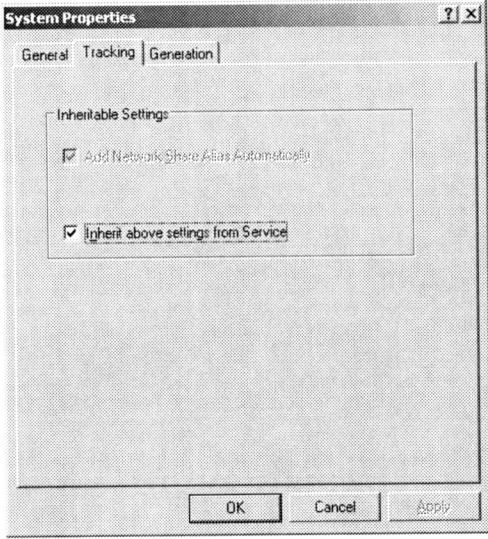

Figure 11-5. *The Tracking tab*

Figure 11-6 shows the Generation tab.

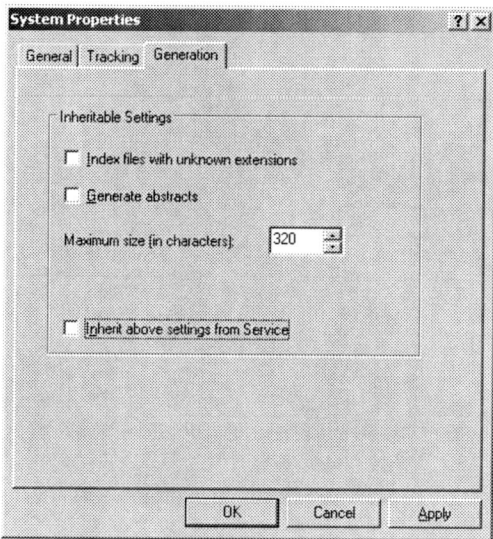

Figure 11-6. *The Generation tab*

Aside from the abstract generation setting, all of the options on these tabs require a restart of the catalog in order to be recognized. Simply right-click the appropriate catalog within the Indexing Service snap-in and select Stop and then Start to do this. If you change the abstract generation setting, you need to stop and restart the overall Indexing Service itself; see the previous instructions for a procedure to do that.

Directory and Location Selection

Upon adding a new catalog and configuring its properties, you also need to define the directories to be included or excluded from its indexing activities. Specifying included directories includes any subdirectories of that particular directory. You can choose to exclude individual directories within an included parent directory, but you cannot include individual directories within an excluded parent directory—the directory will appear to be included, but it will not be indexed.

How does security play into the indexing process? The Indexing Service is completely compatible with any NTFS permissions you apply to files and folders; if a user's current security privileges won't allow him to see a file that is stored on a local NTFS volume, the Indexing Service won't return that file within the results of a query. If a catalog is configured to index a remote UNC share, then any protected files still won't be able to be accessed by the user, but the file will be included in the results of the search. Additionally, encrypted files are not indexed at all. If a file included in a catalog is encrypted after it is indexed, it will be removed from the index upon the next indexing (this doesn't happen right away).

You can block the service from indexing a particular file or folder also through adjusting that object's attributes. Right-click the appropriate file or folder, choose Properties, and then click the Advanced button on the General tab. This raises the Advanced Attributes dialog box, as shown in Figure 11-7.

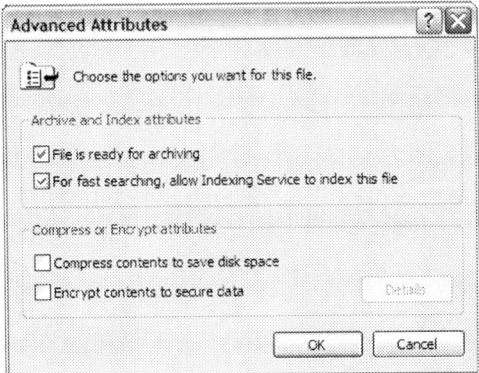

Figure 11-7. *The Advanced Attributes dialog box*

Under Archive and Index Attributes, uncheck the second option, and the folder won't be indexed by the service.

Also, note that the operating system that hosts drives being indexed also affects the operation of the Indexing Service in the following ways:

- FAT volumes hosted remotely on machines running operating systems other than Windows NT, 2000, or Server 2003 will need to be rescanned periodically to detect modified files.

- Volumes on any file system hosted on Novell NetWare servers or UNIX systems can be indexed, but there is no permission validation on files stored on those services.

- Novell NetWare volumes will need to be rescanned periodically also to detect modified files.

To include or exclude directories from a catalog's indexing processes:

1. Open the Indexing Service console.

2. Right-click the appropriate catalog in the right pane, and then from the New menu, select Directory.

3. The Add Directory dialog box appears, as shown in Figure 11-8. In the Path box, enter the location of the directory you're either including or excluding. This can be either a local path or a network (UNC) path.

4. If you are specifying a path to a remote computer, supply a valid username and password in the Account Information section.

5. Finally, select whether to include or exclude this particular directory in the index in the Include in Index section to the right of the box.

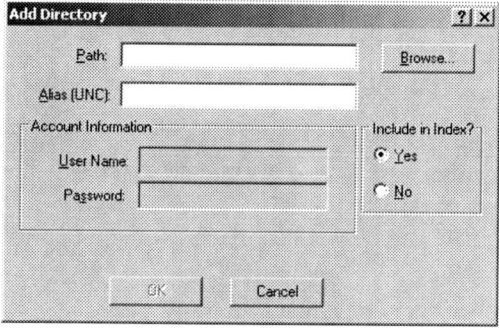

Figure 11-8. *The Add Directory dialog box*

Initiating Scans

Full scans involve making a complete list of all documents contained in a catalog. When the Indexing Service is first installed, it of course conducts a full scan, but these types of scans are also made when directories are added to a catalog and as part of the error recovery process. On the other hand, incremental scans—which only look for changed documents within a catalog—are done automatically upon a restart of the Indexing Service to determine what documents may have changed while it was inactive.

If you have a heavy load on your server from a large number of modified files, you may want to manually initiate either a full or an incremental scan. To do so:

1. Open the Indexing Service console.

2. In the left pane, select the appropriate catalog.

3. In the right pane, double-click Directories.

4. Select the directory for which you'd like to initiate a scan.

5. From the Action menu, select All Tasks and then either Rescan (Full) or Rescan (Incremental) depending on which operation you want.

6. Confirm your choice by clicking OK.

The scan will then proceed.

Indexing New Web Sites

When you create a new web site with IIS, it isn't automatically indexed when you create a catalog for it. If you want the content of the web site to be indexed, follow these steps:

1. Open the Indexing Service console.

2. Select the relevant catalog and right-click it in the left or right pane. Choose Properties.

3. Navigate to the Tracking tab.

4. In the drop-down box at the bottom of the screen, select the web site to index, and then click OK.

5. Open the IIS Manager console (see Chapter 7 for detailed instructions on administering IIS).

6. Right-click the relevant web site in the left pane, and then select Properties from the context menu.

7. Navigate to the Home Directory tab.

8. Check the Index This Resource box, and then click OK.

9. Restart the Indexing Service.

The new catalog is now active and will begin indexing the site you specified.

Indexing PDF Files

While the Indexing Service and Windows Server 2003 does not come bundled with a filter that can index the contents and properties of PDF files, Adobe—the manufacturer of Acrobat—has made available a free filter that you can install that will enable that functionality. You can find this filter at `http://www.adobe.com/support/downloads/detail.jsp?ftpID=1276`, and you will need to have a login and password for the Adobe web site (which is free, although you must register and provide your e-mail address) to download it.

To install the PDF filter:

1. Open the Indexing Service console.

2. Stop the Indexing Service.

3. Double-click the ifilter50.exe file that you downloaded from the Adobe web site.

4. The installation process will commence. You can accept the default location to install the filter product, unless you have a reason to change it.

5. Once the installation process finishes, start the Indexing Service.

6. Initiate a new scan, as described in the previous section.

If, for some reason, after that procedure PDF files are still not being indexed, check the registry to make sure that the Indexing Service knows that the PDF filter is present and where it can find it. Stop the Indexing Service, and then open the Registry Editor and navigate to the `HKEY_LOCAL_MACHINE\SYSTEM\CurrentControlSet\Control\ContentIndex` key. In the right pane, double-click the DLLsToRegister key, look to see if PDFFILT.DLL is present, and make sure the path is correct. (If you accepted the default entries during the filter installation process, the path is `C:\Program Files\Adobe\PDF IFilter 5.0`.)

Controlling Merges

There may be a time in your organization when a significant number of documents within your corpus are modified. In this instance, it may be beneficial to initiate a master merge yourself, rather than waiting for the automatic master merge to occur in the evening.

To initiate a master merge manually:

1. Open the Computer Management applet within Control Panel.

2. Expand the Indexing Service node in the left pane.

3. Right-click the appropriate catalog where the changed documents are represented, and select Merge from the All Tasks menu. This is shown in Figure 11-9.

4. Confirm your choice to merge the catalog by clicking Yes. Remember that this is a CPU- and time-intensive operation.

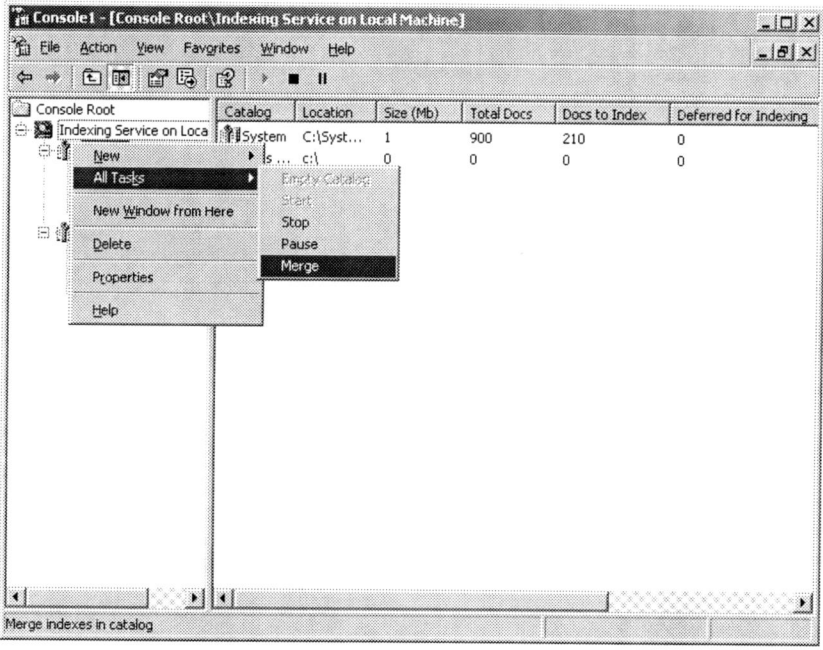

Figure 11-9. *Controlling merges*

You may also find it convenient to change the scheduled time for master merges to occur. Perhaps your lowest CPU load occurs at 3 a.m. and not at midnight, as the service comes pre-configured. To change this time, you'll need to edit the registry. Follow these steps:

1. Open the Registry Editor (selecting the Run command from the Start menu and entering **regedit** is an easy way).

2. Navigate to the HKEY_LOCAL_MACHINE\SYSTEM\CurrentControlSet\Control\ContentIndex key.

3. In the right pane, double-click the MasterMergeTime window.

4. In the Data box in the resulting DWORD Editor window, enter a value that represents the number of minutes past midnight that the master merge process should begin. This should be a number between 0 and 1439. For our example—to begin at 3 a.m. instead of midnight—enter **180**. Be sure Decimal is selected.

5. Click OK.

Configuring Queries

There are several interfaces to the Indexing Service. Perhaps the easiest and most accessible is simply using the Search command off the Start menu, as shown in Figure 11-10.

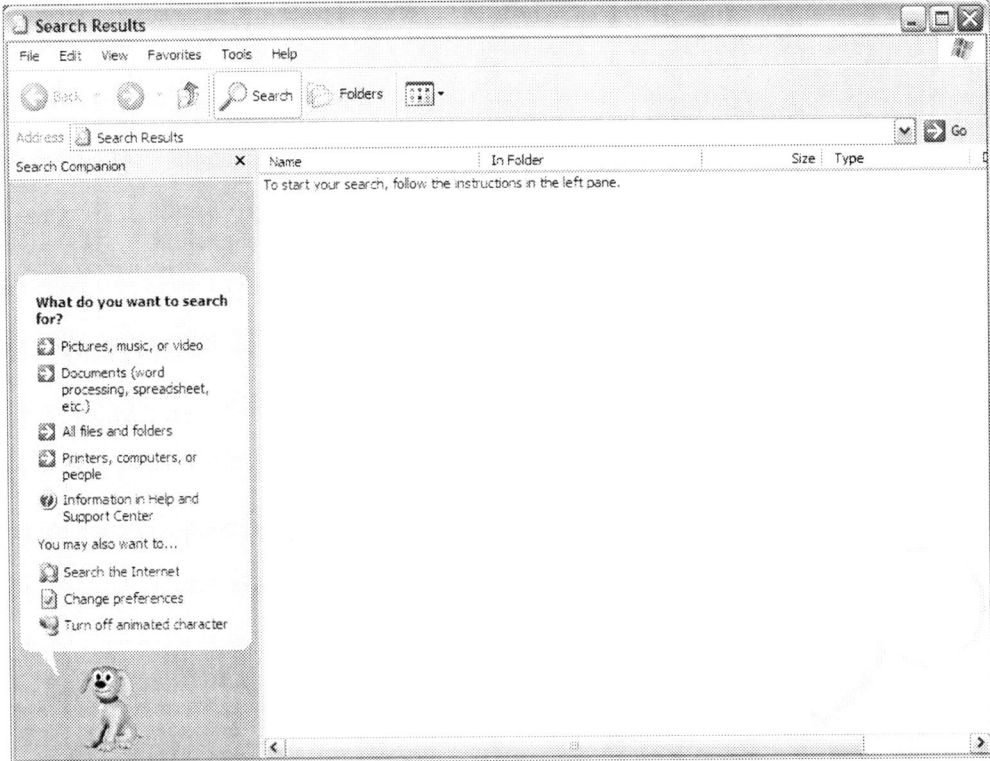

Figure 11-10. *Searching from the Start menu*

When using this interface, choose the option to search for files and folders, and then enter either a filename, a word or string of text from a file, or some other criteria in the box provided. The Indexing Service will then work its magic, displaying results sometimes as much as ten times faster than an ordinary search done with Windows without the Indexing Service present.

There is also a "Query the Catalog" interface found within the Indexing Service console, as shown in Figure 11-11.

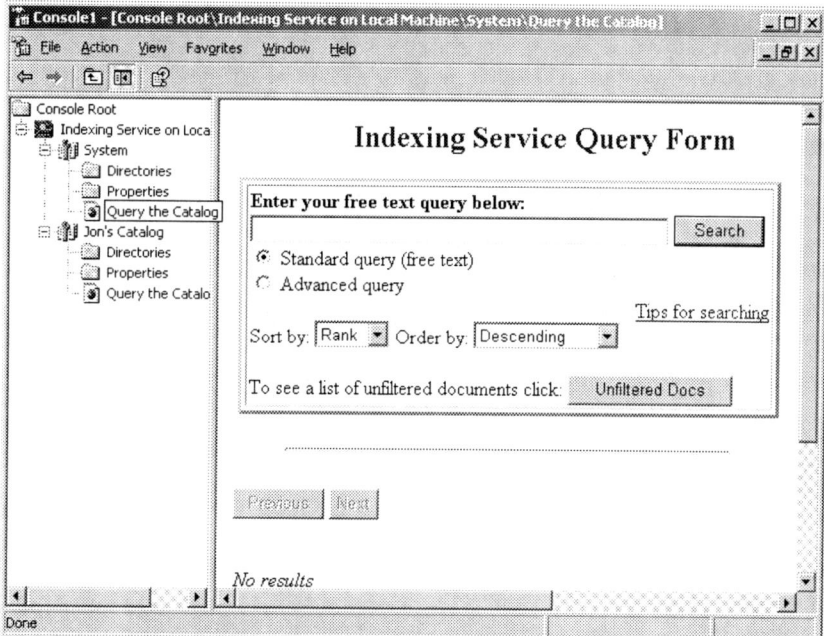

Figure 11-11. *The "Query the Catalog" interface*

The main advantage of the Query the Catalog form is the wider availability of search criteria. Using this page, you can search for words and phrases, search for words and phrases that are near other words and phrases, search for strings within text properties (like a document summary in Microsoft Word), search within certain document formats, use operators like <, <=, =, =>, >, and != against a fixed data point (useful for comparing against a date, a time, a size, or the like), use Boolean operators, use wildcard operators, use regular expressions, and rank results by how close the match is to the query. It's certainly quite a list.

If you'd like to create your own custom query form, that's simple to do as well. A basic form might consist of the following:

```
<h1>Indexing Service Query</h1>

<p>Enter the term for your search, and then click Submit.</p>

<form method="POST" action="/scripts/querydemo.idq">
<p><input type="text" name="CiRestriction" size="75">
<input type="submit" value="Submit" name="B1">
<input type="reset" value="Reset" name="B2"></p>
</form>
```

A custom query form has one requirement: it must post back to the Internet data query file (IDQ), which simply configures the correct query parameters for a search. There is a standard format for an IDQ file, shown here:

```
[Query]
# CiCatalog=d:\ <= COMMENTED OUT - default registry value used
CiColumns=filename,size,rank,characterization,vpath,DocTitle,write
CiRestriction=%CiRestriction%
CiMaxRecordsInResultSet=200
CiMaxRecordsPerPage=35
CiScope=/
CiFlags=DEEP
CiTemplate=/iissamples/issamples/ixtourqy.htx
CiSort=rank[d]
CiForceUseCi=true
```

Let's take a closer look at each part of the IDQ file:

- **[Query]**: Identifies the following information as a query restriction.

- **CiCatalog=d: **: Points to the index to use. In the preceding case, the statement is commented out, so a default is used.

- **CiColumns=filename,size,rank,characterization, vpath,DocTitle,write**: Indicates the kind of information to return in the result set.

- **CiRestriction=%CiRestriction%**: Indicates the query terms to search for. In this case, the CiRestriction form parameter is used, which matches the variable name of the text box used in the example form previously.

- **CiMaxRecordsInResultSet=200**: Sets the maximum number of results to be returned; in this example, 200.

- **CiMaxRecordsPerPage=35**: Determines how many results are shown on each web page returned. In this case, 35 results will be shown per web page.

- **CiScope=/**: Tells where to start the query. In this example, the query starts at the root of the virtual directory space. You can list more than one virtual directory in your scope by separating the directories with a comma (,). For example: CiScope=/docs,/work,/school.

- **CiFlags=DEEP**: Instructs the query to search all subdirectories within the scope.

- **CiTemplate=/iissamples/issamples/ixtourqy.htx**: Indicates which file to use to format the results; in this case, Ixtourqy.htx.

- **CiSort=rank[d]**: Tells how to sort the results. This example calls for results to be listed in descending ([d]) rank order; that is, the results are listed in order from the file with the most hits to the file with the least hits.

- **CiForceUseCi=true**: This is an optional variable that, when set to TRUE, forces the Indexing Service to search the content index even if it is out of date.

Note If you use a sort method other than rank descending, you only receive a subset of the total set of matching documents, and that subset may be different upon every successive query. The only surefire, consistent rank sorting method is rank descending, as described previously.

If you are receiving an error like "No documents matched the query" when using a custom query form, there's a few things to try. For one, check the .idq file that is being used for the query, and make sure the line CiCatalog is pointing to the correct catalog location. If you are using a custom catalog, be sure to point this entry somewhere; otherwise, you are searching in the default catalog, which isn't what you want.

Also, if you are trying to search content on an IIS-hosted web site, make sure the Index This Resource check box is ticked for that particular site. Open the IIS Manager console, right-click the relevant web site in the left pane, and then select Properties from the context menu. Navigate to the Home Directory tab, check the Index This Resource box, and then click OK. Finally, restart the Indexing Service.

You may also be impeded from viewing some documents because of permissions. The Indexing Service scans and indexes using the System local account and must have at least Read permissions on the files you want indexed; otherwise, the service can't read them and they're not indexed. The service also needs Full Control permissions for the root folder of the drive that houses the catalog, and it also needs Full Control on the CATALOG.WCI directory—this is located within the catalog directory. Additionally, if your users are attempting to search for documents, the users may not be allowed to access them, and thus those documents would not show up in the search results (if those documents are hosted on an NTFS volume).

Adjusting Performance Options

Trying to adjust performance for the Indexing Service and to issue recommendations is tantamount to aiming at a moving target: there are several variables that significantly affect the performance of the service, including the obvious ones: corpus size, amount of memory available, and amount of physical disk space present. Testing, on an informal basis, has revealed that indexes with 150,000 documents or less tend to not require a special hardware emphasis: the stock hardware that runs SBS 2003 should be a sufficient base for such a small corpus. Above that "magic" number, however, and you may need to look at expanding hardware on the machine running the Indexing Service in order to improve performance.

There are a couple of knobs to adjust within the Indexing Service to configure a certain level of performance based on system load; these adjustments are sometimes a quick fix to avoid needing a hardware upgrade. However, it's important to realize that in the majority of cases, the service works in the background and configures itself to consume an appropriate number of resources; these options will only make a noticeable difference in either very high or very low load situations.

With that disclaimer out of the way, let's turn to adjustments. For one, you can adjust the level at which the Indexing Service thinks it runs on the server—this can sometimes make the service a better player among the other processes jockeying for CPU time on your machine.

To try this:

1. Open the Indexing Service console.

2. Right-click the Indexing Service node in the left pane, and select Stop.

3. Now, from the Action menu, select All Tasks and then choose Tune Performance.

4. The Indexing Service Usage screen appears, as shown in Figure 11-12.

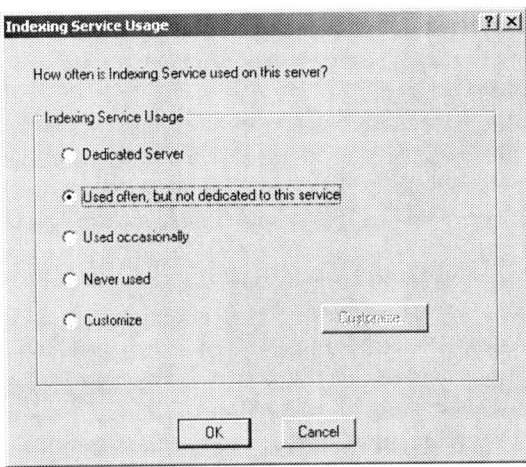

Figure 11-12. *The Indexing Service Usage screen*

On this screen, simply select the option that adequately fits this machine's usage profile:

- Dedicated Server, which provides "instant" indexing and "high load" querying

- Used often, but not dedicated to this service, which uses "lazy" indexing and "moderate load" querying

- Used occasionally, which specifies "lazy" indexing and "low load" querying

- Never used, which completely turns off the indexing service

- Customize, which brings up a separate dialog box, shown in Figure 11-13.

Then, you can configure the second option: the Desired Performance screen allows you to adjust individually the indexing and querying settings for the service to use. You can choose between lazy, moderate, and instant indexing and low load, moderate load, and high load querying.

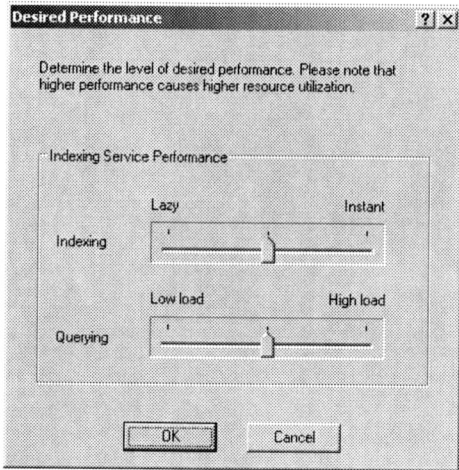

Figure 11-13. *The Customize screen*

Conclusion

The Indexing Service catalogs documents without needing them reformatted to a special, proprietary format, allowing Microsoft Office file formats, including the common Word and Excel documents, and those types of files indexed by the service to be available immediately and without any sort of special processing required. This lets you find the files you need quickly, with minimal effort.

Index

forums.apress.com

FOR PROFESSIONALS BY PROFESSIONALS™

JOIN THE APRESS FORUMS AND BE PART OF OUR COMMUNITY. You'll find discussions that cover topics of interest to IT professionals, programmers, and enthusiasts just like you. If you post a query to one of our forums, you can expect that some of the best minds in the business—especially Apress authors, who all write with *The Expert's Voice*™—will chime in to help you. Why not aim to become one of our most valuable participants (MVPs) and win cool stuff? Here's a sampling of what you'll find:

DATABASES
Data drives everything.

Share information, exchange ideas, and discuss any database programming or administration issues.

INTERNET TECHNOLOGIES AND NETWORKING
Try living without plumbing (and eventually IPv6).

Talk about networking topics including protocols, design, administration, wireless, wired, storage, backup, certifications, trends, and new technologies.

JAVA
We've come a long way from the old Oak tree.

Hang out and discuss Java in whatever flavor you choose: J2SE, J2EE, J2ME, Jakarta, and so on.

MAC OS X
All about the Zen of OS X.

OS X is both the present and the future for Mac apps. Make suggestions, offer up ideas, or boast about your new hardware.

OPEN SOURCE
Source code is good; understanding (open) source is better.

Discuss open source technologies and related topics such as PHP, MySQL, Linux, Perl, Apache, Python, and more.

PROGRAMMING/BUSINESS
Unfortunately, it is.

Talk about the Apress line of books that cover software methodology, best practices, and how programmers interact with the "suits."

WEB DEVELOPMENT/DESIGN
Ugly doesn't cut it anymore, and CGI is absurd.

Help is in sight for your site. Find design solutions for your projects and get ideas for building an interactive Web site.

SECURITY
Lots of bad guys out there—the good guys need help.

Discuss computer and network security issues here. Just don't let anyone else know the answers!

TECHNOLOGY IN ACTION
Cool things. Fun things.

It's after hours. It's time to play. Whether you're into LEGO® MINDSTORMS™ or turning an old PC into a DVR, this is where technology turns into fun.

WINDOWS
No defenestration here.

Ask questions about all aspects of Windows programming, get help on Microsoft technologies covered in Apress books, or provide feedback on any Apress Windows book.

Printed in the United States
206554BV00004B/63-66/A

9 781590 594650